Cognitive Behavioural Coach

Cognitive Behavioural Coaching in Practice explores various aspects of coaching from within a cognitive behavioural framework. Michael Neenan and Stephen Palmer bring together experts in the field to discuss topics including:

- procrastination
- stress
- performance
- self-esteem
- perfectionism
- goal selection
- Socratic questioning.

This highly practical book is illustrated throughout with lengthy coach–coachee dialogues that include a commentary of the aims of the coach during the session. It will be essential reading for both trainees and professional coaches whether or not they have a background in psychology. It will also be useful for therapists, counsellors and psychologists who want to use coaching in their everyday practice.

Michael Neenan is Associate Director of the Centre for Stress Management, London, an accredited cognitive behavioural therapist and author (with Windy Dryden) of *Life Coaching: A Cognitive-Behavioural Approach*.

Stephen Palmer is Honorary Professor of Psychology at City University and Director of its Coaching Psychology Unit. He is Founder Director of the Centre for Coaching, London, UK.

Essential Coaching Skills and Knowledge
Series Editors: Gladeana McMahon, Stephen Palmer & Averil Leimon

The **Essential Coaching Skills and Knowledge** series provides an accessible and lively introduction to key areas in the developing field of coaching. Each title in the series is written by leading coaches with extensive experience and has a strong practical emphasis, including illustrative vignettes, summary boxes, exercises and activities. Assuming no prior knowledge, these books will appeal to professionals in business, management, human resources, psychology, counselling and psychotherapy, as well as students and tutors of coaching and coaching psychology.

www.routledgementalhealth.com/essential-coaching-skills

Cognitive Behavioural Coaching in Practice

An Evidence Based Approach

Edited by Michael Neenan and Stephen Palmer

Routledge
Taylor & Francis Group

LONDON AND NEW YORK

First published 2012
by Routledge
27 Church Road, Hove, East Sussex BN3 2FA

Simultaneously published in the USA and Canada
by Routledge
711 Third Avenue, New York NY 10017

Routledge is an imprint of the Taylor & Francis Group, an Informa business

Typeset in New Century Schoolbook by
RefineCatch Limited, Bungay, Suffolk
Printed and bound in Great Britain by
TJ International Ltd, Padstow, Cornwall
Paperback cover design by Lisa Dynan

British Library Cataloguing in Publication Data
A catalogue record for this book is available from the British Library

Library of Congress Cataloging-in-Publication Data
Cognitive behavioural coaching in practice : an evidence based approach/
edited by Michael Neenan and Stephen Palmer.
    p. cm.
Includes bibliographical references and index.
ISBN 978-0-415-47262-3 (hbk.) — ISBN 978-0-415-47263-0 (pbk.)
1. Personal coaching. 2. Cognitive-behavioral therapy. I. Neenan,
Michael. II. Palmer, Stephen, 1955–
    BF637.P36C64 2012
    158'.3—dc23

                                            2011021202

                            ISBN: 978–0–415–47262–3 (hbk)
                            ISBN: 978–0–415–47263–0 (pbk)
                            ISBN: 978–0–203–14440–4 (ebk)

Contents

Dedications

To my wonderful son, Laurence

Michael

To my father, Ronald Palmer (1930–2011)

Stephen

Editors and contributors

Editors

Michael Neenan is Associate Director, Centre for Coaching and Centre for Stress Management, Blackheath, London, UK. He has a private practice as a therapist, coach and supervisor. He also runs resilience-building programmes for various companies. Michael, along with several others, developed cognitive behavioural coaching (CBC) – adapting the empirically driven cognitive behavioural therapy (CBT) for the coaching world. His books include (with Windy Dryden) *Life Coaching: A Cognitive Behavioural Approach* (2002), *Cognitive Therapy in a Nutshell* and *Rational Emotive Behaviour Therapy in a Nutshell* (2011, 2nd editions). The book he had the most pleasure writing was *Developing Resilience: A Cognitive Behavioural Approach* (2009).

Stephen Palmer is Founder Director of the Centre for Coaching, London, UK and Managing Director of the International Academy for Professional Development. He is an Honorary Professor of Psychology at City University London and Founder Director of their Coaching Psychology Unit. He is Honorary President of the International Society for Coaching Psychology and was the first Honorary President of the Association for Coaching and the first Chair of the British Psychological Society Special Group in Coaching Psychology. He is the UK Coordinating Co-editor of the *International Coaching Psychology Review* and Executive Editor of *Coaching: An International Journal of Theory, Research and Practice*. He has authored or edited over 35 books, including: *Handbook of Coaching Psychology* (with Whybrow, 2007), *The Coaching Relationship: Putting People First* (with McDowall, 2010) and *Developmental Coaching: Life Transitions and Generational Perspectives* (with Panchal, 2011). In 2008 the British Psychological Society's Special Group in Coaching Psychology gave him the 'Lifetime Achievement Award in Recognition of Distinguished Contribution to Coaching Psychology'.

Contributors

Tim Anstiss is a medical doctor specialising in health and well-being improvement, motivational interviewing and behavioural medicine. A former international pole vaulter and decathlete, Tim has a Diploma in Occupational Medicine, a masters degree in sports medicine and is a member of the Faculty of Sports and Exercise Medicine.

Patrizia Collard is a senior lecturer at the University of East London. Her interests include CBT and integrative psycho-therapy. She is a mindfulness trainer and coach, motivational speaker, writer and conference organiser. She is accredited and registered with a number of professional bodies.

Windy Dryden is Professor of Psychotherapeutic Studies at Goldsmiths College, University of London and is the author of many books, including *Coping with Life's Challenges: Moving on from Adversity* (Sheldon Press, 2010).

Kristina Gyllensten is a registered counselling psychologist, a chartered psychologist, a CBT psychotherapist and coach. She is Honorary Research Fellow and Deputy Director of the Coaching Psychology Unit, City University London. Her particular interests are workplace stress, stress management and cognitive therapy and coaching, on which she has co-authored a number of articles and chapters.

Gladeana McMahon holds a range of qualifications as a therapist and coach and is Life Fellow and Chair of the Association for Coaching, UK. She is also a fellow, accredited coach and therapist with a range of professional bodies (info@gladeanamcmahon.com).

Alanna O'Broin is an executive coach. Formerly an investment analyst and Fund Manager, Alanna is a chartered and registered psychologist. She has a private coaching and therapy practice, and is conducting doctorate research on the coaching relationship, on which she has published a number of co-authored articles and book chapters. Alanna is an International Board Member of *Coaching: An International Journal of Theory, Research and Practice*.

Siobhain O'Riordan is a trainer, examiner and supervisor on graduate/postgraduate coaching and coaching psychology programmes. She is an Honorary Research Fellow and Deputy Director of the Coaching Psychology Unit at City University London and Editor of *The Coaching Psychologist*. She is Chair of the International Society for Coaching Psychology.

Jonathan Passmore is an executive coach, trainer and coach supervisor. He has worked in the public, voluntary and private sectors including for PricewaterhouseCoopers and IBM Business Consulting. Jonathan has published 30 coaching research papers, 14 books and delivered over 90 coaching conference papers around the world. He received the Association of Coaching Global Award in 2010 for his work in coaching research and practice.

Alison Whybrow has a strong coaching practice and partners with organisations keen to use coaching to shift business performance and culture. Alison is a key contributor to a Masters programme in Professional Coaching Practice and supervises the practice of Coaches and Coaching Psychologists. Alison is a speaker and writer, having published a number of papers and chapters in the field of coaching and coaching psychology. Alison edited the *Handbook in Coaching Psychology* (with Palmer, 2007). Alison is a Chartered and Registered Psychologist.

Helen Williams is a coaching psychologist specialising in solution focused cognitive behavioural coaching. She gained 10 years of commercial experience working with SHL, and has since co-authored several publications on coaching in organisations and cognitive behavioural coaching.

Preface

You can guess that with the recent success story of cognitive behavioural therapy it was almost inevitable that it would start to be adapted and applied to other fields such as coaching. Yet that is a myth and not the reality. Going back to the 1980s cognitive behavioural and rational emotive therapy was not particularly popular and was still slowly building up an evidence base. However, practitioners who also worked in organisations as trainers or consultants saw its great potential to help employees manage stress, enhance performance and increase resilience or hardiness. From the mid-1980s the co-editors of this book were adapting the cognitive behavioural approach for use in the UK workplace and subsequently in New Zealand. It certainly needed adapting because often therapeutic terminology was rejected by course delegates. The approach was used in group and one-to-one work.

But there was a catch. The research into the application of cognitive behavioural therapy to a range of clinical disorders raced ahead in the 1990s whilst research into the use of the cognitive behavioural approach in non-clinical settings such as the workplace for coaching or training purposes was almost non-existent. Only in the last 10 years has the research into the cognitive behavioural approach being used beyond the therapeutic arena really started to gain momentum and gradually an evidence base is building up, underpinning its use in coaching at work as well as personal coaching.

This book brings together authors who are experienced practitioners, some of whom are researchers too. We would like to take this opportunity to thank them for the insights they have shared with us. We hope that this book helps to inform cognitive behavioural coaching practice.

Michael Neenan
Stephen Palmer

Foreword

Coaching is inevitably a goal-directed activity. Clients come to see coaches because they want to achieve certain goals in their work or personal lives. In essence, regardless of the coach's preferred theoretical or explanatory framework, the coach's role is to help clients identify their preferred outcome and to facilitate the development of a self-regulatory process that will help the client move towards that outcome, helping the client delineate specific action steps and then helping them monitor, evaluate and, if necessary, change their actions in order to make better progress towards their goals – a straightforward process of goal-directed self-regulation.

Clearly, in order for clients to create purposeful, positive change – real and lasting change – the client needs to have the thoughts, feelings and behaviours that can best support them in making such changes. It is also important that the environment or context supports these changes, and it is the role of the coach to help the client to design or structure these domains accordingly.

This, then, is the very core of the coaching process. It is also the core of the cognitive behavioural approach, and is why the cognitive behavioural approach is fundamental to coaching.

Indeed, virtually every aspect of coaching can be clearly and concisely explained in cognitive behavioural terms: from the notion of goals being internalised representations of desired states or outcomes (Austin and Vancouver, 1996), to the psychological and behavioural processes associated with the self-control required for purposeful positive change (Carver and Scheier, 1998), to the constructs of hope and pathways thinking (Snyder, Rand and Sigmon, 2002), resilience (Maddi, 2005), self-concordance (Sheldon, 2004) and self-reflection and insight (Grant, Franklin and Langford, 2002) – all essentially cognitive behavioural constructs.

There is little doubt that, besides being a comprehensive 'biopsychosocial' theory of human behaviour (Froggatt, 2006), cognitive behavioural theory can provide a wide range of useful and effective techniques for changing thoughts, feelings and behaviours. Indeed, there is a wealth of research attesting to the effectiveness of the cognitive behavioural approach in a wide range of domains, primarily with clinical or counselling populations and to a lesser extent in relation to sports, health and work related issues – and much of that research, theory and practice has great relevance for the goal and solution orientation of the coaching enterprise.

The challenge for coaches who wish to utilise the existing evidence base accumulated in the cognitive behavioural tradition is to be able to express and use these concepts in a non-pathological fashion – in a way that resonates for coaching clients, in a way that is constructive and positive, rather than in a way that focuses on repairing or fixing dysfunctionality. When this is done well, when coaching clients learn to constructively view their thinking from different perspectives and work with a well-trained cognitive behavioural coach to develop insight and greater behavioural choice, then grand things can happen. Indeed, there is now a growing body of coaching-specific research indicating that cognitive behavioural approaches to coaching are highly effective, not just at facilitating goal attainment but also in enhancing resilience, well-being and insight (Grant, Passmore, Cavanagh and Parker, 2010).

Evidence based coaching is becoming a reality, and this book marks an important milestone in helping coaches and clients alike to develop a greater understanding of the cognitive behavioural approach to coaching. Enjoy!

Anthony M. Grant
Director, Coaching Psychology Unit
School of Psychology
University of Sydney

References

Austin, J. T. and Vancouver, J. B. (1996) Goal constructs in psychology: Structure, process, and content. *Psychological Bulletin, 120*(3): 338–375.

Carver, C. S. and Scheier, M. F. (1998) *On the Self-Regulation of Behavior.* Cambridge, UK: Cambridge University Press.

Froggatt, W. (2006) *A brief intoduction to cognitive-behaviour therapy.* Retrieved on 1 January 2008, from http://www.rational.org.nz/

Grant, A. M., Franklin, J. and Langford, P. (2002) The Self-Reflection and Insight Scale: A new measure of private self-consciousness. *Social Behavior and Personality, 30*(8): 821–836.

Grant, A. M., Passmore, J., Cavanagh, M. J. and Parker, H. (2010) The state of play in coaching today: A comprehensive review of the field. *International Review of Industrial and Organisational Psychology, 25*: 125–168.

Maddi, S. R. (2005) On hardiness and other pathways to resilience. *American Psychologist, 60*(3): 261–262.

Sheldon, K. M. (2004) *Optimal Human Being: An Integrated Multi-Level Perspective.* Mahwah, NJ: Lawrence Erlbaum Associates, Inc.

Snyder, C. R., Rand, K. L. and Sigmon, D. R. (2002) *Hope Theory: A Member of the Positive Psychology Family.* New York: Oxford University Press.

Introduction

Michael Neenan and Stephen Palmer

These seem to be the boom years for coaching: growing media interest in the subject; increasing use of coaching for personal, professional and organisational growth; and the rush of people wanting to train as coaches. Coaching has definitely passed the fad phase of its existence (*The Economist* in 2003 stated that 'having an executive coach is all the rage') and has established itself as an enduring resource for personal and professional development: 'Executive coaching during this period [from the first edition of the book in 2001] has grown and become mainstream in many business sectors worldwide. Coach-training organizations have also grown and thrived across the globe. It looks like coaching is here to stay' (Peltier, 2010: xv). Many of the coaching approaches are adaptations of psychological models used in therapy, such as psychodynamic, cognitive behavioural, person-centred, solution-focused and gestalt. Our coaching focus is a cognitive behavioural one. Cognitive behavioural coaching (CBC) derives from the work of two leading cognitive behavioural theorists, researchers and therapists: Aaron Beck, who founded cognitive therapy (CT), and Albert Ellis, who developed rational emotive behavioural therapy (REBT). Collectively, these two approaches come under the banner of cognitive behavioural therapy (CBT). We would define CBC as:

> A collaborative, goal-directed endeavour using multimodal learning methods to help individuals develop their capabilities and remove any psychological blocks that interfere with this process.

The central message of the cognitive behavioural approach is usually traced back to the Stoic philosophers, Epictetus and Marcus Aurelius, but a modern source will do equally well: 'The meaning of things lies not in things themselves, but in our attitudes towards them' (Antoine de Saint Exupéry, French writer and aviator, 1900–1944). By exploring our attitudes to events rather than focusing excessively on the events themselves, we can understand better why we react in some of the self- and goal-defeating ways that we do. Through this exploration, we can learn to widen our perspective in order to see that there are more productive ways of dealing with our difficulties and reaching our goals. Auerbach (2006: 103) states that a cognitive coach is 'a thought partner. As a thought partner, I help my clients think with more depth, greater clarity, and less distortion – a cognitive process. Coaching is largely a cognitive method' but, as he elaborates, emotions are not neglected in this process and without a solid working alliance cognitive methods alone will not usually have much positive effect on the coachee.

Coaching and CBT have the same aim: problem resolution – closing the performance gap in coaching and the amelioration of unhelpful thoughts, feelings and behaviours in CBT. Other similarities between CBC and CBT include: staying mainly in the here and now to understand coachees' presenting issues and then moving towards the future to help them achieve their goals (not all therapies are backward-looking, as many coaching books claim); setting an agenda in each session; encouraging belief and behaviour change; carrying out and reviewing between-session goal-oriented tasks; seeing the relationship as a collaborative partnership in problem-solving and resilience-building; and helping to foster an experimental approach to change. The ultimate aim of CBC and CBT is to help people to become their own self-coach or therapist.

A key difference between CBC and CBT is that people seeking coaching usually focus on achieving personal and/or professional fulfilment, not on psychological difficulties that significantly impair their well-being or functioning. However, some research studies 'have found that between 25 and 50% of those seeking coaching have clinically significant levels of anxiety, stress, or depression' (Grant, 2009: 97), therefore emotional problems may get in the way of coaching (Dryden, 2011). With their understanding and treatment of psychological disorders, cognitive behavioural therapists who have moved into coaching, after a period of transitional training (Auerbach, 2001; Sperry, 2004), would be more likely than coaches without a background in mental health to recognise when it would be appropriate to refer a coachee for therapy.

We believe that some distinctions between therapy and coaching are overstated – therapy often gets dismissed as just repairing weakness and dysfunction, while coaching is focused on unlocking potential, improving performance, enhancing well-being and delivering results. A client who comes to therapy for help with their panic attacks or obsessive–compulsive disorder is seeking results (overcoming the problem), which will lead to enhanced well-being, improved performance at work or home and unlock some of the potential previously inhibited by the problem. Indeed, from a CBT perspective, when clients are gaining in confidence as a self-therapist (i.e. independent problem-solver), the therapist then conceptualises their role as more of a coach supporting clients' self-directing learning. Therefore, promoting coaching does not have to be carried out at the expense of diminishing what therapy has to offer.

CBT's emphasis (or, more accurately, Beck's cognitive therapy) 'on empirical research, its theoretical base, and its coherence as a therapeutic intervention have meant that, at this stage, it is better validated as an effective treatment for a range of disorders than any other psychological therapy' (Bennett-Levy, Butler, Fennell, Hackman, Mueller and Westbrook, 2004: 2; Salkovskis, 1996). Does the success of CBT in treating clinical problems translate into similar success in coaching with individuals focused on personal and professional development? This is an important question. Over a decade ago it was a leap of faith for practitioners who had adapted the cognitive behavioural approach to the field of coaching as little research had been undertaken. However, since 2001, researchers have been building up an evidence base for cognitive behavioural and solution-focused cognitive behavioural coaching. The research indicates that the approach reduces:

- anxiety;
- stress;

- depression;
- perfectionism;
- self-handicapping.

The approach has also been found to enhance:

- goal-striving;
- well-being;
- hope;
- resilience;
- cognitive hardiness;
- sales performance;
- core self-evaluation;
- 'significant' personal and professional value;
- global self-rating of performance;
- emotional management.

The research has included qualitative, quantitative and single-case design studies (Beddoes-Jones and Miller, 2007; Grant, 2001, 2003, 2008; Grant, Curtayne and Burton, 2009; Green, Oades and Grant, 2006; Gyllensten, Palmer, Nilsson, Regnér and Frodi, 2010; Kearns, Forbes and Gardiner, 2007; Kearns, Gardiner and Marshall, 2008; Libri and Kemp, 2006; Spence and Grant, 2007) and manualised coaching programmes have been developed and researched (Grant and Greene, 2001; Grbcic and Palmer, 2007; Greene and Grant, 2003). Practitioners have been writing about CBC for some years and have focused on the theory and practice, illustrating various models, techniques and strategies applied to life and workplace coaching (e.g. Anderson, 2002; Ducharme, 2004; Edgerton and Palmer, 2005; Ellam and Palmer, 2006; Good, Yeganeh and Yeganeh, 2010; Neenan and Palmer, 2001; Neenan and Dryden, 2002; Palmer, 2007; Palmer and Gyllensten, 2008; Palmer and Szymanska, 2007; Williams and Palmer, 2010; Williams, Edgerton and Palmer, 2010).

Practitioners have also adapted the cognitive behavioural frameworks and models such as SPACE and PRACTICE to different cultures and languages by working with their colleagues in other countries (e.g. Dias, Edgerton and Palmer, 2010; Dias, Gandos, Nardi and Palmer, 2011; Syrek-Kosowska,

Edgerton and Palmer, 2010). For example, in Brazil SPACE becomes FACES and in Poland it becomes SFERA, whereas PRACTICE becomes POSTURA or POSITIVO in Brazil and Portugal. This is an important development because often coaching frameworks have been translated into other languages and acronyms such as GROW or SPACE, which are supposed to represent the model, become meaningless and no longer an *aide-memoire* for the coach or coachee.

So, what has CBC got to offer? In Chapter 1, Neenan examines a rational emotive behavioural approach to tackling procrastination and shows how the coach moves between the psychological and practical aspects of problem-solving. Although the reader can dip into any chapter of this book that interests them, for readers who are relatively new to CBC this chapter would be a good starting point because it covers the basic approach. Anstiss and Passmore in Chapter 2 look at how, among other things, motivational interviewing (MI) can 'roll with resistance' to change in order to help the person become more motivated to improve performance. Miller and Rollnick (2009) describe MI as 'a collaborative, person-centered form of guiding to elicit and strengthen motivation for change' (p. 137). This method or tool may be necessary at the beginning stage of CBC if a coachee is reluctant to move forward, even though at one level they want to move forward. In Chapter 3, O'Broin and Palmer consider ways to enhance the coaching relationship by discussing the published research on the subject and what can be learnt from sports coaching and psychology. Neenan in Chapter 4 focuses on Socratic questioning and asks if its essential purpose is to point coachees in predetermined directions or foster new and surprising possibilities, and he stresses the importance of asking good questions because questioning is the major part of a coach's verbal activity. In Chapter 5, Palmer and Williams focus on the major drawback of raising low self-esteem – it still makes a person's worth conditional upon achieving a desirable outcome – and propose, as an alternative, teaching unconditional self-acceptance whereby the performance is decoupled from the self. Neenan and Dryden in Chapter 6 look at resilience: what it is, the attributes that underpin it and some of the ideas that undermine resilience building.

In Chapter 7, Gyllensten and Palmer discuss using coaching to tackle stress and enhance performance, particularly highlighting stress theory and practice. In Chapter 8, Collard and McMahon show how CBC is fused with mindfulness meditation (i.e. purposeful, non-judgemental attention to being in the present moment) and how this approach is applied to people whose difficulties do not fall within medical or therapy contexts. In the final chapter, based on their research, Whybrow and O'Riordan explore to what extent companies are using coaching to improve performance and engagement among employees.

It is worth noting that the CBC approach described in this book is not identical to the Cognitive Coaching[SM] practised in the United States (see Costa and Garmston, 1997). Cognitive Coaching[SM] is generally used within the teaching profession whereas CBC is used for a range of issues in a variety of settings and is applied across professions. Cognitive Coaching[SM] has also built up a good evidence base, which can also inform CBC practice.

Where appropriate, chapters contain an annotated coach–coachee dialogue to make explicit the reasons for the coach's interventions – to get inside the coach's mind, so to speak. At the end of each chapter we have included discussion issues to aid personal reflection and debate with colleagues and students. Recommended reading has also been included.

We hope that this book will stimulate your interest in CBC by providing a showcase for the range of issues that this coaching approach deals with.

Discussion issues

- Are the boom years for coaching over?
- Is cognitive behavioural coaching identical to cognitive behavioural therapy?
- Are the distinctions between therapy and coaching overstated?
- Does cognitive behavioural coaching offer anything different to other forms of coaching?

References

Anderson, J. P. (2002) Executive coaching and REBT: Some comments from the field. *Journal of Rational-Emotive and Cognitive-Behavior Therapy*, *20*(3/4): 223–233.

Auerbach, J. E. (2001) *Personal and Executive Coaching: The Complete Guide for Mental Health Professionals*. Ventura, CA: Executive College Press.

Auerbach, J. E. (2006) Cognitive coaching. In D. R. Stober and A. M. Grant (Eds.), *Evidence Based Coaching Handbook: Putting Best Practices to Work for Your Clients*. Hoboken, NJ: Wiley.

Beddoes-Jones, F. and Miller, J. (2007) Short-term cognitive coaching interventions: Worth the effort or a waste of time? *The Coaching Psychologist*, *3*(2): 60–69.

Bennett-Levy, J., Butler, G., Fennell, M., Hackman, A., Mueller, M. and Westbrook, D. (2004) *Oxford Guide to Behavioural Experiments in Cognitive Therapy*. Oxford: Oxford University Press.

Costa, A. and Garmston, R. (1997) *Cognitive Coaching: A Foundation for Renaissance Schools*, 3rd edn. Norwood, MA: Christopher-Gordon.

Dias, G., Edgerton, N. and Palmer, S. (2010) From SPACE to FACES: The adaptation of the SPACE model of cognitive behavioural coaching and therapy to the Portuguese language. *Coaching Psychology International*, *3*(1): 12–16.

Dias, G., Gandos, L., Nardi, A. E. and Palmer, S. (2011) Towards the practice of coaching and coaching psychology in Brazil: The adaptation of the PRACTICE model to the Portuguese language. *Coaching Psychology International*, *4*(1): 10–14.

Dryden, W. (2011) *Dealing with Clients' Emotional Problems in Life Coaching*. London: Routledge.

Ducharme, M. (2004) The cognitive-behavioral approach to executive coaching. *Consulting Psychology Journal: Practice and Research*, *56*, 214–224.

Edgerton, N. and Palmer, S. (2005) SPACE: A psychological model for use within cognitive behavioural coaching, therapy and stress management. *The Coaching Psychologist*, *1*(2): 25–31.

Ellam, V. and Palmer, S. (2006) To achieve, or not to achieve the goal – that is the question: Does frustration tolerance influence goal achievement in coaching clients? *The Coaching Psychologist*, *2*(2): 27–32.

Good, D., Yeganeh, B. and Yeganeh, R. (2010) Cognitive behavioural executive coaching: A structure for increasing leadership flexibility. *OD Practitioner*, *42*(3): 18–23.

Grant, A. M. (2001) Coaching for enhancement performance: Comparing cognitive and behavioural approaches to coaching.

Paper presented at *3rd International Spearman Seminar: Extending Intelligence: Enhancement and New Constructs*, Sydney. Retrieved on 30 December 2007, from http://www.psych. usyd.edu.au/coach/CBT_BT_CT_Spearman_Conf_Paper.pdf

Grant, A. M. (2003) The impact of life coaching on goal attainment, metacognition and mental health. *Social Behavior and Personality*, *31*(3): 253–64.

Grant, A. M. (2008) Personal life coaching for coaches-in-training enhances goal attainment and insight, and deepens learning. *Coaching: An International Journal of Research, Theory and Practice*, *1*(1): 47–52.

Grant, A. M. (2009) Coach or couch? *Harvard Business Review*, *87*(1): 97.

Grant, A. M. and Greene, J. (2001) *Coach Yourself: Make Real Changes in Your Life*. London: Momentum.

Grant, A. M., Curtayne, L. and Burton, G. (2009) Executive coaching enhances goal attainment, resilience and workplace well-being: A randomised controlled study. *Journal of Positive Psychology*, *4*(5): 396–407.

Grbcic, S. and Palmer, S. (2007) A cognitive-behavioural self-help approach to stress management and prevention at work: A randomized controlled trial. *The Rational Emotive Behaviour Therapist*, *12*(1): 41–43.

Green, L. S., Oades, L. G. and Grant, A. M. (2006) Cognitive-behavioral, solution-focused life coaching: enhancing goal-striving, well-being, and hope. *Journal of Positive Psychology*, *1*(3): 142–149.

Greene, J. and Grant, A. M. (2003) *Solution-Focused Coaching: Managing People in a Complex World*. London: Momentum.

Gyllensten, K., Palmer, S., Nilsson, E.-K., Regnér, A. M. and Frodi, A. (2010) Experiences of cognitive coaching: A qualitative study. *International Coaching Psychology Review*, *5*(2): 98–108.

Kearns, H., Forbes, A. and Gardiner, M. (2007) Intervention for the treatment of perfectionism and self-handicapping in a non-clinical population. *Behaviour Change*, *24*: 157–172.

Kearns, H., Gardiner, M. and Marshall, K. (2008) Innovation in PhD completion: The hardy shall succeed (and be happy!). *Higher Education Research and Development*, *27*(1): 77–89.

Libri, V. and Kemp, T. (2006) Assessing the efficacy of a cognitive behavioural executive coaching programme. *International Coaching Psychology Review*, *1*(1): 9–20.

Miller, W. R. and Rollnick, S. (2009) Ten things that motivational interviewing is not. *Behavioural and Cognitive Psychotherapy*, *37*(2): 129–140.

Neenan, M. and Dryden, W. (2002) *Life Coaching: A Cognitive-Behavioural Approach*. Hove, UK: Brunner-Routledge.

Neenan, M. and Palmer, S. (2001) Cognitive behavioural coaching. *Stress News*, *13*(3): 15–18.

Palmer, S. (2007) PRACTICE: A model suitable for coaching, counselling, psychotherapy and stress management. *The Coaching Psychologist*, *3*(2): 71–77.

Palmer, S. and Gyllensten, K. (2008) How cognitive behavioural, rational emotive behavioural or multimodal coaching could prevent mental health problems, enhance performance and reduce work related stress. *Journal of Rational Emotive and Cognitive Behavioural Therapy*, *26*(1): 38–52.

Palmer, S. and Szymanska, K. (2007) Cognitive behavioural coaching: An integrative approach. In S. Palmer and A. Whybrow (Eds.), *Handbook of Coaching Psychology: A Guide for Practitioners*. Hove, UK: Routledge.

Peltier, B. (2010) *The Psychology of Executive Coaching: Theory and Application*, 2nd edn. New York: Routledge.

Salkovskis, P. M. (1996) *Frontiers of Cognitive Therapy*. New York: Guilford Press.

Spence, G. B. and Grant, A. M. (2007) Professional and peer life coaching and the enhancement of goal-striving and well-being: An exploratory study. *Journal of Positive Psychology*, *2*(3): 185–194.

Sperry, L. (2004) *Executive Coaching: The Essential Guide for Mental Health Professionals*. Hove, UK: Brunner-Routledge.

Syrek-Kosowska, A., Edgerton, N. and Palmer, S. (2010). From SPACE to SFERA: Adaptation of the SPACE model of cognitive behavioural coaching and therapy to the Polish language. *Coaching Psychology International*, *3*(2): 18–20.

Williams, H. and Palmer, S. (2010) CLARITY: A cognitive behavioural coaching model. *Coaching Psychology International*, *3*(2): 5–7.

Williams, H., Edgerton, N. and Palmer, S. (2010) Cognitive behavioural coaching. In E. Cox, T. Bachkirova and D. Clutterbuck (Eds.), *The Complete Handbook of Coaching*. London: Sage.

Recommended reading

Neenan, M. and Dryden, W. (2002) *Life Coaching: A Cognitive-Behavioural Approach*. Hove, UK: Brunner-Routledge.

Palmer, S. and Whybrow, A. (2007) *Handbook of Coaching Psychology: A Guide for Practitioners*. Hove, UK: Routledge.

Peltier, B. (2010) *The Psychology of Executive Coaching: Theory and Application*, 2nd edn. New York: Routledge.

1

Understanding and tackling procrastination

Michael Neenan

Introduction

Coaching aims to bring out the best in people in order to help them achieve their desired goals. While a lot of the coaching literature is full of exciting promises of unleashing your potential, reinventing yourself or living your dream life by implementing dynamic action plans, the 'unexciting' side of coaching can involve tackling some of the usual change-blocking problems familiar to therapists, such as perfectionism, procrastination, excessive self-doubt, lack of persistence and self-depreciation. Unless these psychological blocks are overcome, little progress is likely to be made in achieving the person's coaching goals. Therefore, the coach needs to be competent in addressing both the psychological and practical aspects of change.

A theoretical model for understanding and tackling psychological blocks in general and procrastination in particular is rational emotive behavioural therapy (REBT; Ellis, 1994), founded in 1955 by the late Albert Ellis, an American clinical psychologist. (REBT is one of the approaches within the field of CBT.) A capsule account of the REBT approach follows. The approach proposes that rigid and extreme thinking (irrational beliefs) lies at the core of psychological disturbance. For example, faced with a coachee who is sceptical about the value of coaching, the coach makes himself very anxious and over-prepares for each session by insisting: 'I must impress her with my skills [rigid belief – why can't he let the coachee make up her own mind?], because if I don't this will prove I'm an incompetent coach' (an extreme view of his role to adopt if the coachee is unimpressed). Rigid thinking takes the form, for example, of must, should, have to and got to. Derived from these rigid beliefs are three major and extreme conclusions: awfulising (nothing could be worse and nothing good can come from negative events), low frustration tolerance (LFT; frustration and discomfort are too hard to bear) and depreciation of self and/or others (a person can be given a single global rating [e.g. useless] that defines their essence or worth).

What lies at the core of psychological health is flexible and non-extreme thinking (rational beliefs). Flexible thinking is couched in non-dogmatic preferences, wishes, wants and desires, and flowing from these flexible beliefs are three major non-extreme beliefs: anti-awfulising (things could always be worse and valuable lessons can be learnt from coping with adversity), high frustration tolerance (HFT; frustration and discomfort are worth bearing in order to achieve your goals) and acceptance of self and/or others (individuals are too complex to be given a single global rating but aspects of the person can legitimately be rated, e.g. bad timekeeping doesn't make *you* a bad person). The concepts of the REBT approach have been applied for over 30 years to tackling problems in the workplace (DiMattia, 1991; Ellis, 1972; Dryden and Gordon, 1993a) and, more recently, to coaching (Anderson, 2002; Kodish, 2002; Neenan and Dryden, 2002a).

When the REBT approach is used outside of a therapy context it is more advantageous to call it rational emotive behavioural coaching (REBC), although some practitioners prefer to use the shorter name of rational coaching (see Palmer, 2009). REBT terms such as 'irrational' and 'disturbance' can be reframed as performance-interfering thoughts and/or self-limiting beliefs or any permutation on problematic thinking that coachees are willing to endorse.

What is procrastination?

Procrastination can be described as putting off until later what our better judgement tells us ought (preferably) to be done now, thereby incurring unwanted consequences through such dilatory behaviour. The 'putting off' occurs because the person is actively seeking more interesting or pleasurable activities to engage in rather than experiencing *now* the discomfort or difficulty associated with doing the avoided tasks. It is important to distinguish between procrastination and planned delay: in the latter case there are legitimate reasons for postponing action, such as collecting more information before making an important decision (although this can segue into procrastination if the person becomes worried about making the wrong decision). Also, it would be incorrect to dismiss procrastination as mere laziness because the latter is a disinclination to exert oneself while the former frequently involves carrying out other tasks (i.e. being busy) in order to avoid getting on with the priority task that requires action now.

Procrastination is often described as 'the thief of time'. As procrastination is, in essence, lack of self-management, a more personal way of describing it is to see yourself stealing your own time through your continuing inaction (Neenan and Dryden, 2002b). Another view of procrastination is that you give away your time free of charge – time that you might pay anything for on your deathbed to stay alive a little longer. So much time can be wasted through procrastination that you might believe you have several lives to lead instead of only one. People who become increasingly frustrated about their procrastination habits fear that they are wasting their lives, yet avoid doing what would help them to make more productive use of their time. This is what Knaus (1998: 7) calls the fundamental procrastination paradox: 'When we try to buy time by procrastinating, we condemn ourselves to running out of time.'

Some surveys suggest that up to 20% of the adult population are chronically affected by procrastination (Persaud, 2005). Dryden (2000a) distinguishes between chronic situation-specific procrastination (e.g. constantly missing deadlines for filing tax returns) and chronic cross-situational procrastination that affects a number of important areas of a person's life (e.g. avoiding whenever possible tedious or boring tasks that require more than minimal effort to complete them). Chronic procrastination can have high costs:

> It has been associated with depression, guilt, low exam grades, anxiety, neuroticism, irrational thinking, cheating and low self-esteem. As a result, procrastination probably accounts for much of why many never realize their full potential and so it can be an extremely disabling psychological condition.
>
> (Persaud, 2005: 237)

In essence, chronic avoidance usually means chronic suffering (Lazarus, Lazarus and Fay, 1993).

What stops productive action?

Hauck (1982: 18) comments that poor self-discipline is an unsurprising human trait as 'avoiding a difficult situation seems like the most natural course to take because we are so easily seduced by immediate satisfactions'. Freeman and DeWolf (1990: 234) state that 'immediate enjoyment is what procrastination is all about. Ice cream instead of struggle'. Adair (1988: 14) suggests that 'it is the vice of people who like to consider work rather than actually do it'. Dryden (2000b) observes that procrastination is often a behavioural way of protecting yourself from experiencing an unpleasant emotional state, such as feeling highly irritated if you start working on a boring task you wish you did not have to do. Sapadin and Maguire (1996: 10) state that 'procrastination is caused by an internal conflict' and have identified six fundamental procrastination styles:

1 **The perfectionist** is reluctant to start or finish a task in case it proves to be less than perfect and therefore is seen to fail in his own and/or others' eyes.
2 **The dreamer** wants life to go smoothly and avoids difficult challenges. Grandiose ideas are not translated into achievable goals. Ill at ease with daily reality, she retreats into fantasy.
3 **The worrier** fears things going wrong and being over-whelmed by events (lots of 'What if . . .?' catastrophic

thinking); risk or change is avoided and he has little confidence in his ability to make decisions or tolerate discomfort.

4 **The defier** is resistant and argumentative towards others' instructions or suggestions because this means she is being told what to do or other people are trying to control her. An indirect form of defiance is passive-aggressiveness, such as saying 'yes' to others' requests when the person really means 'no' because she is not prepared to take on the responsibility of doing them within the allotted time.

5 **The crisis-maker** likes to display bravado in declaring he cannot get motivated until the eleventh hour or this is when he does his best work; 'living on the edge' gives him an adrenaline rush. He has a low threshold for boredom in his life. Leaving things until the last minute often means that they do not get done on time or opportunities are missed.

6 **The overdoer** takes on too much work without establishing what her priorities are; time is managed inefficiently, leading to some work not being done, done poorly or finished later than agreed.

Sapadin and Maguire (1996) suggest that individuals display a mix of procrastination styles: some are more prominently displayed than others. From the REBT perspective, underpinning these various procrastination styles there are likely to be found ego disturbance and discomfort disturbance beliefs (Dryden and Neenan, 2004). Ego disturbance relates to the demands that we impose on ourselves and the consequent negative self-ratings that we make when we fail to live up to these demands. An ego disturbance belief likely to be found in perfectionists is: 'I must do the task extremely well or else I'm a failure.' Discomfort disturbance or low frustration tolerance (LFT) is related to the domain of human comfort and occurs when we make demands that comfortable life conditions must exist and, when they do not, to see these difficult or unpleasant conditions as unbearable. A discomfort disturbance belief likely to be found in dreamers is: 'I shouldn't have to work hard to fulfil my dreams. I can't stand having to get my mind around all those boring details.' Of course, clients can have both types of beliefs underpinning their procrastination. For example, with perfectionists, as well as fear of failure, some may have LFT beliefs related to their need to reach their high standards *effortlessly* (e.g. 'I shouldn't have to struggle!').

Can procrastination ever be justified? Hauck (1980: 138) suggests that self-discipline can be abandoned if you have a terminal illness or are facing a firing squad in the morning: 'Not to live life to the fullest when you are fairly certain life will be brief is folly.' Apart from these situations, it is better to get the work done first before you slacken your self-discipline.

The common denominator of procrastination

According to Dryden and Gordon, the 'one thing all people who procrastinate have in common ... is a clear-cut emotional problem' (1993b: 59). Individuals might not be aware of their own emotional problem because of their avoidance behaviour, which protects them from experiencing it. In order to 'release' this emotion, they can face the situation in imagination or actuality and identify the irrational beliefs maintaining their procrastination by using the ABCs of the REBT approach:

Situational **A** = activating event, such as imagining giving a presentation to a group of colleagues.

Critical   **A** = what the person is most troubled/upset about regarding the presentation: 'Not being able to answer all of the questions.'

B = irrational beliefs: 'I must be able to answer all of the questions because if I can't this will prove I'm a phoney or I don't know my subject.'

C = consequences, such as the following:

- emotional: rising anxiety;
- behavioural: highly agitated, leans on table for support;
- cognitive: dwells on what being exposed as a 'phoney' will do to her reputation and career;
- physical: heart pounding, sweating, light-headedness, trembling;
- interpersonal: withdrawing from her colleagues in coffee and lunch breaks.

By exposing herself in imagination to giving the presentation (A) the person's critical A is located, which triggers her irrational beliefs (B), which then largely determines her reactions at C. By avoiding the presentation, the coachee remains safe from being exposed as a 'phoney' but, at the same time, she sees herself as a 'phoney' for avoiding doing something she knows she is good at: 'Phoney if I do and phoney if I don't.' Within the ABC model, it is of fundamental importance to teach coachees the difference between two types of thinking: A→C thinking, where events or others make you feel and behave in the way that you do (e.g. 'Giving a presentation makes me anxious and agitated'); and B→C thinking, where you largely upset yourself by the irrational beliefs you hold about events or others, as shown in the ABC model above.

A→C thinking is likely to keep you feeling helpless in the face of events because you believe they have to change before you can, while B→C thinking frees you from this perceived helplessness by demonstrating that *you*, not events, largely determine how you feel and act (Dryden and Neenan, 2006). By changing your beliefs you can change your feelings and actions. The coach needs to monitor closely, but not obsessively, when the coachee is slipping back into A→C thinking instead of using B→C thinking and point out this cognitive slippage.

Some cautions in tackling procrastination

The coach may overly focus on the consequences of her coachee's procrastination by exploring his feelings about it (e.g. 'I feel angry and guilty about missing the deadline for the report. I've let people down'), thereby unwittingly helping to perpetuate his procrastination instead of uncovering what the coachee said to himself *at* the time in order to delay finishing the report *on* time (e.g. 'Why should I have to do another one so soon after finishing the last one?'). This investigation would have revealed his procrastination as an act of rebellion against what he saw as his boss's mistreatment of him.

What can seem perplexing to the coach is the coachee's reply when asked how she would feel if she got on with the task: 'Great' (but no action is forthcoming). Why is she depriving herself of experiencing this feeling by her continuing inaction? Anticipating feeling 'great' is insufficiently motivating because she still has to face starting the task, which usually means a discomfort phase to contend with that currently acts as a deterrent to action (e.g. 'There is so much information to sift through. I'll feel overwhelmed, get angry and frustrated and give up'). So it is important for the coach not to take feeling 'great' at face value and thereby expect constructive action to occur – emotional disturbance still blocks the way! Even if the coachee forces herself to complete this particular task through a reluctantly self-imposed deadline and is mightily relieved once it is finished, her disturbance-inducing thinking is likely to be unmodified (e.g. 'I hated doing it. I felt terrible. I shouldn't have to put myself through that again'). As Grieger and Boyd (1980: 36) point out, focusing on 'practical problems before emotional problems tends to rob clients of their motivation to solve their emotional problems, leaving them more comfortable yet still disturbed'.

Rewards might seem an obvious incentive to complete tasks but some individuals might become dependent on them, particularly if the tasks are onerous, and thereby avoid developing the intrinsic motivation to get the job done without a carrot being dangled in front of their noses (no reward, no action). In my experience, some individuals can become so reward-fixated that they give themselves a treat in anticipation of doing the work, or they do not do it and then reward themselves again for pledging to do it tomorrow; they spend too much time thinking of new and more exciting rewards to give themselves because they have become jaded with the routine ones; or they rush the job to get the reward instead of focusing on the quality (usually poor) of the work being done. If coachees want to break the procrastination habit, then they need to be really clear why they want to change and be prepared to commit themselves to the sustained effort involved in changing ingrained behaviours – that is, developing intrinsic motivation. Rewards can only add to or enhance such motivation, not replace it.

Some coachees can be very articulate about the reasons for their procrastination, which impresses the coach who then assumes it is the prelude to forthcoming action, and so respectfully listens and listens and listens ... but nothing happens. What the coach wants to be impressed with is action, not articulacy, and therefore he encourages the coachee to start carrying out an avoided behaviour *in the session* (e.g. making notes for an article) and maintaining the new behaviour between the sessions (finishing the article and sending it off to the publisher within an agreed timescale).

Tackling procrastination

Dryden (2000a) specifies four key stages to overcoming procrastination: becoming aware of one's procrastination; developing goal-directed behaviour to carry out currently avoided tasks; making a commitment to tolerate short-term discomfort in order to achieve longer-term gains; and being persistent in maintaining an anti-procrastination outlook. I will use a person from my coaching practice to illustrate progress through these stages.

Awareness

Paul (not his real name) was a therapist who wanted to move into coaching and enrolled on some courses to learn more about the subject. Having completed the training, he continually put off finding people to coach, saying 'the conditions have to be right before I make my move' and 'maybe I need more training, maybe I'm running before I can walk'. As Knaus (1998: 68) asks in relation to generating awareness regarding one's present behaviour: 'How do you know when you need to stop doing one thing and start doing something else?' One clue to answering this question was Paul's agitation about not 'getting on with it' (i.e. seeking people to coach), which his rationalisations for the delay could not ease. Imagery is a good technique to 'bypass defenses of rationalization and intellectualization' (Weishaar, 1993: 117), therefore I asked Paul to imagine making an immediate start in seeking coachees and how did he feel in doing so?

Paul: If I was going to start now, I would feel pretty anxious.

Coach: What is anxiety-provoking in your mind about starting now?
    [This is to focus his attention on searching for the beliefs driving his anxiety.]

Paul: Well, I'll have to put myself out there, you know, find people to coach, start proving myself.

Coach: And if you do that . . .?
    [This is called conjunctive phrasing – removing the full stop at the end of the coachee's sentence and inserting a conjunction such as 'and' or 'if'. This is done to nudge along the coachee's thinking.]

Paul: I don't feel completely confident about coaching people.

Coach: And if you don't feel completely confident about coaching people . . .?
    [Continuing with conjunctive phrasing to refine the cognitive aspects of his anxiety.]

Paul: Then I'll fall flat on my face because they will see my lack of confidence. My clients will think that I don't know what I'm doing, they've wasted their money.

Coach: And if they do think that . . .?
    [What is the meaning for him of their putative thinking.]

Paul: Then I'll be a failure, never make it as a coach.

Coach: Is that what you're most anxious about: if you don't feel completely confident about your coaching skills, then you'll be revealed as a failure and your coaching career will be over?

          [This summary is to check if the coachee's critical A – what he is most anxious about in this situation – has been revealed.]

Paul: Yes, that's it, but I can't see a way forward at the present time.

The coachee's critical A triggered his irrational beliefs (B), 'I must be completely confident about my coaching abilities before I see any clients because if I don't give value for money, then I'll be a failure', which, in turn, drove his anxiety (C). In REBT terms, this is a rigid must leading to an extreme conclusion (self-depreciation) if the must is not met, which is likely to be the case as musts are infrequently met (Neenan and Dryden, 2002b).

Paul was able to see how his irrational beliefs maintained his procrastination: he was demanding to feel completely confident *before* taking on clients instead of realising that confidence develops over time through practising his coaching skills with clients. To be even more accurate, courage comes before confidence: without taking risky and uncomfortable steps into the unknown, confidence will not be given the chance to develop. However, awareness does not necessarily lead to action, as Paul had already read a book on procrastination that he said was very insightful but 'somehow the book didn't give me the kick-start I needed'. Coaching would show him how to self-administer the 'kick-start' as well as keep the process of change going.

Goals

In order to develop an action plan for change, Paul needed to pinpoint a clear, specific, measurable goal that was within his control to achieve. Initially, he said his goal was to 'stop procrastinating'. This goal was stated negatively (i.e. what he does not want to do) rather than in positive terms of what he wants to do. As Cormier and Cormier (1985: 223) observe:

> When the goal is stated positively, clients are more likely to encode and rehearse the things they want to be able to do rather than the things they want to avoid or stop. For example, it is fairly easy to generate an image of yourself watching TV. However, picturing yourself *not* watching TV is difficult [emphasis in original].

Paul put his goal in positive terms 'to become a coach' but this was a general directive for change rather than specifying the goal in concrete and measurable terms. After discussion to concentrate his thinking, he said his goal was 'to have at least two fee-paying clients within the next three months'.

Commitment

When a person states his goals for change, this does not automatically mean that he has committed himself to carrying out the hard work to achieve them – his commitment may be to lip service instead of active service. As Leahy (2006) points out, once the goal has been established, the person needs to ask herself two key questions: 'What do I have to do to get it?' and 'Am I willing to do it?' In coaching as well as therapy, some individuals want a largely effort-free progress towards their goals. Grieger (1991: 60) states that effecting change is 'a 24-hour-a-day, seven-day-a-week thing'. While this view may sound extreme, it can be used as a yardstick by coachees to measure their level of effort. If they want to make gains, then they need to embrace the daily discomfort of working on their difficulties *now* – no discomfort dodging! – in order to feel relatively comfortable later about continuing the work of change (Ellis, 2002). Also, the person is committing himself to 'the possibilities that change may bring, even when there is no existing evidence to support this. The coachee has to commit to the unknown' (Zeus and Skiffington, 2002: 131). The unknown is neutral and only turned into something fearful, dull or exciting depending on the coachee's perception of what the future might hold.

Paul said he took responsibility for carrying out the work to bring about the changes he wanted. The next step was to teach him to dispute (D) his procrastination-perpetuating irrational beliefs. This disputing process occurs after the ABCs of the problem have been established. Disputing relies primarily on five points to help coachees see the self-defeating nature of their beliefs (Dryden and Neenan, 2004):

1 **Rigidity versus flexibility** – rigid beliefs allow no other outcome than the one demanded, whereas flexible beliefs support your goal-directed efforts while acknowledging the possibility of setbacks and activating contingency plans if needed.
2 **Extremism versus non-extremism** – extreme appraisals of self, others or events are harsh and unbalanced, whereas non-extreme appraisals are balanced and compassionate, seeing oneself, others and events in the round.
3 **Logic** – this looks at the internal coherence of your beliefs: No matter how much you prefer something to occur or not to occur, does it follow logically from your preferences that this event therefore must or must not occur?
4 **Empiricism** – this looks at the realistic basis of your beliefs: Do they correspond with the world as it actually is (empirical reality) or with your demands of how the world must be?
5 **Pragmatism** (often the most effective dispute in both therapy and coaching) – this looks at the concrete consequences of holding on to your irrational beliefs: Where are they getting you?

Through this examination of Paul's irrational beliefs he was able to construct a rational alternative that helped him to manage better his considerable doubts about his coaching skills: 'I realise that my confidence as a coach will develop over time, not overnight, through practice and good supervision and maybe some clients will think I'm not value for money. If that happens, I will remind myself that I have no immunity from such experiences but what I won't do is call myself a failure based on these experiences; instead I will accept myself as a fallible person who is striving to improve his competence as a coach.' This rational alternative to his irrational belief was lengthy and elaborate as it needed to take a rounded view of his development as a coach in stark contrast to the all or nothing quality of his irrational beliefs. In time, Paul condensed his wordy rational belief to the terse: 'Confidence comes with doing, reflection and feedback, so get on with it!'

An orderly sequence of goal-directed action steps coupled to timely completion dates was agreed with Paul, such as establishing a minimum number of cold calls to Human Resources (HR) departments per week, preparing a coaching brochure, giving a presentation on the benefits of coaching to a local Chamber of Commerce meeting, practising coaching on some willing friends, seeking advice from experienced coaches. Paul said he would 'try' to carry out these steps. When people say they'll 'try', this suggests little effort or responsibility on their part to effect change and lacks the commitment that 'doing' denotes (Paul had been trying to overcome his procrastination without success, so it was important not to reproduce in coaching a failed strategy). A way to teach coachees the difference between trying and doing is to ask them if at the end of the session they will try to leave the room or actually leave it. Trying will keep them in the room for some time, maybe indefinitely, while doing means they will have left it in seconds. Doing, coupled with a careful review of what has been done, learnt and what needs to be done next, is much more likely to bring results than trying, which can become a vicious circle of constantly reviewing failed attempts at task completion. While Paul understood and accepted that 'doing gets the job done', he still faltered over its implementation.

Persistence

It can be easy for some coachees to think that an initial surge of productivity in tackling their procrastination heralds the end of their 'I'll do it tomorrow' attitudes. However, they can easily run out of steam after several days of effort and then find themselves reaching for their familiar excuses for inaction. As Ellis (1991: 10) has repeatedly stated: 'The power in people's "willpower" consists of their strong *determination* to change themselves *plus* persistent *work and practice* to carry out this determination' (italics in original). Paul started to lose momentum with his anti-procrastination plan, particularly with regard to cold calling HR departments in local businesses to promote his coaching practice – he made cold calling a 'hot' (i.e. emotionally charged) issue:

Paul: I'm getting demoralised with this cold calling business.

Coach: It can be a hard grind, but how are you demoralising yourself about it up here (tapping head)?

[Turning the coachee's attention towards his own thinking to start the investigation.]

Paul: I'm not demoralising myself. It's just what happens when people are not interested in your services.

Coach: Is it their job to help you set up your private practice?

[This is to remind him that setting up his private practice is his responsibility, not the shared responsibility of anyone he contacts for work.]

Paul: True, but it's still not nice being rejected every day.

Coach: Are they rejecting you or your services?

[Is the coachee able to see the difference?]

Paul: Well, it feels like it's both.

Coach: Feelings are not necessarily facts: when they turn down your services, do they say they are also rejecting you or is that the part you add on?

[The coach's hypothesis is that the coachee is rejecting himself when companies reject his services.]

Paul: Well, I didn't think of it like that. Of course they don't say 'we're rejecting you as well'. When I put the phone down, I think I'm a failure for not getting any work.

Coach: With that belief in mind, how does it affect subsequent phone calls?
          [Bringing the coachee back to the issue of self-demoralisation and its consequences.]

Paul: Well, I lose confidence in myself, just go through the motions on the phone; in fact, I often rush my spiel to get it over with and feel quite relieved, only temporarily though, when it's over. I hardly sound inspiring on the phone. I find ways to avoid the phone calls. I dread them. That failure belief is still with me.

Coach: Now, we've discussed that belief change occurs over time, not overnight. Do you remember some of the important steps in belief change?
          [Attempting to elicit the information from the coachee to assess his level of understanding of change processes. The coach does not want to do the coachee's thinking for him by telling him.]

Paul: If I want to get my new beliefs from here to here (pointing to his head, then his heart), I need to put them into practice every day, experience and tolerate the discomfort involved in change, keep pushing myself until I'm thinking and acting in the new way.

Coach: Experiencing some daily goal-directed discomfort is a sign of progress. What about the old beliefs?
          [Thinking in new ways does not mean that the old beliefs will slip quietly away.]

Paul: I know they're going to still trouble me but it is important to keep reminding myself of the unwanted consequences I'm getting if I hold on to them, so keep disputing those beliefs. But it's still a struggle to do it when there's no success!

Coach: No *immediate* success. Something I would like you to consider is the difference between failure and failing. Failure is the outcome of this process of seeking work as a coach; failing can be seen as the steps in this process, each step an attempt at finding clients. Failing doesn't have to mean failure; it can also mean that success is the outcome of a series of failings – you eventually get your first client. So, using this distinction, currently you're failing, but your efforts haven't ended in failure.

[The coach supplies some didactic input to bolster the coachee's efforts to find clients as well as giving him a 'break' from answering questions as this can be wearisome if it is the only mode of learning.]

Paul: I like that. That's a very interesting distinction to make – I never would have thought of that.

Coach: So what do you propose to do before our next session?

[Securing the coachee's commitment to carrying out further goal-directed steps.]

Paul: I'm going to put a sign by the phone, 'Only my services are being rejected, not me!', and keep at it by telling myself that by failing I can end up eventually succeeding.

Through such techniques, Paul was able to refocus his energies on working towards his three-month goal, which, at the end of this period, resulted in three fee-paying clients, one more than he had hoped for. By the end of coaching he had developed a new and effective (E) rational outlook, the last stage in the ABCDE model of identifying and over-coming psychological blocks to change: he accepted (without liking it) the uncertainty and hard work involved in setting up a coaching practice, and strove (not always successfully) to accept himself irrespective of the difficulties he encoun-tered in this endeavour.

In order to maintain their gains from coaching, coachees need to develop a 'maintenance message' which is a 'lifelong responsibility to protect your progress from your own forget-fulness, inaction or neglect' (Neenan and Dryden, 2006: 75). Coachees can spend a few minutes every day going over the benefits of their new beliefs; additionally, procrastination is likely to reappear from time to time and this can be dealt with by coachees searching for and disputing the rigid and extreme beliefs that have slipped back into their thinking.

Paul's maintenance message was 'Persevering Paul', which encapsulated the key REBT principles of striving for high frustration tolerance and self-acceptance, which, when internalised, helped to reduce the frequency, intensity and duration of his emotional difficulties. Paul's vulnerability to future episodes of procrastination was likely to be his doubts about his confidence and competence if a coachee was dissatisfied with his performance or cancelled appointments: 'I should be a better coach than I am and then this wouldn't happen.' He needed to remind himself on these occasions that no coach is immune from experiencing these events and that the criteria for evaluating his performance should be reasonable and realistic, not grandiose ('I should feel really confident all the time, have perceptive answers to all their questions and be seen as an outstanding coach'). His longer-term goal was to develop his coaching practice so that eventually there would be a 60 : 40 percentage split between his coaching and therapy clients, respectively. Booster sessions were agreed to monitor Paul's progress towards this goal.

Conclusion

Often the same problems appear in coaching as in therapy. This chapter has focused on the all too common problem of procrastination and how the REBT approach can help coaches, particularly those without a professional background in psychology, to understand both the factors maintaining it and what needs to be done to overcome it. To change a behavioural pattern such as procrastination 'requires *work*, and typically lots of it. Ironic as it may seem, the problem of avoiding work can only be solved by doing *more work*' (Knaus, 1993: 37; Knaus, 2010). This involves uncovering and then disputing vigorously the irrational beliefs, which insist that a task or situation, for whatever reason, is too difficult to face. By internalising an anti-procrastination outlook, coachees are then much less likely to squander their time – an irreplaceable resource, unlike cars, food or clothes – and, instead, harness it to the pursuit of important life goals.

Discussion issues

- Does coaching focus too much on 'selling' the exciting possibilities of change, thereby underplaying the hard work required to achieve this change?
- Many therapy approaches are adapted for coaching purposes. Is there a real difference in this adaption or is it just therapy in disguise?
- What do you think of the idea that there is always an emotional problem underpinning procrastination?
- What might be some of the strengths and limitations of rational emotive behavioural coaching?

References

Adair, J. (1988) *Effective Time Management*. London: Pan Books.

Anderson, J. P. (2002) Executive coaching and REBT: Some comments from the field. *Journal of Rational-Emotive and Cognitive-Behavior Therapy*, 20 (3/4): 223–233.

Cormier, W. H. and Cormier, L. S. (1985) *Interviewing Strategies for Helpers: Fundamental Skills and Cognitive Behavioural Interventions*, 2nd edn. Monterey, CA: Brooks/Cole.

DiMattia, D. J. (1991) Using RET effectively in the workplace. In M. E. Bernard (Ed.), *Using Rational-Emotive Therapy Effectively: A Practitioner's Guide*. New York: Plenum Press.

Dryden, W. (2000a) *Overcoming Procrastination*. London: Sheldon Press.

Dryden, W. (2000b) *Invitation to Rational-Emotive Psychology*, 2nd edn. London: Whurr.

Dryden, W. and Gordon, J. (1993a) *Peak Performance: Become More Effective at Work*. Didcot, UK: Mercury Business Books.

Dryden, W. and Gordon, J. (1993b) *Beating the Comfort Trap*. London: Sheldon Press.

Dryden, W. and Neenan, M. (2004) *Rational Emotive Behavioural Counselling in Action*, 3rd edn. London: Sage.

Dryden, W. and Neenan, M. (2006) *Rational Emotive Behaviour Therapy: 100 Key Points and Techniques*. Hove, UK: Routledge.

Ellis, A. (1972) *Executive Leadership: A Rational Approach*. New York: Albert Ellis Institute for REBT.

Ellis, A. (1991) Using RET effectively: Reflections and interview. In M. E. Bernard (Ed.), *Using Rational-Emotive Therapy Effectively: A Practitioner's Guide*. New York: Plenum Press.

Ellis, A. (1994) *Reason and Emotion in Psychotherapy* (revised and updated). New York: Birch Lane Press.

Ellis, A. (2002) *Overcoming Resistance*, 2nd edn. New York: Springer.

Freeman, A. and DeWolf, R. (1990) *Woulda, Coulda, Shoulda: Overcoming Regrets, Mistakes, and Missed Opportunities*. New York: Harper Perennial.

Grieger, R. and Boyd, J. (1980) *Rational-Emotive Therapy: A Skills-Based Approach*. New York: Van Nostrand Reinhold.

Grieger, R. M. (1991) Keys to effective RET. In M. E. Bernard (Ed.), *Using Rational-Emotive Therapy Effectively: A Practitioner's Guide*. New York: Plenum Press.

Hauck, P. (1980) *Brief Counseling with RET*. Philadelphia, PA: Westminster Press.

Hauck, P. (1982) *How To Do What You Want To Do*. London: Sheldon Press.

Knaus, W. J. (1993) Overcoming procrastination. In M. E. Bernard and J. L. Wolfe (Eds.), *The RET Resource Book for Practitioners*. New York: Albert Ellis Institute for REBT.

Knaus, W. J. (1998) *Do It Now! Break The Procrastination Habit*, 2nd edn. New York: Wiley.

Knaus, W. (2010) *End Procrastination Now! Get it Done with a Proven Psychological Approach*. New York: McGraw-Hill.

Kodish, S. P. (2002) Rational emotive behaviour coaching. *Journal of Rational-Emotive and Cognitive-Behavior Therapy*, *20*(3/4): 235–246.

Lazarus, A., Lazarus, C. and Fay, A. (1993) *Don't Believe It For a Minute: Forty Toxic Ideas That Are Driving You Crazy*. San Luis Obispo, CA: Impact Publishers.

Leahy, R. L. (2006) *The Worry Cure*. London: Piatkus.

Neenan, M. and Dryden, W. (2002a) *Life Coaching: A Cognitive-Behavioural Approach*. Hove, UK: Brunner-Routledge

Neenan, M. and Dryden, W. (2002b) *Cognitive Behaviour Therapy: An A–Z of Persuasive Arguments*. London: Whurr.

Neenan, M. and Dryden, W. (2006) *Rational Emotive Behaviour Therapy in a Nutshell*. London: Sage.

Palmer, S. (2009) Rational coaching: A cognitive behavioural approach. *The Coaching Psychologist*, *5*(1): 12–18.

Persaud, R. (2005) *The Motivated Mind: How To Get What You Want From Life*. London: Bantam Books.

Sapadin, L. and Maguire, J. (1996) *It's About Time: The Six Styles of Procrastination and How to Overcome Them*. New York: Penguin.

Weishaar, M. E. (1993) *Aaron T. Beck*. London: Sage.

Zeus, P. and Skiffington, S. (2002) *The Coaching at Work Toolkit*. Sydney: McGraw-Hill Australia.

Recommended reading

Knaus, W. (2010) *End Procrastination Now! Get it Done with a Proven Psychological Approach.* New York: McGraw-Hill.

Neenan, M. and Dryden, W. (2002) *Life Coaching: A Cognitive-Behavioural Approach.* Hove, UK: Brunner-Routledge.

2

Motivational interviewing

Tim Anstiss and
Jonathan Passmore

Introduction

In this chapter we will explore the use of motivational interviewing (MI) as a tool for coaches seeking to facilitate change
in their coachees. In the first section we will explore the
background to MI before moving on to consider the principles that underpin the approach. It is argued that whilst MI
is not strictly cognitive behavioural, it shares some overlap
with both cognitive behavioural and humanistic approaches
and is a very useful style for the cognitive behavioural coach
to be able to move into when required, as well as being an
excellent style for facilitating engagement with coaching. In
the final section, we will focus on illustrating the approach
through examples using detailed transcripts and commenting
on these interactions to provide a detailed insight for coaches
on how the approach may be used for real.

Background

Motivational interviewing is 'a person-centered method of
guiding to elicit and strengthen personal motivation for
change' (Miller and Rollnick, 2009). It has been proven to be
effective in helping people change a wide range of health
related behaviours, including smoking, drinking, substance
misuse, drug-taking, dietary management, sexual health,
physical activity and medication-taking (Burke, Arkowitz
and Menchola, 2003). We argue that MI is an efficient method
of helping people change that can be used by a range of

practitioners, working with clients with different health and performance problems, and in a wide range of settings from organisational to life and health management.

One reason why MI may be proving to be so powerful is that it works in harmony with the coachee's own natural change processes. It aims to provoke intrinsic motivation to change within the individual, in contrast with many approaches that seek to impose an external force for change. Such external forces often result in resistance and withdrawal from counselling or coaching. Motivational interviewing develops intrinsic motivation through building a powerful relationship with the client, including using specific skills and strategies for building empathy, reducing resistance, developing 'change talk' and building client or coachee confidence.

The approach has a spirit, which has been characterised as being collaborative, evocative and autonomy-supporting. Motivational interviewing is done with clients rather than to them, with practitioner and client working in partnership to explore issues and discover the best way forward. 'Expert' advice is rarely given, and certainly not given unless asked for. The approach seeks to evoke arguments in favour of change – as well as options, goals and plans for change – from the client and has an optimistic view of human nature. Practitioners believe that clients have an inner wisdom and a tendency to move towards health, success and well-being that can be discovered and tapped into. The approach both respects and helps develop client autonomy, accepting that they are the active decision-maker, and that decision-making itself is good for a person (even when the decision may not be optimal). The ability of a practitioner to manifest this spirit has been shown to help predict both client responsiveness to treatment and treatment outcome (Gaume, Gmel and Daeppen, 2008).

The approach seems to be in harmony with Ryan and Deci's self-determination theory (Ryan and Deci, 2000), which suggests that human beings have three psychological needs – for autonomy, competence and relatedness – and that when these needs are met human beings are likely to move towards improved health and functioning. Motivational interviewing helps to provide clients with each of these three psychological needs, or nutriments.

Sharing with humanistic approaches an emphasis on non-judgemental listening and the development of accurate empathy, MI is more focused than humanistic approaches on behaviour change and is more directed – for instance towards the exploration and resolution of ambivalence, and the elicitation and selective development of change talk (Miller and Rollnick, 2002).

The principles of MI

The principles of the MI approach (Miller and Rollnick, 2002; Rollnick, Miller and Butler, 2007) may be summarised around the acronym RULE:

- Resist the righting reflex.
- Understand your client's dilemma and motivations.
- Listen to your client.
- Empower your client.

The first is key – developing the ability not to jump in and try to fix the coachee, however much you care and however much you can see what it is they need to do (in your opinion) to get well or be successful. This is one of the issues that many practitioners, especially non-mental health clinicians, have real difficulty with – not least because they are trained to 'diagnose and fix' people within an acute illness model of care. The overall goal – improved coachee health, well-being and functioning – is the same, it is just that in MI the role of the coach is to facilitate the client in 'fixing' themselves. That is not to say that there is not a role for providing clients with expert information and advice, because there is. It is just that this is done in a particular way within an MI framework.

The second principle can also be considered a core task for the practitioner, helping them to bring into play the collaborative spirit of the approach. The approach can be considered a shared conversation and exploration about behaviour change, and in seeking to understand the coachee's dilemma and motivations the practitioner helps the coachee to understand these things too. The coachee should be doing some thinking, and silences are when the 'work' of the approach may be happening, as conflict between coachees' values, goals and behaviours are brought to light in their own mind and they get to see that behaviour change may be the best way to establish or re-establish inner harmony and cohesion.

Reflective listening is a core skill for using the approach. Questions have a role, as do summaries, but if you cannot make reflective listening statements, statements that guess at what the person meant, demonstrate listening and encourage the person to continue, then you probably cannot do MI.

Motivational interviewing empowers coachees in a number of ways, one of which is to specifically target and attempt to build confidence or self-efficacy in their ability to change. Self-efficacy is a predictor of the likelihood of someone initiating change, persisting with it and being successful (Maibach and Murphy, 1995), so it makes a lot of sense to work with a person to develop their self-efficacy, or to 'empower' them.

In addition to the above mentioned spirit and principles, MI practitioners sometimes use several strategies and exercises to help with the core tasks of helping the coachee explore and resolve their ambivalence about behaviour change, decide what to do and how to do it and build up their confidence about being successful. These strategies or tools include:

- Setting the scene.
- Agreeing on the agenda.
- Exploring a typical day.
- Assessing and building importance and confidence.
- Exploring two possible futures.
- Exploring options.
- Agreeing goals.
- Agreeing to a plan – including a plan for preventing relapse.

In this chapter we do not have the space to explore the details behind each of these but they are more fully explored by Rollnick et al. (2007).

Positioning MI as an intervention

In a recent paper entitled 'Ten things that motivational interviewing is not', Miller and Rollnick (2009) state that MI is neither cognitive behavioural therapy nor the transtheoretical model of change. It is also not: a way of tricking people into doing what you want them to do; a 'technique'; the decisional balance tool; assessment feedback; client-centred therapy; easy to learn; practice as usual; or a panacea.

It is argued that cognitive behavioural approaches tend to involve providing coachees with something they are presumed to lack – perhaps new or improved coping skills, more helpful patterns of thinking skills, self-management skills or environmental management skills. Cognitive behavioural practitioners also tend to confirm this skills deficit in the awareness of the coachee, and help them to consciously use a mix of interventions to better manage their thinking, feeling, behaviour and environment in the future.

Motivational interviewing, by contrast, does not involve the teaching of new skills, re-educating, counter-conditioning, changing the environment or installing more rational and adaptive beliefs. That is not to say that these things are not helpful – they are, with the right person at the right time. Rather, MI may be thought of as working with people at an early stage of change, either when they have not been thinking of changing or when they are unsure about whether or not to change and how they might best make the change. And once a person has decided to change, no further help may be necessary – they may be able to just go away and do it. This is the case in a very large number of cases – including in your own life. You just decide to change and you do it without professional help. Sometimes you might need to develop skills in order to change – for instance, to learn to drive a car, overcome chronic shyness, lose weight or deliver great presentations at work. But sometimes deciding to do it is enough for people to get going with change on their own. The focus of MI might be considered to be on this decision-making phase of behaviour change. Cognitive behavioural approaches might be considered to focus on the skills development phases.

Let us take juggling as an example and imagine a coachee who is thinking of developing some kind of circus skill to show her child and his friends at his birthday party. Motivational interviewing might be useful in helping the person decide whether or not the skill should be juggling, as well as how to go about getting better at it. They may then just go away and learn to juggle on their own, or they may decide to enrol in a circus skills course or consult a juggling coach to learn how to juggle. Motivational interviewing is not about teaching people to juggle. It is about helping them decide whether or not they want to juggle, how they might go about it, when they might start, how they will know if they have been successful and what help they might need. It also helps to build up their confidence (self-efficacy) that if they did decide to learn to juggle they would likely be successful.

So whilst MI may not best be considered a cognitive behavioural approach, it can nevertheless be a very helpful approach for cognitive behavioural practitioners to be able to do with their coachees, for a number of reasons. One reason is the frequency with which people receiving a cognitive behavioural approach do not do the things likely to help them, or the things they agreed to do as homework. Moving into an MI style and approach, perhaps using one or more of the MI strategies, might prove an effective and efficient way for helping to improve the likelihood that coachees will make the changes thought likely to be helpful – be they skills practice, goal-setting, behavioural experimentation, response avoidance, thought-capturing or reframing – and it will do this by getting the coachee to argue in favour of making changes, not the practitioner. The coachee will explore the reason why it is important for them to make certain changes and how they might best go about it. Pressure to change from the practitioner will be avoided, since this is likely to lead to increased resistance to change as the coachee naturally tries to demonstrate their autonomy and freedom.

Using MI for real

Motivational interviewing to date has very limited reference within the coaching literature (Anstiss and Passmore, in press; Passmore, 2007; Passmore and Whybrow, 2007; Passmore, Anstiss and Ward, 2009; Passmore, 2011a, 2011b, in press–a, in press-b; Newnham-Kanas, Morrow and Irwin, 2010). These papers have adopted a more theoretical, techniques description or alternatively a case study approach, in contrast with detailed RCT studies conducted in health psychology. In this section we will explore using MI for real, and to bring this alive we have included a series of transcripts, each of which contains a short commentary to illustrate various elements of the MI process. The extracts are drawn sequentially (but sometimes with gaps in between) from a real case involving a coachee presenting with chronic pain who was considering taking more exercise. The coach was an expert in physical activity and exercise programming, having spent several years working in the fitness industry and ending up as group fitness manager for a health club chain. Notice, however, the almost complete lack of any advice-giving about what exercises to do and how to do them from the coach. The approach is almost relentlessly coachee focused. This example has been chosen to give a flavour or feeling of the MI approach to behaviour change.

Setting the scene and agreeing the agenda

Approach

Emphasise personal control and choice, explicitly telling the client that they will not be forced into making any changes they do not want to make – thus minimising resistance and supporting their autonomy. Get their active involvement in the conversation by 'agenda-setting'.

Example

Coach: So, Mary, thank you for coming along today.
Coachee: Okay.
Coach: I understand that your doctor said it would be a good idea for us to have a chat about physical activity. Is that your understanding?
Coachee: Yes. He doesn't think I do enough, really.

Coach: Okay. Right. Well we have about twenty minutes today, to talk about physical activity. And what I really want to do is get an understanding of how you feel about it. What your thoughts are. What I'm certainly not going to do is try and force you into a programme of activity that you're not ready or unable to do. Is that okay?

Coachee: Yes. That's fine.

Coach: Is there anything in particular that you want to talk about today?

Comment

In this example the coach sets the scene, checks the coachee's understanding, communicates his aim (to understand her thoughts and feelings and not to pressure her into change), checks with the coachee that this is okay and then asks if there is anything they want to talk about – and does this all efficiently. These 'setting the scene' and 'agenda-setting' strategies help to create a coachee expectation that they can talk freely (if they want to) about the behaviour without fear of trying to be persuaded or coerced into change. If coachees talk freely about their health behaviour, then the MI practitioner can get on with the core tasks of developing empathy and rapport, helping them to explore and resolve ambivalence about behaviour change, noticing and developing any change talk and building coachee confidence. If coachees feel they are going to be pressured into change they may not 'open up', and if they feel it is all about the practitioner's agenda they may slip towards passivity in the conversation and feel that what concerns them is not as important as what concerns the referring agent or the coach.

Gaining a good understanding of how the behaviour fits into the client's life

Approach

Listen non-judgementally without conveying a sense of the rating or scoring of the behaviour that commonly happens in health assessment. The MI practitioner sometimes uses the 'typical day' strategy to help with this task.

Example

Coach: Is there anything in particular that you want to talk about today?

Coachee: Um ... probably the way of actually accessing some of it. Some of it I find quite difficult to access, and maybe we can talk about that. Maybe you can help me find a way of actually getting to these places or, you know, accessing some of the facilities that are more difficult to access?

Coach: Right. As a way of increasing what you do?

Coachee: Yeah. Yeah.

Coach: Right. Certainly. Well perhaps a good way to get started – because we've never met before – is just to understand where physical activity fits into your life at the moment. And I know that you experience pain.

Coachee: A lot, yeah.

Coach: And so it would be good to get an understanding of that. And the best way to get going, I think, is for you to walk me through a day that's fairly typical in your life. Just so I can understand where physical activity fits in. Would that be okay?

Coachee: Yeah. A typical day is not really what happens in my life. You know, I've been a ... I do quite a lot of travelling around in the car, and that exacerbates pain, so that makes it very difficult. I basically only do one real, what I would call exercise session a week. Where I do an aqua-aerobics class. I help out with an aqua-aerobics class. So for an hour a week. So that's really the only exercise I do. If I go out shopping or something like that, some days it's okay, other days by the time I've got halfway around the supermarket, I can't walk anymore.

Coach: Right. Your pain really influences what you can do.

Coachee: I'm in pain all the time. It just gets worse with walking. I have an artificial leg. That gives me back pain, and I also have some neurological pain from the damage to my spine at the neck. So it's a combination of things that I have a lot of pain which is neurological pain, and then the mechanical pain will come in on top of that, and then I end up just walking out of a supermarket and saying, sorry, can't do it.

Coach: It just gets too much for you.

Coachee: It's all too much, you know, and if I push too far, then I can end up a wreck in a pile of tears in the corner, I just can't do it.

Coach: So you know your limitations. You know what you can do, and when you absolutely need to stop, and it's the pain that influences that.

Coachee: One of the biggest problems is knowing when to stop, because sometimes you're enjoying it, and you're doing it, and it's fine, and then later on you think 'I really shouldn't have done that one'. You know, it's keeping it to a level that is manageable. But sometimes, if you're wanting to go to do some exercise, by the time you've got through all the rigmarole of getting ready and got there, you're so tired. . . .

Coach: You've got to that point already before you've started.

Coachee: You know, and is it worth doing? I mean this is probably part of the barrier that I have. Is all that effort to do it – I get down there and I'm actually so exhausted that the pleasure of doing anything has gone by the time I get there. I do enjoy swimming, that's one thing that I find very, very useful, but it's just getting down to the swimming pool, getting changed, getting in, what to do – five minutes? Sometimes I think, is it worth it?

Coach: Yeah. It's kind of demoralising that you think, I want to do it, because when I actually do it it's enjoyable, and I actually get something positive from it. But by the same token, it requires a lot of investment in terms of your energy, and then when you get to that point, it's all got to stop. And that gets you down.

Comment

The practitioner expresses a desire to understand more about two different (but interrelated) things – the coachee's pain and her physical activity patterns – and sets up the 'typical day' exercise in the standard way. But the coachee says she does not have a typical day. Nevertheless, she starts talking about how the pain and physical activity interact. Knowing that manifesting the spirit and principles of MI is much more important than getting a coachee to follow a particular 'tool' or 'strategy', the practitioner just follows the flow of conversation of the coachee, using several skilful reflective listening statements to check and communicate understanding, help communicate empathy and build rapport – all critical to good outcomes. As the coachee continues to talk, her dilemma is revealed – she enjoys exercise and wants its benefits, but finds it hard to get into a session or activity, or doing the right level.

The final statement by the practitioner is a mini-summary, taking the form of a double-sided reflection. The coach tries to accurately capture both sides of the coachee's ambivalence, and present it back to her. This serves several purposes – showing the coach has been listening, helping the coachee hear things that might be important again and giving the coachee a chance to agree or disagree with the statement and either move on or further clarify what she meant or how she feels about the subject. It helps the coachee feel heard, and feel that her concerns are valid and important.

Building empathy and communicating understanding

Approach

Make frequent use of OARS throughout the conversation: Open questions, Affirmations, Reflective listening statements and Summaries.

Example

Coach: So let me see if I understand you correctly. Your pain is influencing, in your life, a lot of things. It influences what you do [coachee says 'absolutely'], it influences the choices that you have. And that has an effect on you in terms of how you feel about yourself, the psychology, if you like. It gets you down when you're not able to do the things that you like to do, that you want to do. That you enjoy doing.

Coachee: Yes. I mean, it's not just me, it affects my partner as well. Because I can't go and do things, that's restricting him. You know, we like to go to craft fairs, and that's very difficult to do. Even in a wheelchair, I get very uncomfortable, so it limits what both of us can do. So it's not just my life that's limited, it's also other people's, and that's even more demoralising actually. I think that's even harder to take.

Coach: Right. Yeah. There are things that you want to do together, there are things that you enjoy together, and this pain influences. . . .

Coachee: And I'm the one stopping us doing it. And that makes me feel very guilty, so there's a lot of guilt involved as well.

Coach: Yeah. Yeah. And that has an effect on how you feel about yourself.

Coachee: Definitely. Yeah (laughs).

Comment

The summary at the start of this example helps the coachee to feel understood and encourages her to continue to talk.

A skilful reflection by the practitioner ('There are things that you want to do together, there are things that you enjoy together, and this pain influences . . .') brings out new information from the client – that she experiences guilt. A cognitive behavioural practitioner might at this stage be thinking: *Aha, a possibly unhealthy emotion (guilt) and some A→C thinking too ('makes me feel guilty'). Perhaps I might ask her about how helpful this feeling of guilt is, why she has it and explore with them where it comes from – perhaps helping her discover and change any associated irrational beliefs. If she experienced less guilt and reduced her A→C thinking then her health and well-being might improve.* The MI practitioner, however, is more concerned about understanding, and helping the coachee understand, her ambivalence about becoming more physically active – not in helping her change unhelpful thinking patterns. The guilt she feels is part of the motivational picture about not being able to exercise – albeit a little towards the extrinsic end of the motivational spectrum.

Talking about the benefits of changing

Approach

Use open ended questions to have the client talk about the good things related to the behaviour change.

Example

Coach: There's something really positive in it, and I was just wondering if you could describe the last time that you had that sense, that this is a real beneficial thing for me, it's something I'm in . . . I'm in control of.

Coachee: I think Monday. I think part of the . . . part of the thing is I actually help other people in the pool, so I'm working with people who aren't confident in the pool. So I'm actually doing the exercises, but I'm doing it *with* somebody else, and I'm helping somebody else, so that gives me a great deal of sort of, um, I suppose it's kudos, really. I . . . I enjoy doing it, I enjoy seeing how they get on, and to be able to get somebody who's so unconfident in water, to actually leave the side and do exercises, it's a great buzz. You know, I get more out of it than they do, I'm sure.

Coach: You get a sense of achievement.

Coachee: I do.
Coach: In their achievement.
Coachee: Yes, absolutely. And it's – I feel like I'm actually *doing* something and I think that's part of the . . . um. . . .
Coach: You're contributing.
Coachee: Yes, yes, I'm doing something *useful* for a change, and I'm also getting the exercise as well. If I was going on my own, I don't think I'd get quite so much of a kick about it. And I think that because I'm . . . because I'm working *with* other people, and I feel that I would let them down, that's a big, for me a big stimulus for me, getting going and doing it.

Comment

The MI practitioner enquires about the benefits of changing in a number of ways – looking backwards to a time when the behaviour was more common, asking for examples, looking forwards to a time when the behaviour might be happening more, explicitly asking about the good things about changing and the reasons for doing it. In this case the coach asked the coachee to talk more about a recent time when she experienced good feelings associated with the behaviour. Asking the coachee to elaborate is also a strategy that can help to elicit or develop more change talk. The strategy brought out the following from the coachee: that she gets a great buzz from helping others, and a feeling of kudos, achievement and doing something useful. She also told the practitioner some more about her personal motivation for taking exercise. How important do you think feelings of 'usefulness' and 'achievement' are to the health and well-being of someone experiencing chronic pain? In fact they are very important.

Making the transition from phase 1 to phase 2

Approach

At the right time (a slightly intuitive call on the part of the practitioner, when they feel enough exploration has been done, resistance is low, change talk has emerged and they feel the coachee may well be ready to decide whether or not to change) the practitioner summarises key aspects of the coachee story so far and asks the coachee what she thinks she will do. The practitioner continues to manifest the evocative spirit of the approach – drawing the solution out of the coachee, rather than jumping in with unasked-for advice. During phase 2, once a decision has been made to change (or stay the same), the practitioner may start to build coachee confidence and commitment, helping to develop a more concrete plan – who, what, when, where – whilst enquiring about any support that might increase the coachee's confidence (self-efficacy) and help the coachee to be successful. In many ways this is similar to the OW elements of the GROW coaching model.

Example

Coach: Right. So let's see where we're going here. We're sort of nearing the end of the consultation, so let me see if I understand what you've said correctly. Currently you're doing about one session of activity a week [*yes*]. And that's swimming. Something that you enjoy doing [*hmmm-hmmm*], albeit it's sometimes difficult to get to that point [*yup*], and you get a sense of ... that you're in control of this pain. The pain is something that influences what you do, the choices in your life, and you've described how you want to be in control of this pain, and taking more activity is one thing that you [*hmmm, yeah*] can do to control the pain, okay, both in your mind and physically [*hmmm*] as well. And when you do the things that you do, in terms of the swimming, you get a sense of control, and you're adding benefit to other people, which shows that. . . .

Coachee: Yes, yes I do, I think that's a very good way of putting it, yeah.

Coach: And if you were to *increase* the amount that you did, over and above what you're doing, then you feel you would slow down any decline in your condition.

Coachee: That would be the hope (laughs).

Coach: And any programme, if you did decide to change, would need to take account of the fluctuation [*hmmm-hmmm*] in your day-to-day pain [*yes, yes*], and also would need to bear in mind that things are, from your perspective, changing.

Coachee: Yes. I think a constant review. If you're put onto a scheme and told 'go away and do it' that's all very well, but I think you do need to have a constant review and not to be told 'well you're just chronic, and away you go'. You do need to have that facility to come back and say well, this is what I've done [*okay*], and check it out on a regular basis.

Coach: Do you think that's something that we should be doing?

Coachee: Yes I do.

Coach: Would it be a good idea for you to book an appointment to see me again in a period of time?

Coachee: Yes, I think that would be a really good idea.

Coach: What would that period of time be for you, ideally?

Coachee: Um, I think probably three months [*okay, all right*] and then you know, if things were going well, then extend it, or at that stage, if I felt that I needed to talk to you about other things, then perhaps we could shorten it, but I think, you know, to start off on something and say, come back in three months and see how it's going, that might be a way of going forward.

Coach: And what's *it*, then? What would you be prepared to do, given our conversation today. What do you think you'll do?

Coachee: Um, I think I'm going to have to see if I can bully a friend into going swimming with me. That's, uh, I think that might be the way forward.

Coach: Do you have a friend in mind?

Coachee: Yes, I've got another friend who's also, you know, also suffers from pain, and I think the pair of us will probably benefit from doing a little bit of exercise. So maybe, just once a week or something, the two of us get together and do something [*right*], that's a step forward and if it, uh, if we can get into a pattern of it, at least that's another chunk [*all right*] forward.

Coach: So you'd be doing two sessions.

Coachee: Don't want to overdo it (laughs).

Coach: It's got to be right for you.

Coachee: Yeah, that's right.

Coach: And when would you call them?

Coachee: You're putting me on the spot here, aren't you? Um, how about this afternoon?

Coach: You'd do it this afternoon? [*yep*] Okay, all right, with a view to what?

Coachee: Well, to talk through how they feel about doing the same thing [*okay*], and if we could actually do something together [*okay*]. But, uh, you know, it might be good to know if you have other people coming through, and that you talk to, that you know, you could be put in touch with each other or something, I don't know, from the practice point of view, it would be a good idea.

Coach: Yes, we do have groups who meet on a regular basis, and that's something that we could talk about.

Coachee: Yeah, that would be great.

Coach: All right, so should we end it there today?

Coachee: Yes, okay.

Comment

The practitioner somewhat selectively reflects back to the coachee the reasons she came up with for becoming more active. In this way, she gets to hear it several times – in her head, when she first spoke it and when the practitioner reflects it back. It is also very hard for the coachee to argue against reasons she has articulated. The coachee states that a review would be helpful, and is given a degree of control over the frequency and duration of this ongoing support. The coachee also enquires about other forms of community support that might be available, and the practitioner agrees to signpost her towards these. The practitioner gets the coachee to come out with and agree to take some very concrete but do-able steps, including phoning a specific friend this afternoon with a view to going swimming twice a week, and arranging a follow-up session with the practitioner. From starting the conversation unsure about how best to become and stay more active, the coachee has come up with her own solution – drawn out by the coach.

The coach asks a nice open question (two actually) to move the coachee towards making a decision: 'What would you be prepared to do, given our conversation today. What do you think you'll do?' Asking the coachee what she is prepared to do to help herself achieve the benefits she has articulated is a powerful way of developing coachee autonomy as well as encouraging means–end thinking (if I do this, then I expect this will occur).

The coachee also suggests that going swimming with a friend 'might be the way forward'. This is not really change talk – it *might* be the way forward. The coach decides to see if this can be worked up into a commitment, as commitments are more likely to result in actual change. The coach asks 'Do you have a friend in mind?' and then continues to ask open questions until the coachee agrees to call him at a particular time to help her become more active.

There is a slight suggestion of resistance when the coachee states that she does not 'want to overdo it'. The coach skilfully 'rolls with resistance' here, using a simple reflection to ensure that the coachee feels heard and to re-emphasise that the client is in charge: 'It's got to be right for you'.

Conclusion

Motivational interviewing is an evolving, evidence based style of talking with people, with proven efficacy in helping people change a variety of behaviours. It has some overlap with both humanistic and cognitive behavioural approaches, sharing with them a positive view of human nature, but working with and alongside different aspects of the coachee's psyche. The approach is learnable, although, like learning to play a musical instrument, significant practice and feed-back are required for practitioners to become competent in using this sophisticated method.

Cognitive behavioural coaches might benefit from being able to adopt, or drop into, the MI style for several reasons – not least improving coachee engagement with the coaching process and increasing the likelihood that coachees will make the behaviour changes they desire or need to make for improved health, well-being, performance and success.

Discussion issues

- Would you agree with Miller and Rollnick that motivational interviewing is neither cognitive behavioural therapy nor the transtheoretical model of change?
- Reflective listening is considered a core skill for MI. Is it also a core skill of cognitive behavioural coaching?
- Can cognitive behavioural coaches benefit from being able to adopt, or drop into, the MI style?

References

Anstiss, T. and Passmore, J. (in press) *Health Coaching*. London: Karnac.

Burke, B. L., Arkowitz, I. I. and Menchola, M. (2003) The efficacy of motivational interviewing: A meta analysis of controlled clinical trials. *Journal of Consulting Clinical Psychology*, 71: 843–861.

Gaume, J., Gmel, G. and Daeppen, J. B. (2008) Brief alcohol interventions: Do counsellors' and patients' Communication characteristics predict change? *Alcohol and Alcoholism*, 43: 62–69.

Maibach, E. and Murphy, D. A. (1995) Self-efficacy in health promotion research and practice: Conceptualization and measurement. *Health Education Research: Theory and Practice*, 10: 37–50.

Miller, W. R. and Rollnick, S. (2002) *Motivational Interviewing: Preparing People for Change*, 2nd edn. New York: Guilford Press.

Miller, W. R. and Rollnick, S. (2009) Ten things that motivational interviewing is not. *Behavioural and Cognitive Psychotherapy*, 37(2): 129–140.

Newnham-Kanas, C., Morrow, D. and Irwin, J. D. (2010) Motivational coaching: A functional juxtaposition of three methods for health behaviour change—Motivational interviewing, coaching, and skilled helping. *International Journal of Evidence Based Coaching and Mentoring*, 8(2): 27–48.

Passmore, J. (2007) Addressing deficit performance through coaching: Using motivational interviewing for performance improvement in coaching. *International Coaching Psychology Review*, 2(3): 265–279.

Passmore, J. (2011a) MI techniques – Reflective listening. *The Coaching Psychologist*, 7(1): 49–52.

Passmore, J. (2011b) Motivational Interviewing: A model for coaching psychology practice. *The Coaching Psychologist*, 7(1): 35–39.

Passmore, J. (in press-a) MI techniques: Balance sheet. *The Coaching Psychologist*, 7(2).

Passmore, J. (in press-b) MI techniques: Typical day. *The Coaching Psychologist*, 8(1).

Passmore, J. and Whybrow, A. (2007) Motivational interviewing: A specific approach for coaching psychologists. In S. Palmer and A. Whybrow (Eds.), *Handbook of Coaching Psychology: A Guide for Practitioners*. Hove, UK: Routledge.

Passmore, J., Anstiss, T. and Ward, G. (2009) This way out: Motivational interviewing. *Coaching at Work*, 4(2): 38–41.

Rollnick, S., Miller, W. and Butler, C. (2007) *Motivational Interviewing in Health Care: Helping Patients Change Behavior*. New York: Guilford Press.

Ryan, R. M. and Deci, E. L. (2000) Self-determination theory and the facilitation of intrinsic motivation, social development, and well-being. *American Psychologist*, 55: 68–78.

Recommended reading

Anstiss, T. (2009) Motivational interviewing in primary care. *Journal of Clinical Psychology in Medical Settings*, 16(1): 87–93.

Anstiss, T. and Passmore, J. (in press) *Health Coaching*. London: Karnac.

Miller, W. R. and Rollnick, S. (2009) Ten things that motivational interviewing is not. *Behavioural and Cognitive Psychotherapy*, 37(2): 129–140.

Passmore, J. and Whybrow, A. (2007) Motivational interviewing: A specific approach for coaching psychologists. In S. Palmer and A. Whybrow (Eds.), *Handbook of Coaching Psychology: A Guide for Practitioners*. Hove, UK: Routledge.

Rollnick, S., Miller, W. and Butler, C. (2007) *Motivational Interviewing in Health Care: Helping Patients Change Behavior*. New York: Guilford Press.

3

Enhancing the coaching alliance and relationship

Alanna O'Broin and Stephen Palmer

As coaches we strive for effective coaching relationships with our coachees. Much like other helping relationships (Hardy, Cahill and Barkham, 2007), a coaching relationship needs to be established, developed and maintained. The coaching relationship is considered a critical factor in the coaching process (Bluckert, 2005; Kemp, 2009; Lowman, 2005) although research studies reporting its importance in the nascent coaching relationship literature remain scarce (Gyllensten and Palmer, 2007; De Haan, 2008; O'Broin and Palmer, 2010a). There have been a number of comparisons of the coaching relationship with other helping relationships, such as the therapeutic relationship (Hart, Blattner and Leipsic, 2001; Price, 2009; Spinelli, 2008) and coach–athlete relationship (Jowett, O'Broin and Palmer, 2010; O'Broin and Palmer, 2006). Such comparisons and adaptations of existing theories, methods and interventions to coaching practice may prove invaluable (Bachkirova, 2007: 363). However, dedicated coaching theories, comprehensive and inclusive empirical grounding for coaching research and evaluation frameworks have yet to be developed (Fillery-Travis and Lane, 2006; Lowman, 2005; Kauffman and Bachkirova, 2009). Evidence-informed coaching approaches (e.g. Stober and Grant, 2006) suggest that the coach draws on best current knowledge, often in established literature in allied fields of knowledge, theory and practice, in deciding how to deliver coaching to their coachees.

Cognitive behavioural coaching (CBC; Palmer and Szymanska, 2007; Williams, Edgerton and Palmer, 2010) is closely based on the adaptation of cognitive, cognitive behavioural and rational emotive behavioural therapy to coaching (Dryden, 2011; Ducharme, 2004; Neenan, 2008; Neenan and Dryden, 2002; Palmer and Gyllensten, 2008). Ultimately the aim of CBC is for the coachee to become his/ her own self-coach (Neenan, 2006).

This chapter delineates a CBC perspective on the coaching relationship, drawing from published research in the coaching, working alliance, cognitive behavioural therapy and sports coaching and psychology literature. Negotiating and building an optimal coaching alliance, being explicit on views and the coach as self-coach are three primary themes explored to demonstrate how the coaching relationship can be enhanced and developed. The chapter also focuses on problem areas within the coaching relationship and how these can be addressed, using examples of coachee and coach thoughts and beliefs and coach–coachee dialogue.

A coaching alliance or a coaching relationship?

Negotiating and building an optimal coaching alliance

The coaching relationship is a broad concept incorporating any and all motivations and activities of the coachee and coach (Palmer and McDowall, 2010). Since not all relationships are likely to bring change (Castonguay and Beutler, 2006), focusing on relationship factors repeatedly linked to positive outcome, such as the working alliance (Horvath, 2006), is the strategy adopted here. Transferable to other change situations, the pantheoretic working alliance (Bordin, 1979) emphasises three interrelated features – goals, tasks and bonds – associated with purposive, collaborative work. O'Broin and Palmer (2010b) take up the theme of collaboratively creating the coaching alliance, suggesting that its explicit discussion, agreement and renegotiation over time can help to create the clarity and transparency vital for trust and respect in the coaching relationship.

In the left-hand column of Table 3.1 are five broad factors considered important in establishing, developing

Table 3.1 Key coaching alliance factors and their emphasis in the CBC alliance

Coaching alliance factors	Emphasis in CBC alliance
Active alliance negotiation	Collaborative and explicit negotiation and renegotiation by coach and coachee of goals, tasks and bonds
Alliance-fostering strategies	Explicit about views and model of coaching
Different conceptual approaches to the relationship	Coach as self-coach working with coachees to ultimately become their own self-coach
Awareness and management of interpersonal dynamics	A focus on coach and coachee's coaching-enhancing interpersonal dynamics and coaching-interfering blocks where appropriate
Renegotiation of any disruptions	Coaching-interfering interactions of coach and coachee's thinking, feeling and behaviour identified, acknowledged, discussed, validated and challenged where appropriate

Adapted and extended from Bordin (1979) and Hatcher and Barends (2006).

and maintaining a coaching alliance in any conceptual framework. Within each of these broader factors, those aspects particularly emphasised in a CBC perspective are shown in the right-hand column. A detailed discussion of differing conceptual approaches to the coaching alliance is beyond the scope of this chapter. However, it is noteworthy that other approaches may emphasise and/or reframe these individual aspects to a greater or lesser degree.

Turning to the three interrelated features of the coaching alliance, there needs to be a clear mutual understanding and agreement on goals, tasks and bonds.

Goals

The coach and coachee need to agree on the coaching goals and how to work towards achieving them. Coachees may also have mediating goals, which are stepping stones to the achievement of outcome goals. It is vital that the coachee understands the link between, and rationale for, the achievement of mediating goals in reaching their outcome goals. Finally, the coach has goals that they set themselves during the coaching process, often linked to the coachee's goals and reflecting the coachee's stage of change, preferences and individual differences.

Tasks

Aside from the *content* of the coaching tasks, a coaching alliance perspective on tasks requires that the coachee understands the nature and requirements of completing their own tasks, the rationale for the tasks of their coach and how their coach's tasks relate to their own. The coach has a role to play in ensuring that the coachee is able and willing to undertake and complete their tasks.

Bonds

Tailoring the alliance to the individual rather than applying a blanket approach may improve outcome effectiveness (Norcross, 2002; Norcross and Wampold, 2011). This 'bespoke' approach to therapy was also discussed by Lazarus (1989), with the therapist behaving as an 'authentic chameleon', able to adapt their relational style to their client's needs. CBC encourages a collaborative and explicit outlook to the use of the coaching model in working towards the coachee's goals. This chapter argues that this outlook extends to the views, beliefs, attitudes, feelings and behaviours of the coach and coachee where such dynamics add to, and detract from, the collaborative purposive work of the coaching alliance.

Bordin (1979) described the broad affective bond involving liking, trust and respect, as well as a second, narrower bond concept – the 'work-supporting bond' (Hatcher and Barends, 2006) supporting the goals and tasks and linking the three interrelated features to the core alliance issue of joint purposive work. The work-supporting bond in coaching (see O'Broin and Palmer, 2010c) suggests that the coach and coachee seek an optimal level of bond for

the particular coachee in the specific context and renegotiate this bond over time, as feelings that the dyad have
towards each other may change during coaching (Bluckert,
2006). Which variables should the coach consider varying?
Dryden's (2008a) discussion of the bond provides two
suggested areas applicable to the coaching alliance:

1 **Adapting according to the coachee's 'stage of
   change'.** Applied to a wide range of problem behaviours
   and individual and organisational change, the stages of
   change model (Prochaska and DiClemente, 1983) proposes
   a cyclical change process through six overlapping stages.
   Depending on the coachee's current stage, the interventions of the coach need to adapt to the coachee's requirements in that stage (Grant, 2006: 172).

2 **Adapting according to the coachee's interpersonal
   preferences and relational style.** Dryden (2008b)
   outlines formal/informal relational style, influence preferences and degree of reactance/dependence, also advocating asking the client their explicit preferences, in
   determining how to tailor one's approach. General questions such as 'What things could I do that would be particularly helpful to you – and why would they be helpful?'
   and relational style questions such as 'Would it help you
   most if I was relatively formal or informal in our interactions – and why?' can assist in explicitly negotiating and
   building the bond in the alliance.

Being explicit about the views of coaching

Turning to our second theme, in an expanded model of the
working alliance Dryden (2006, 2008a) adds 'views' as a
fourth feature (highly applicable to explicit negotiation of
the coaching alliance). These 'views', held by coach and
coachee, range from views on practicalities (frequency,
length, cost, venue for meetings, cancellation, contact and
access policy to each other) to the nature of the coachee's
block, how the block may be best addressed, how the coach
conceptualises and understands the coachee and the
coachee's views on coaching. These views require explicit

discussion and agreement as part of the formation of a coaching alliance, much as the goals, tasks and bond features do. Discussion will help to clarify the similarities or differences of the views. Differences require acknowledgement, discussion and negotiation, the outcome being either that the coaching relationship proceeds or, if a shared understanding cannot be reached, that the coach refers the coachee on.

Once the relationship has proceeded, Dryden (2008a) suggests an in-session 'reflective process' whereby the dyad explicitly discusses and deals with any doubts, misunderstandings or disruptions in the alliance as they occur, in order to seek to prevent irretrievable ruptures and renegotiate solutions to disruptions. The alliance may be strengthened by resolution of such threats. Similarly, Spinelli (2008) alludes to the tendency for coaches to use contracts as an explicit means of stating their preferred methods, as well as the requirement for flexibility in coaching frameworks for the conditions under which coaching can take place.

Coach as self-coach

The third theme, of the coach as self-coach, draws upon findings first from the coaching relationship literature. Along with increasing examination of interpersonal dynamics, the impact of the use of the self (Bluckert, 2006) and the presence of the coach (Spinelli, 2008) on the coachee have been highlighted.

Cox and Bachkirova (2007), in a study investigating how coaches dealt with difficult emotional situations, found that it was important for coaches to be aware of how emotions can help or hinder the coachee's progress, and of their own responses, biases and limitations. Similarly, Day, De Haan, Sills, Bertie and Blass (2008) found that critical moments of experienced coaches resulted in either reported coachee insight or a distancing or breakdown, influenced by the ability of the coach to contain the coachee's and their own emotions. Taking up the theme of biases, Kemp (2008, 2009) has highlighted the apparent centrality of coach self-management and the coaching alliance in working with executive coachees, citing examples of cognitive biases that may negatively influence the coaching relationship and advocating the use of supervision for increasing awareness and dealing with such coach constructs.

Themes and parallels from sport coaching and psychology (Gordon, 2007; O'Broin and Palmer, 2006; Peltier, 2001) are also instructive here. The 3 + 1Cs coach–athlete relationship model (Jowett, 2005, 2007) operationalises the dyad's feelings, cognitions and behaviours through constructs of Closeness, Commitment and Complementarity. Associated meta-perspectives are measured through its Co-orientation construct. The model can be used to relationally analyse the effectiveness of coach–athlete relationships over time.

The theme of 'coach as self-coach' involves the coach intentionally applying the CBC approach to establishing, developing, improving and maintaining the coaching alliance (see Figure 3.1). The processes here are synergistic, with mention of CBC's 'radar' that 'would be monitoring all areas of coaching to detect whether any beliefs, explicitly or subtly subscribed to, are having an adverse impact on a client's progress' (Neenan, 2008: 13). These processes include the coach identifying and challenging where appropriate:

- coaching-interfering thoughts, feelings and behaviours in themselves relating to their relationship with a specific coachee;
- coaching-interfering thoughts, feelings and behaviours in their coachee relating to the coaching relationship and/or themselves as coach;
- the interaction of their own and their coachee's unhelpful thinking styles, feelings and behaviours in the dynamics of the coaching alliance.

The coach is also involved in *encouraging* corresponding coaching-enhancing thoughts, feelings and behaviours.

Multiple factors such as general self-reflection on the use of conceptual, technical or management skills unrelated *directly* to the coaching alliance dynamics are also part of

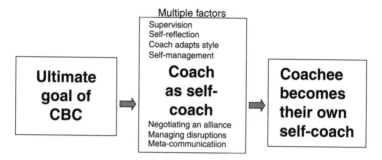

Figure 3.1 A CBC Perspective on the 'Coach as Self-Coach' in the Coaching Alliance (adapted and extended from Palmer and Szymanska, 2007)

the 'coach as self-coach' concept but are outside the scope of this discussion.

Dealing with some common difficulties in the coaching alliance

Despite collaboration, problems can and do occur, particularly as the alliance changes over time and with the recognised need (Stober and Grant, 2006) to maintain challenge in the change process. These problems may involve:

- Disruptions, such as confrontation or withdrawal in the coaching relationship.
- Misunderstandings between coachee and coach.

Inappropriate use of interpersonal skills: The relationship in cognitive behavioural therapy

Historically practitioners using cognitive behavioural frameworks have tended to place less emphasis on relationship than on technical aspects of the approach (see Leahy, 2008; Thwaites and Bennett-Levy, 2007). Recognition in psychotherapy outcome research of the need to understand the nature of participant, relationship *and* technical factors that work individually, and in interaction, to induce positive outcome (Beutler and Castonguay, 2006) has increased interest in the relationship in the cognitive behavioural therapy tradition (Gilbert and Leahy, 2007). Holtforth and Castonguay (2005) suggested that the therapy relationship was in continuous interaction with technique, either as a facilitator of application of technique or as the object of technique when it comes to fostering or dealing with disruption in the working alliance. The work by Bennett-Levy and colleagues (Bennett-Levy, 2006; Bennett-Levy and Thwaites, 2007; Bennett-Levy, McManus, Westline and Fennell, 2009), particularly on interpersonal skill development within a cognitive therapy model, highlights the importance assigned to such relationship factors in training, supervision and self-reflection of cognitive therapists. The importance of the relationship in combination with technique is echoed in a study by Gyllensten and Palmer (2007), who found that coachees in an organisational setting rated a good coaching relationship, techniques, learning skills and working towards and achieving goals as important aspects of coaching.

'Tuning out' instead of 'tuning in'

Interpersonal *perceptual* skills, including the overlapping skill-set of empathy, mindfulness and reflection-in-action (Bennett-Levy, 2006), are receptive skills of the coach. Deficits in perceptual skills involve the inability of the coach to 'tune in' to the coachee's verbal and non-verbal indicators and process; although they are difficult skills to measure, they are crucial elements of coaching, as in therapy (Greenberg and Goldman, 1988). Deficits can arise from a variety of sources ranging from attentional resource limitations, lack of confidence, over-technical emphasis, lack of capacity for empathic attunement to the triggering of representations of significant others from past relationships. The inability of the coach to question effectively can exacerbate the difficulty in tuning in. By focusing on information lying outside the coachee's key goals and aims, time may be wasted and the coachee may disengage, become less collaborative and ultimately withdraw, derail or pay lip-service to the coaching process.

Let us see how a coach uses his interpersonal perceptual skills effectively at an early stage in the coaching programme to tune in to his coachee's focus:

Coach: So, it seems you are finding the people-management side of your new role difficult and stressful? [Coach summarises and paraphrases coachee's initial description of problem.]

Coachee: Yes, that's right. I don't enjoy the responsibility of it.

Coach: What is it about not enjoying the responsibility of people-management that you find difficult and stressful?
[Here the coach probes for the precise individual meaning for the coachee.]

Coachee: Well ... I find it hard when I'm put in a position where I have to pull up members of my team when they get it wrong. I don't like confrontation.
[Whilst the coach has elicited that the difficulty appears to be with confrontation, more detail may clarify further the coachee's specific concerns.]

Coach: How do you experience finding it hard to pull up team members?

Coachee: I feel tense and worried. Sometimes I put off doing it altogether.

Coach: And what is it about *confrontation* with a team member that is difficult or stressful?

Coachee: (Sheepishly) I don't want my team to think I'm a dragon particularly as I've worked with some of them as my peers. They might end up hating my guts.
[Here the coachee chose to focus on the *effects* of confrontation. By probing further, the coach has uncovered the coachee's beliefs about self and others.]

Active discussion and negotiation of the coaching alliance as part of the assessment process (Palmer and Szymanska, 2007), and being explicit about the coaching process, should assist in pre-empting many such problems and/or provide 'permission' for the dyad to spotlight and address issues arising. Incidences of coachee lack of engagement, mood change, change of voice tone, use of language, attitudes towards agenda-setting and in-between session assignments may provide fruitful indicators to the coach regarding the accuracy (or inaccuracy) of their 'tuning-in' process.

Feeling but not conveying empathy

Interpersonal *relational* skills are active coach communication skills, such as expressing empathy, warmth, genuineness or compassion to the coachee. Deficits in relational skills involve an inability of the coach to convey their feelings about the coachee's emotional experience and frame of reference. Accurate empathy includes both emotional and cognitive aspects. Empathy has been conceptualised in the therapeutic empathy model (Thwaites and Bennett-Levy, 2007) with four main components – empathic attitude/stance, empathic attunement, empathic communication skills and empathic knowledge – although empathic communication has received most attention from cognitive behavioural theorists.

In our career coaching example below, the coach conveys empathy to her coachee, who feels under pressure to follow the family tradition:

Coachee: (Heatedly) I've told my Dad repeatedly that I don't want to be a pharmacist. He just doesn't listen and I feel like I'm hitting my head against a brick wall.

Coach: I see, it feels like it's *so* hard, so frustrating for you, trying to get your Dad to listen and understand how you feel about studying media studies and how much you *really don't want* to be a pharmacist.

[Here the coach's response is interchangeable with the coachee's statement, and she adds her emotional understanding by her choice of language and emphasis on how hard it is for the coachee.]

Coachee: (Excitedly) Yes, it's so hard because Dad just doesn't get it. I've always got good grades, I've never let my parents down. I don't like having to get angry with him about it. (Sighs) I wish he would trust me for once instead of pushing me in the career direction that he thinks is best.

Coach: So, you've tried really hard to do well and meet your parents' expectations, and now you are angry that your Dad isn't trusting you to choose wisely yourself which career direction to follow. To get angry with him like that I imagine must have been hard for you? What was it like for you?

Coachee: This is the first time that I've got really angry like this. I'm disappointed that he can't see that this is important to me. Sure I want to do well, it's not just about succeeding as a pharmacist. I believe there are other ways of being successful, other choices.

[The second exploratory coach response encouraged the coachee to differentiate his experience and discover new meaning. It focused on the leading edge of the coachee's experience of not being heard when he is trying to do well.]

The coach–coachee dialogue illustrates the importance of the balance of understanding (conveying empathy and compassion) and exploratory (drawing the coachee's focus to the leading edge of awareness) responses (Greenberg, 2002). Some technical elements of the CBC model, such as regular coachee and coach feedback and Socratic questioning, can in themselves promote empathic communication and assist the coaching alliance.

Supervision and self-supervision may assist the coach in raising their awareness of deficits in interpersonal skills, particularly if audio- or audiovisual recordings of coaching sessions are available, using roles plays, imaginal work (being in the coachee's shoes) and self-reflection.

Coaching-interfering thoughts, feelings and behaviours of the coachee

Here, the question for the coach might be 'What are the issues (if any) that push my coachee's buttons about the coaching or about me as their coach?' Issues detracting from or disrupting the alliance may include: the style, presence, attitude or behaviour of the coach; not being listened to; lack of accurate empathy; lack of appropriate focus of the coaching from the coachee's perspective; or other interpersonal aspects of the relationship.

Technique, technique, technique

By challenging the coachee's thinking, perhaps in a forceful or technique-focused way (Neenan, 2008) or by being judgemental (Dryden and Neenan, 2004) rather than responding appropriately to the particular situation and to the coachee's emotional response, the coach can inadvertently create a hostile coachee reaction. This can result in uncooperative and 'Yes, but . . .' behaviour in the coachee, who may think 'My coach is criticising me . . . by criticising my thinking'. Verbal (such as sarcastic or abrupt comments) or non-verbal indicators (such as change of body position or facial expression) may alert the coach to these coachee responses.

Gentle probing by the coach for the coachee's specific meaning, awareness of the coachee's emotional reaction, immediacy in examining the meaning of these responses, exploring the coachee's meta-cognitions (beliefs about meaning of thoughts) and meta-emotions (emotional reactions to their emotions) and emotionally attuning to and validating the coachee's feelings about their thinking are all likely to encourage alternative thinking, and they help to engender a more collaborative alliance. In the example below the coachee is describing his feelings after a strategy meeting with his manager and the organisation's overseas subsidiaries:

Coachee: I feel like a failure after the way I totally blew that meeting.
Coach: How do you think you blew the meeting?
Coachee: I got distracted by an argument between two of my colleagues and failed to make my point about the new projections for the Irish subsidiary effectively.

Coach: And what was it about getting distracted and not making the point about the new projections effectively that left you feeling that you'd failed?

Coachee: I felt stupid that I'd failed to convince them by not making the point effectively. It's not like me to make a mistake like that. Usually I'm on the ball.

Coach: It sounds like you rarely make a mistake like that. However, if you do, you feel like a failure.

Coachee: Yeah, I do feel a failure.

Coach: What would your manager say if you told him that you thought you'd totally blown the meeting and felt like a failure.

Coachee: (Thoughtfully) He . . . wouldn't think I'd totally blown the meeting.

Coach: What would prevent him from thinking you'd blown the meeting?

Coachee: Well, actually I did gain commitment from my colleagues on a project that I was promoting, which my manager has been keen on progressing.

Coach: So how do you think your manager would evaluate your performance in the meeting overall?

Coachee: Oh, he'd probably say I'd done okay. That I'd salvaged something from it. Maybe 7/10 for effort.

Coach: I see, and would he consider you a failure if you'd salvaged something from the meeting and got 7/10 for effort?

Coachee: No, he wouldn't. Okay, maybe it's true that . . . I didn't blow the meeting . . . (smiling) and I retrieved something from it, so I didn't actually fail.

Using ongoing feedback, as well as inviting the coachee to give explicit feedback in the session when feeling invalidated, are strategies that the coach can use in adapting their approach to the coachee's needs. Ventilation and validation of the coachee's feelings are unhelpful if they alone become the purpose of the work (Dryden and Neenan, 2004). Instead, the aim is for mutual understanding and then for the coachee to use this understanding to move forward in the change process.

Coaching-interfering thoughts, feelings and behaviours of the coach

The coach too can experience coaching-interfering thoughts, feelings and behaviours. The coach's attitudes, beliefs and assumptions are also likely to impact on their interpersonal perceptual and relational skills. Let us take examples of coaching-interfering thoughts, feelings and behaviours, respectively.

Coachee must meet my outcome measures

Here we have an example of an all-or-nothing cognitive thinking bias (O'Broin, 2008) exhibited by the coach. Coach thought: 'This isn't good enough. My coachee isn't going to achieve their goal at this rate.' Either the coachee is 'successful' or a 'failure' according to the thinking bias of the coach. Similarly, this example suggests the *demanding standards* coach schema, with accompanying coach beliefs such as: 'The coachee *must* meet my outcome measures. I *have* to have a good outcome with all my coachees or it will reflect badly on me.'

Although no measures have been undertaken at this time with coaches, *demanding standards* was the most common schema found among trainee CBT therapists (Haarhoff, 2006), with *special, superior person* and *excessive self-sacrifice* being the second and third most common schemas.

Fear of negative evaluation by the coachee

Take coaching-interfering feelings, for example a coach working for the first time with a senior executive in a FTSE 100 company. Here the coach's fear of negative evaluation by the coachee may lead to feelings of incompetence, helplessness or need for approval. Neenan's (2008) example of coach beliefs could apply here: 'I've got to ask continually incisive questions to impress my client and not let any silences occur as this indicates incompetence.' Feeling incompetent, however, is not tantamount to being incompetent (Thériault and Gazzola, 2008). Once coaches recognise the nature and source of their self-doubts and that such feelings can be part of the coaching process, they are in a better position to mobilise them for greater understanding of the coachee's process and their own self-management (Kemp, 2008). Emotion can then be used effectively as a guide to the coach's thinking and action. Personal theories that coaches hold about emotion may also be relevant (Cox and Bachkirova, 2007; Cremona, 2010), particularly if the coach holds negative beliefs about difficult emotions.

Behaving in a pleasant, well-meaning way

Moving on to coaching-interfering behaviour, let us highlight the coach being 'nice' to the coachee. Examples of this behaviour include: avoiding 'difficult' techniques and situations for fear of upsetting or displeasing the coachee; lack of boundaries in time-keeping or cancellations; and failing to press or challenge the coachee's thinking or behaviour where appropriate. This *excessive self-sacrifice* schema is not only observed in trainee CBT therapists, but is also the most frequently observed in all therapists (Haarhoff, 2006). Whilst the coach's intentions may be well-meaning, this behaviour can prevent or delay progress. Often, being explicit or direct about the issue is more appropriate and is likely to bring discussion and renegotiation of the issue, leading to an effective solution.

Coach: So, we talked in our last session about using role play for you to practise your assertiveness techniques in preparation for your team meeting next month.

Coachee: (Avoiding eye contact and shifting in chair) I feel too nervous. I can't face role playing the meeting yet. Let's wait until I feel more confident.

Coach: Sometimes practising a task helps to build confidence even if we aren't confident in attempting it in the first place. How about undertaking the role play for five minutes – I'll time it and if you are still as nervous after five minutes, we'll move on to another of the areas we have discussed.

[Here the coach encourages the coachee to engage in role play even if she is not confident, on the basis that attempting the task may aid achievement and increase confidence. The coach's approach also conveys the message that he thinks the coachee is capable of undertaking the task.]

Coachee: Oh . . . okay, just for five minutes then . . .

Interaction of coaching-inhibiting thoughts, feelings and behaviours

The interaction of coaching-interfering thoughts, feelings and behaviours of the dyad can produce problem cycles impairing the work of the coaching alliance.

Collusion

Taking collusion as an example, what do we do if our coachee does not complete between-session assignments? If we ignore the coachee's behaviour, we are effectively training the coachee that between-session assignment tasks are unimportant (see Dryden, 2008a), thereby potentially threatening the coaching alliance. So first the coach can reflect on and challenge their own thinking, feeling and behaviour, perhaps in this instance around abandonment and rejection sensitivity if the coachee is pressed on not completing the assignment. Second, we may seek clarification from the coachee on why they have avoided the task.

In the example below, the coaching work focuses on the coachee increasing his assertiveness with his manager as part of the goal of improving his sales performance. The coach asks the coachee about the between-session assignment of initiating a meeting with his manager to discuss criteria for sales targets.

Coach: How did the task from last week go?
              [Coach confronting her own feelings of anxiety, aware that last session the coachee had excused himself from completing his between-session assignment and she had not pressed him on this.]

Coachee: (Irritated) I told you before, these assignments won't work. I didn't do it.

Coach: How did you stop yourself from doing it?

Coachee: I . . . bottled out basically. I started thinking my manager would get really angry, he might refuse my request, might even consider demoting me, or worse . . .
              [Coachee exhibiting catastrophic thinking.]

Coach: What might be worse?
              [Encouraging coachee to make his ultimate concern explicit.]

Coachee: I might lose my job and I've got a mortgage to pay!

Coach: So, is it that you think that being assertive with your manager could result in losing your job, or are there other concerns about being assertive with him?
              [Seeking further explicit clarification about the coachee's thinking/feelings/behaviour.]

Coachee: I'm also concerned that my manager might think badly of me. We've always had a good relationship even though he's got a volatile personality and has been pretty short with other team members who stand up to him. I don't like confrontation.
              [Here the coachee is exhibiting rejection sensitivity and a need for approval from the manager.]

Coach: So, is carrying on going along with him likely to improve or detract from your sales performance?
              [Reminding coachee of the coaching goal and the implications of continuing with unchanged behaviour and beliefs.]

Coachee: (Soberly) It's not going to improve my sales performance.

Coach: And would assertively discussing criteria for sales targets improve or detract from your sales performance?

Coachee: It would improve it if I could just *do* it rather than worrying about what my manager might think of me!

Coach: Do you want to look at ways of tackling your worries about assertively discussing criteria for sales targets?

[Seeking coachee's commitment to change via this route.]

Coachee: Yes, definitely.

Coach: Okay then, how can you start to tackle your worries about assertively discussing the criteria for sales targets with your manager?

Coachee: I . . . well, I could use the thought-challenging skills that we've talked about.

Interacting rule based thinking of coachee and coach

A further possible contributory factor in the case of interacting thinking, feelings and behaviours is schematic 'overmatch' (Leahy, 2008) – that *both* coachee and coach demonstrate similar schemas that detrimentally interact. In the above example this caused the coach to avoid difficult topics that might lead to confrontation or to avoid putting limits on the coachee. The coachee's behavioural response is to continue to avoid. The coachee could think that the coach thinks them incapable of completing the task and that the task is too difficult to be accomplished.

Alternatively, a mismatched schema of the coach and coachee can involve a conflict in the schema or core beliefs, which can impact negatively on the coaching alliance. This iterative interpersonal process, whereby two individuals follow their own rule based thinking, has been conceptualised within game theory models in the therapeutic (Leahy, 2007) and the coaching context (O'Broin and Palmer, 2007, 2010b).

By recognising rule based thinking patterns problems can be identified, averted and, where appropriate, addressed using cognitive, experiential, emotion-focused and emotional schema techniques in the coaching relationship. Such rule based patterns emphasise the need for the coach to be able to adapt or 'tailor' their approach to the needs of the particular coachee.

Let us use the example of a coach working with a newly promoted, highly ambitious executive coachee on team leadership capabilities. The coachee's directive management style has helped to achieve high profits for his organisation relative to their sector; however, his behaviour has isolated him from several staff members and is at odds with his organisation's culture.

Coachee: I want to see tangible results from this coaching, in six months. I hope you can deliver.

Coach: (Smiling) We'll both be working towards your goals, so I anticipate we'll make a good team.
[The coach feels an initial defensiveness, as if she needs to justify herself to the coachee. Noticing the aggressiveness and directiveness of the coachee's remark, she chooses to deflect it by reinforcing the collaborativeness of coaching – and their need for team work to achieve the coachee's goals, akin to the coachee's goals in developing leadership capabilities.]

Coachee: I hope so. Now what's on the agenda?
[The coach is aware that the coachee is attempting to direct the coaching process.]

Coach: If you remember when we discussed the CBC model, we talked about negotiating an agenda every session. So we *both* have the opportunity to put our items relating to your goals on the agenda for discussion. What would *you* like to put on today's agenda?
[Here the coach continues to emphasise a collaborative approach and that both coach and coachee are required to provide input and nego-tiate the agenda and the process, and that she will not be providing the 'answers' at the request of the coachee.]

The coach's 'radar' has picked up information about the coachee's style and interpersonal communication that she may choose to return to or check out further with the coachee later in the session. The coach has become aware of the coachee's dominance-seeking behaviour, so will avoid reciprocating with the 'submissive' behaviour that the coachee's behaviour could unwittingly provoke, and that perhaps is the reaction of some of his colleagues. In tailoring the base of influence of her approach to the particular coachee, the coach will also be aware of and work with the coachee's potential aversion to being 'controlled'.

Conclusion

The coaching relationship is a critical aspect of the coaching process, regardless of conceptual approach. In viewing the coaching relationship through the lens of a CBC perspective (see also O'Broin and Palmer, 2009), we have highlighted in this chapter explicitly negotiating and renegotiating a collaborative, optimal coaching alliance (including the coach and coachee's views of the coaching) for the specific coachee in the specific context. Also emphasised is the concept of the 'coach as self-coach', referring to the ability of the coach to apply the CBC approach to the dynamics of the coaching alliance, particularly in identifying and working towards modifying coaching-interfering thinking, feeling and behaviour in themselves and their coachee.

In discussion of these themes for enhancing and developing an optimal alliance and later addressing problems in the coaching alliance, it has become apparent that the cognitive behavioural dynamics of coachee (Cavanagh and Grant, 2004) and coach (Kemp, 2008) individually and in interaction are an important factor. What is also clear is the need for self-management and adaptability of the coach to the coachee's style of relating and changing needs, as part of the broader coaching process seeking to help coachees achieve their realistic goals and ultimately become their own self-coach.

Discussion issues

- How can a cognitive behavioural coaching (CBC) perspective on the coaching relationship enhance the coaching alliance in practice?
- Discuss examples of situations when it might be appropriate to renegotiate goals, tasks and bonds with your coachees.
- In what ways and when might you adapt your relational style to improve the bond and alliance with your coachees?
- Describe ways in which the coaching alliance and techniques may interact, or when the quality of the alliance reflects the effect of the coach's appropriate use of techniques when working within a CBC approach.
- Compare and contrast the broad affective bond and the work-supporting bond, using examples to highlight where these might overlap and differ over time.
- How might you work with coachees in the event of a disruption in the alliance in the form of (a) confrontation, (b) withdrawal or (c) misunderstanding?

References

Bachkirova, T. (2007) Role of coaching psychology in defining boundaries between counselling and coaching. In S. Palmer and A. Whybrow (Eds.), *Handbook of Coaching Psychology: A Guide for Practitioners*. Hove, UK: Routledge.

Bennett-Levy, J. (2006) Therapist skills: A cognitive model of their acquisition and refinement. *Behavioural and Cognitive Psychotherapy*, *34*: 57–78.

Bennett-Levy, J. and Thwaites, R. (2007) Self and self-reflection in the therapeutic relationship: A conceptual map and practical strategies for the training, supervision and self-supervision of interpersonal skills. In P. Gilbert and R. L. Leahy (Eds.), *The Therapeutic Relationship in the Cognitive Behavioral Psychotherapies*. Hove, UK: Routledge.

Bennett-Levy, J., McManus, F., Westline, B. E. and Fennell, M. (2009) Acquiring and refining CBT skills and competencies:

Which training methods are perceived to be most effective? *Behavioural and Cognitive Psychotherapy, 37*: 571–583.

Beutler, L. E. and Castonguay, L. G. (2006) The task force on empirically based principles of therapeutic change. In L. G. Castonguay and L. E. Beutler (Eds.), *Principles of Therapeutic Change that Work*. Oxford: Oxford University Press.

Bluckert, P. (2005) Critical factors in executive coaching – the coaching relationship. *Industrial and Commercial Training, 37*(7): 336–340.

Bluckert, P. (2006) *Psychological Dimensions of Executive Coaching*. Milton Keynes, UK: Open University Press.

Bordin, E. S. (1979) The generalizability of the psychoanalytic concept of the working alliance. *Psychotherapy: Theory, Research and Practice, 16*: 252–260.

Castonguay, L. G. and Beutler, L. E. (2006) Common and unique principles of therapeutic change: What do we know and what do we need to know? In L. G. Castonguay and L. E. Beutler (Eds.), *Principles of Therapeutic Change that Work*. Oxford: Oxford University Press.

Cavanagh, M. J. and Grant, A. M. (2004) Executive coaching in organizations: The personal is the professional. *International Journal of Coaching in Organisations, 2*: 6–15.

Cox, E. and Bachkirova, T. (2007) Coaching with emotion: How coaches deal with difficult emotional situations. *International Coaching Psychology Review, 2*(2): 178–189.

Cremona, K. (2010) Coaching and emotions: An exploration of how coaches engage and think about emotion. *Coaching: An International Journal of Theory, Research and Practice, 3*(1): 46–59.

Day, A., De Haan, E., Sills, C., Bertie, C. and Blass, E. (2008) Coaches' experience of critical moments in the coaching. *International Coaching Psychology Review, 3*(3): 207–218.

De Haan, E. (2008) *Relational Coaching: Journeys towards Mastering One-to-One Learning*. Chichester, UK: Wiley.

Dryden, W. (2006) *Counselling in a Nutshell*. London: Sage.

Dryden, W. (2008a) The therapeutic alliance as an integrating framework. In W. Dryden and A. Reeves (Eds.), *Key Issues for Counselling in Action*. London: Sage.

Dryden, W. (2008b) Tailoring your counselling approach to different clients. In W. Dryden and A. Reeves (Eds.), *Key Issues for Counselling in Action*. London: Sage.

Dryden, W. (2011) *Dealing with Clients' Emotional Problems in Life Coaching*. London: Routledge.

Dryden, W. and Neenan, M. (2004) *The Rational Emotive Behavioural Approach to Therapeutic Change*. London: Sage.

Ducharme, M. J. (2004) The cognitive-behavioral approach to executive coaching. *Consulting Psychology Journal: Practice and Research, 56*(4): 214–224.

Fillery-Travis, A. and Lane, D. (2006) Research: Does coaching work or are we asking the wrong question. *International Coaching Psychology Review*, *1*(1): 23–35.

Gilbert, P. and Leahy, R. L. (2007) *The Therapeutic Relationship in the Cognitive Behavioral Psychotherapies*. Hove, UK: Routledge.

Gordon, S. (2007) Sport and business coaching: Perspective of a sport psychologist. *The Australian Psychologist*, *42*(4): 271–282.

Grant, A. M. (2006) An integrated goal-focused approach to executive coaching. In D. R. Stober and A. M. Grant (Eds.), *Evidence-Based Coaching Handbook: Putting Best Practices to Work for your Clients*. Hoboken, NJ: Wiley.

Greenberg, L. S. (2002) *Emotion-focused Therapy: Coaching Clients to Work Through Their Feelings*. Washington, DC: American Psychological Association.

Greenberg, L. S. and Goldman, R. L. (1988) Training in experiential therapy. *Journal of Consulting and Clinical Psychology*, *56*: 696–702.

Gyllensten, K. and Palmer, S. (2007) The coaching relationship: An interpretive phenomenological analysis. *International Coaching Psychology Review*, *2*(2): 168–177.

Haarhoff, B. A. (2006) The importance of identifying and understanding therapist schema in cognitive therapy training and supervision. *New Zealand Journal of Psychology*, *35*(3): 126–131.

Hardy, G., Cahill, J. and Barkham, M. (2007) Active ingredients of the therapeutic relationship that promote client change: A research perspective. In P. Gilbert and R. L. Leahy (Eds.), *The Therapeutic Relationship in the Cognitive Behavioral Psychotherapies*. Hove, UK: Routledge.

Hart, V., Blattner, J. and Leipsic, S. (2001) Coaching versus therapy. *Consulting Psychology Journal: Practice and Research*, *53*(4): 229–237.

Hatcher, R. L. and Barends, A. W. (2006) How a return to theory could help alliance research. *Psychotherapy: Theory, Research, Practice, Training*, *43*(3): 292–299.

Holtforth, M. G. and Castonguay, L. G. (2005) Relationship and techniques in cognitive-behavioural therapy: A motivational approach. *Psychotherapy*, *42*(4): 443–455.

Horvath, A. O. (2006) The alliance in context: Accomplishments, challenges and future directions. *Psychotherapy: Theory, Research, Practice, Training*, *43*(3): 258–263.

Jowett, S. (2005) The coach–athlete partnership. *The Psychologist*, *18*(7): 412–415.

Jowett, S. (2007) Interdependence analysis and the 3 + 1Cs in the coach–athlete relationship. In S. Jowett and D. Lavalee (Eds.), *Social Psychology in Sport*. Champaign, IL: Human Kinetics.

Jowett, S., O'Broin, A. and Palmer, S. (2010) On understanding the role and significance of a key two-person relationship in sport and executive coaching. *Sport and Exercise Psychology Review*, *6*(2): 19–30.

Kauffman, C. and Bachkirova, T. (2009) Spinning order from chaos: How do we know what to study in coaching research and use it for self-reflective practice? *Coaching: An International Journal of Theory, Research and Practice*, *2*(1): 1–9.

Kemp, T. (2008) Self-management and the coaching relationship: Exploring coaching impact beyond models and methods. *International Coaching Psychology Review*, *3*(1): 32–42.

Kemp, T. (2009) Is coaching an evolved form of leadership? Building a transdisciplinary framework for exploring the coaching alliance. *International Coaching Psychology Review*, *4*(1): 105–109.

Lazarus, A. A. (1989) *The Practice of Multimodal Therapy*. Baltimore, MD: John Hopkins University Press.

Leahy, R. L. (2007) Schematic mismatch in the therapeutic relationship. In P. Gilbert and R. L. Leahy (Eds.), *The Therapeutic Relationship in the Cognitive Behavioral Psychotherapies*. Hove, UK: Routledge.

Leahy, R. L. (2008) The therapeutic relationship in cognitive-behavioral therapy. *Behavioural and Cognitive Psychotherapy*, *36*: 769–777.

Lowman, R. L. (2005) Executive coaching: The road to Dodoville needs paving with more than good intentions. *Consulting Psychology Journal*, *57*(1): 90–96.

Neenan, M. (2006) Cognitive behavioural coaching. In J. Passmore (Ed.), *Excellence in Coaching: The Industry Guide*. London: Kogan Page.

Neenan, M. (2008) From cognitive behaviour therapy to cognitive behaviour coaching (CBC). *Journal of Rational-Emotive-Cognitive-Behavior Therapy*, *26*: 3–15.

Neenan, M. and Dryden, W. (2002) *Life Coaching: A Cognitive-Behavioural Approach*. Hove, UK: Brunner-Routledge.

Norcross, J. C. (2002) *Psychotherapy Relationships that Work*. Oxford: Oxford University Press.

Norcross, J. C. and Wampold, B. E. (2011) Evidence-based therapy relationships: Research conclusions and clinical practices. *Psychotherapy*, *41*(1): 98–102.

O'Broin, A. (2008) All-or-nothing thinking: Using thinking skills to re-appraise performance-interfering thinking. *International Coaching Psychology Review*, *3*(3): 250–252.

O'Broin, A. and Palmer, S. (2006) Win-win situation? Learning from parallels and differences between coaching psychology and sport psychology. *The Coaching Psychologist*, *2*(3): 17–23.

O'Broin, A. and Palmer, S. (2007) Re-appraising the coach–client relationship: The unassuming change agent in coaching. In S. Palmer and A. Whybrow (Eds.), *Handbook of Coaching Psychology: A Guide for Practitioners*. Hove, UK: Routledge.

O'Broin, A. and Palmer, S. (2009) Co-creating an optimal coaching alliance: A cognitive behavioural coaching perspective. *International Coaching Psychology Review*, 4(2): 184–194.

O'Broin, A. and Palmer, S. (2010a) Exploring key aspects in the formation of coaching relationships: Initial indicators from the perspective of the coachee and the coach. *Coaching: An International Journal of Theory, Research and Practice*, 3(2): 124–143.

O'Broin, A. and Palmer, S. (2010b) Building on an interpersonal perspective on the coaching relationship. In S. Palmer and A. McDowall (Eds.), *The Coaching Relationship: Putting People First*. Hove, UK: Routledge.

O'Broin, A. and Palmer, S. (2010c) The coaching alliance as a universal concept spanning conceptual approaches. *Coaching Psychology International*, 3(1): 3–6.

Palmer, S. and Gyllensten, K. (2008) How cognitive behavioural, rational emotive behavioural or multimodal coaching could prevent mental health problems, enhance performance and reduce work related stress. *Journal of Rational-Emotive-Cognitive-Behavioral Therapy*, 26: 38–52.

Palmer, S. and McDowall, A. (2010) *The Coaching Relationship: Putting People First*. Hove, UK: Routledge.

Palmer, S. and Szymanska, K. (2007) Cognitive behavioural coaching: An integrative approach. In S. Palmer and A. Whybrow (Eds.), *Handbook of Coaching Psychology: A Guide for Practitioners*. Hove, UK: Routledge.

Peltier, B. (2001) Lessons from athletic coaches. *The Psychology of Executive Coaching: Theory and Application*. Hove, UK: Brunner-Routledge.

Price, J. (2009) The coaching/therapy boundary in organizational coaching. *Coaching: An International Journal of Therapy, Research and Practice*, 2(2): 135–148.

Prochaska, J. O. and DiClemente, C. C. (1983) Stages and processes of self-change of smoking: Toward an integrative model of change. *Journal of Consulting and Clinical Psychology*, 51: 390–395.

Spinelli, E. (2008) Coaching and therapy: Similarities and divergencies. *International Coaching Psychology Review*, 3(3): 241–249.

Stober, D. R. and Grant, A. M. (2006) Toward a contextual approach to coaching models. In D. R. Stober and A. M. Grant (Eds.), *Evidence Based Coaching Handbook: Putting Best Practices to Work for your Clients*. Hoboken, NJ: Wiley.

Thériault, A. and Gazzola, N. (2008) Feelings of incompetence in therapy: Causes, consequences and coping strategies. In W. Dryden and A. Reeves (Eds.), *Key Issues for Counselling in Action*. London: Sage.

Thwaites, R. and Bennett-Levy, J. (2007) Conceptualizing empathy in cognitive-behaviour therapy: Making the implicit explicit. *Behavioural and Cognitive Psychotherapies, 35*: 591–612.

Williams, H., Edgerton, N. and Palmer, S. (2010) Cognitive behavioural coaching. In E. Cox, T. Bachkirova and D. Clutterbuck (Eds.), *The Complete Handbook of Coaching*. London: Sage.

Recommended reading

De Haan, E. (2008) *Relational Coaching: Journeys towards Mastering One-to-One Learning*. Chichester, UK: Wiley.

O'Broin, A. and Palmer, S. (2007) Re-appraising the coach–client relationship: The unassuming change agent in coaching. In S. Palmer and A. Whybrow (Eds.), *Handbook of Coaching Psychology: A Guide for Practitioners*. Hove, UK: Routledge.

Palmer, S. and McDowall, A. (2010) *The Coaching Relationship: Putting People First*. Hove, UK: Routledge.

4

Socratic questioning

Michael Neenan

Introduction

A significant part of a coach's verbal activity is devoted to asking questions in order to, among other things, gather assessment information, clarify points, reveal core values, establish goals, develop action plans and pinpoint and tackle blocks to change. However, asking vague or general questions may not elicit much relevant information as they have a rather aimless quality instead of a particular purpose in a specific context. For example, when reviewing action assignments compare the following questions: 'How are things since I last saw you?' and 'Did you carry out the agreed task?'. The first question has the potential to make the session diffuse and discursive, while the second is likely to concentrate the coachee's mind on discussing his goal-directed tasks and maintaining continuity from the previous session. Further questions might be if he completed the task, 'Did you learn anything from it?' and, if he did not carry out the task, 'How did you stop yourself from doing it?' (this question emphasises personal responsibility more than 'What stopped you . . .?'). Also, as coaching is usually a short-term endeavour it is important to try and make every question count. Therefore, for the aforementioned reasons, not all questions are equally useful; so the focus in this chapter is on using questions that are likely to make a greater impact in a shorter space of time.

A Socratic stance in coaching is likely to achieve this aim. Derived from the Greek philosopher Socrates, this stance focuses on asking a person a series of questions to help promote reflection; this, in turn, is likely to produce knowledge that is currently outside of her awareness and thereby enable her to develop more helpful perspectives and actions in tackling her difficulties. Through this method people are able to reach their own conclusions rather than being told what these should be by the questioner. However, questions other than Socratic ones are useful at times. Here are some examples: closed questions to focus the person's reply, 'Have you decided which issue to work on first?', or confirm what the other person has said, 'Therefore, is the sticking point for you your manager's refusal to apologise?' (Luecke, 2004); direct questions to gather assessment information, 'How many times this month have you been late for meetings?'; and leading questions to test the coach's assumptions, 'It sounds as if you're more worried than excited about the promotion?'. It is important that coaches do not become 'stuck' in Socratic mode. DiGiuseppe (1991) has criticised using Socratic questioning as the only method of learning if it becomes obvious to the coach that some coachees would clearly benefit from direct explanations of how to solve their problems. Once a potential solution has been offered, the coach can revert to a Socratic style by asking for comments on the proposed solution.

Socratic questioning is a cornerstone of cognitive behavioural therapy (CBT; Padesky and Greenberger, 1995), which focuses on how changing our thinking leads to emotional and behavioural change. Naturally enough, Socratic questioning has the same importance in cognitive behavioural coaching (CBC; Neenan, 2006; Neenan and Dryden, 2002).

Changing minds or guiding discovery?

While Socratic questioning is much discussed in the CBT literature, Padesky (1993: 2) asks the intriguing question: 'Is the primary purpose of Socratic questioning to change minds or guide discovery?' Changing minds is using questions to steer a person towards giving answers that you want to hear, so the predetermined conclusions are built into the questions you ask, while guiding discovery is based on a genuine curiosity about where the questioning will lead, what might be uncovered and what the person will do with this material. For example, consider a person who is reluctant to give his opinions at meetings in case he is ridiculed. A changing minds approach might ask: 'Do you have any evidence that you will be ridiculed if you give your opinions?' Reply: 'Not really.' The logical next step from the coach's viewpoint is for the coachee to speak up and see what happens; if no one laughs at him then his fears are unfounded, or reassure him that if he does get some negative responses it will not be as bad as it seems (the coach is pushing him towards her perceived solution). Changing minds can give the impression that the coach has nothing to learn from the coachee, while the coachee might believe that his viewpoint is being disregarded by the coach rather than being taken seriously by her (Westbrook, Kennerley and Kirk, 2007).

A guided discovery approach would want to pursue the personal meaning of being ridiculed and why it is such a troubling issue for him – this is where *his* focus is: 'If my colleagues ridicule me, then I'll lose their respect and won't be taken seriously.' Subsequent questions to illuminate the issue further might be: 'How do you know you have their respect to lose or are taken seriously?'; 'Could you lose this respect by remaining silent in the meetings?'; 'Is there a way of reconciling your stated goal of speaking up in meetings with accepting the possibility of being ridiculed?'; 'Can you be made to feel inferior without your consent?' The coach is encouraging the person to take a wider view of the situation rather than the constricted one he has adopted so that other possibilities can emerge to tackle this issue.

Padesky (1993: 11) favours guided discovery over changing minds in CBT: 'There is no [one] answer. There are only good questions that guide discovery of a million different individual answers.' The former approach would be the one I support in coaching although, in my teaching experience, some coaches seek to change minds in order to convince themselves of their competence (alternatively, the changing minds approach might have been the only method they were taught). Guided discovery is, for these coaches, unpredictable, wishy-washy and, most importantly, unlikely to deliver the 'quick wins' they are seeking (achieving some results rapidly). Changing minds is the coach's agenda for coachee change, while guided discovery is allowing the coachee's agenda to take shape.

However, having said all that and at the risk of contradicting myself, I believe that the differences between changing minds and guiding discovery can be overstated: both approaches are aimed at changing beliefs but the former is mainly coach-led while the latter is a joint enterprise rather than coachee-led – the coach is, after all, *guiding* the coachee's discovery. This brings to mind Jeffrey Auerbach's (2006) description of his cognitive coaching role as a 'thought partner' – clarifying and enhancing the person's goal-directed thinking. Changing minds and guided discovery can be seen as endpoints on a scale, with the coach moving up and down the scale as necessary. In my own case, I favour guided discovery more but this will depend on the coachee's preferences for a particular coaching style, how many sessions we have, the exigencies of the moment, my desire to maintain flexibility of response to changing circumstances and, unfortunately, my own impatience at times to move coaching along at my timetable instead of the coachee's.

Is it good enough?

So, what are good questions to ask in guiding discovery? As a philosopher might say, 'It all depends on what you mean by "good".' Good Socratic questions I would suggest are:

- **Concise** – thereby maintaining the coachee's introspective focus.
- **Clear** – reducing potential coachee confusion or misunderstanding by avoiding prolixity or jargon.
- **Open** – inviting participation and exploring ideas.
- **Purposeful** – you can explain the reasons for the questions you have asked.
- **Constructive** – promoting insight and/or action.
- **Focused** – on the coachee's current concerns.
- **Tentative** – not assuming that the coachee can answer your question.
- **Neutral** – not signalling the answer you want to hear.

For example, 'Do you know what you are worried about in giving your presentation to the board?' This question will help the person to maintain her introspective focus on discovering what is troubling her, as opposed to a convoluted one that is likely to pull her away from this focus as she struggles to understand the coach (e.g. 'So we know it's something about worry. Giving a presentation can be a daunting prospect that would probably cause concerns in most, if not indeed in all, people who do it. Worry itself is a source of important information about the self. So I'm wondering if it's about apprehension of a possibly adverse outcome, such as giving a less than impressive performance or not being able to answer a tough question, or could it be something else? What could be going on here do you think?'). Coaching should strive to be a vagueness-free zone, so purge the verbiage! Some coaching books (e.g. Megginson and Clutterbuck, 2005) give lists of good questions to ask, which can be helpful in increasing your own store; however, merely parroting memorised questions to 'impress' your coachees is not a good idea, whereas providing yourself with reasons for the questions you ask *is* because it shows you are thinking keenly about what you are asking.

Erosion of expertise

Being highly proficient at what you do does not necessarily mean that you can explain in detail the mechanics of what you do. Experienced coaches, like experienced therapists, are likely to operate according to tacit procedural knowledge in asking what they perceive to be good questions:

> Procedural knowledge is the knowledge of 'how to' and 'when to' – rules, plans, and procedures – which leads to the direct application of skills. The procedural knowledge of experienced therapists is often tacit – they just 'do it'. Like experts in other fields . . . the cognitive strategies of therapists change over the course of development. . . . Their knowledge 'chunks' and problem solving strategies become progressively elaborated and refined, and they build a formidable repertoire of

representative when-then rules, plans, procedures and skills.

(Bennett-Levy, 2006: 59)

Trainees watching expert coaches in action or reading coach–coachee dialogues in books usually ask, 'How did she know to ask that question at that moment?' or 'Why that question rather than this one?'. Being told that 'Experience teaches you what and when to ask' does not illuminate the when-then rules in action and you might come to believe that the 'mysteries' of asking good questions are only known to the 'coachnoscenti'. Megginson and Clutterbuck (2005: 106) ask if intuition can be developed: 'There is no simple and easy answer to that question. In all coaching and mentoring sessions, asking the appropriate and "right" questions already has a strong intuitional aspect to it.' Not providing explanations in coaching books for the rationales underpinning the question-asking skills of the experts assumes that maybe the readers are picking it up through osmosis! Along with running commentaries on coach–coachee dialogues in books, demystifying intuition should also involve coaches audio-recording sessions to provide analyses in supervision of their questioning styles and how they can be improved (e.g. by listening to a session tape the coach realises that she is not rigorous enough in reviewing an action assignment and allows the coachee's reply of 'It went well' to suffice). The intuition of the expert can have its drawbacks, as Ericsson, Prietula and Cokely (2007: 119) point out:

> It's very easy to neglect deliberate practice [pushing yourself to undertake tasks that are beyond your current level of competence and comfort]. Experts who reach a high level of performance often find themselves responding automatically to specific situations and may come to rely exclusively on their intuition. This leads to difficulties when they deal with atypical or rare cases, because they've lost the ability to analyze a situation and work through the right response. Experts may not recognize this creeping intuition bias, of course, because there is no penalty until they encounter a situation in

which a habitual response fails and maybe even causes damage. Older professionals with a great deal of experience are particularly prone to falling into this trap, but it's certainly not inevitable.

I once ran a CBT workshop for a group of very experienced and mainly older executive coaches who said they were committed to Socratic questioning of the guided discovery route but none of them audio-recorded (or audiovisually recorded) their sessions. How could they be so sure? 'Intuition' and 'you just know' were the favourite replies. During the pairs' exercises, which were part of the course, I went round the room to see how they were getting on with them and my overwhelming impression was that many coaches were directive in their questioning (I am certainly not implying that this was how they were all the time). In order to make intuition more informed than biased, deliberate practice is the key (Ericsson et al., 2007; for a detailed discussion of the powers and perils of intuition, see Myers, 2004). The deliberate practice I suggested to the executive coaches was regular audio-recording of their sessions and explaining to their supervisors the reasons for the choice, phrasing and ordering of the questions. This suggestion did not go down well because, from the comments I received, it would push them into their discomfort zone and question their assumed intuitive expertise.

What's in a question?

James and Morse (2007: 508) suggest 'a tripartite distinction of questions':

1 **Types** (e.g. open, closed, short, long, simple, complex, leading, direct).
2 **Functions** (e.g. to gather information about presenting issues, examine and change unhelpful beliefs, develop action plans, establish goals, build and deal with any difficulties in the coaching relationship, gain feedback both during and at the end of sessions). If the function of the questions is to examine and help change unhelpful beliefs, it is important that the coach does not slip into

the role of a courtroom prosecutor and try to 'expose' inconsistencies in his coachee's thinking, thereby forcing reluctant belief change on to her. If there are such inconsistencies, let them emerge through the coachee's realisation.

3 **Sequencing of questions in a logical order**. In CBC, questions are asked to help the coachee not only to identify beliefs and behaviours that block change but also to develop new beliefs and behaviours that are likely to promote change.

In the following example, I will explain the reasons for the logical order of my questions. The coachee is a new manager who micromanages the tasks he has delegated, leaving his team members believing that they 'can't be trusted'. He wants to stop micromanaging but finds it difficult to let go:

Coach: What might happen if you did let go?
              [This is to make his concern explicit.]
Coachee: If I let go, they might make a mess of things, which I'll have to clear up, which will then add to my workload. I'm busy enough.
Coach: Is that the issue: increased workload for you if they 'make a mess of things'? Or are there other concerns connected to this issue?
              [This is to clarify if further exploration is required.]
Coachee: I also worry what my manager will think if my team are messing up, but the main issue is the increased workload for me if things go wrong. That's the one I want to work on.
Coach: Okay. Do you think micromanagement increases or decreases your own workload?
              [In business coaching, this is a key question to focus coachees' minds on the pragmatic consequences of retaining their current beliefs and behaviour – do they lead to increased productivity, performance and profit?]
Coachee: Well, delegation is supposed to reduce your workload, but it's not working like that?
Coach: Do you want it to work like that?
              [This is seeking his commitment to change.]

Coachee: Yes. My micromanaging is keeping me on the back foot with important work of my own, but there's still that worry of letting go.

Coach: What shall we look at first: ways of letting go so you can get on with your own important work or your worry about doing it?
[This is gaining a clear session focus.]

Coachee: Letting go.

Coach: How do you start doing that?
[Concentrating his mind on initial action steps.]

Coachee: Instead of micromanaging, step back.

Coach: How far and doing what instead?
['Step back' is vague.]

Coachee: I could have regular meetings, say weekly, to determine progress. I don't want to lose control of the projects though.

Coach: Who's ultimately in control of the delegated tasks and accountable for the results of the team?
[This is to remind him of what he appears to have forgotten.]

Coachee: I am. I retain overall control.

Coach: So what effects might this have on your team when you step back?
[Broadening his view to take in potential team benefits.]

Coachee: I know they'll welcome my not breathing down their necks.

Coach: Could there be other maybe more important benefits?
[Effective delegation is not just stepping back.]

Coachee: Let me see ... giving people a chance to show their abilities, develop their potential, see who could step into my shoes when I'm away, that sort of thing.

Coach: What about someone struggling with a task – will you automatically take it over to get it done?
[Stepping back can easily be changed to micromanaging again when problems arise. Has he considered this?]

Coachee: That would be my first thought, but on second thoughts I would try to let the person work it out for herself. Coach them like you're coaching me.

Coach: What might be the differences between a micro-managed team and a coached one?

[Pulling the information together to see if a new perspective is emerging.]

Coachee: A micromanaged team is stifled and resentful, I can vouch for that, but a coached one, which seems a better way to do things, is bound to keep on improving.

Coach: Has what we've discussed made any impact on your worry?

[This is to ascertain if thinking differently has made any change in how he feels.]

Coachee: I haven't been worried while we were talking about making improvements but now I'm focused on it, I'm still worried somewhat but there is an excitement and risk about doing things differently. Instead of being obsessed with how the team is doing I can get on with my own work and catch up. Making a mess of things is more likely to occur if I fall behind with my own work.

Coach: I forget who said it, but something like leaders gain authority by giving it away.

[Hoping to reinforce his new approach.]

Coachee: I like that. You know most of what we talked about today I already knew but I was afraid to do it. The answers are there if you look hard enough.

Coach: So what do you propose to do before our next session?

[This is to see if good intentions will be translated into results-focused action.]

Coachee: Have a meeting with the team to explain and implement my new approach to delegation.

Of course, you may disagree with my sequencing of questions and the reasons for them but it is important to provide a sound basis for your line of questioning rather than simply relying on instinct or 'just feeling my way along'. In the next sections, further examples of Socratic questioning are presented.

Dealing with some common difficulties in coaching

'I don't know'

This familiar reply has a number of meanings (this list is not meant to be exhaustive):

1 **Lack of knowledge**. The coach has asked a question that she assumed the coachee could answer, such as 'What do you want from coaching?' instead of 'Do you know what you want from coaching?'. Making assumptions without checking them can become pervasive. Coaches are likely to see some individuals who are high achievers in life and, because of this impressive track record, may assume that they all naturally understand what is involved in initiating and maintaining change with regard to their current difficulties. Not so. We all have our blind spots. As Hanna (2002: 43) observes, one of the fundamental mistakes made in therapy (and I would extend this observation to coaching) 'is to assume that clients understand change processes. If they did, then change might be accomplished much easier and quicker on a routine basis'. Questions that elicit 'I don't know' are not Socratic and are likely to force the coachee into a cognitive cul-de-sac, increase the irritation levels of both coach and coachee and put the relationship under strain. Every time you make an uncorroborated assumption, note down a 'UA' on a piece of paper and see how many 'UAs' you have collected by the end of the week. Like professional philosophers, never assume. Check with your coachees!

2 **Lack of mental effort**. If your hypothesis is that your coachee has not expended much thinking time on your question, then in order to test it ask him to verbalise how he processed your question:

Coachee: What's the point of doing that?
Coach: To find out what you did to try and answer the question.

> *Coachee*: If the information doesn't come to mind then it doesn't come to mind. What else can I say?
>
> *Coach*: Do you mean if the information doesn't come to mind immediately or over time?
>
> *Coachee*: Well, I suppose if it isn't in my mind straight-away then I don't really search for it.
>
> *Coach*: What might be the implications for your coaching goals of not searching for it?
>
> *Coachee*: Well, I'm not going to make progress.
>
> *Coach*: Do you want to make progress?
>
> *Coachee*: Of course I do.
>
> *Coach*: So how do you go about searching for an answer to my question without saying 'I don't know'?
>
> *Coachee*: Ask me the question again and this time I will really concentrate on it.

When 'I don't know' is based on lack of mental effort, it can be very useful to drop the phrase from the sessions so it can no longer be used as a bolt-hole (but watch out for the emergence of a substitute such as 'I'm not sure'). It is important that you do not answer the question yourself and thereby strengthen the coachee's tendencies towards not making much mental effort. You can ask the coachee after several minutes of silence if he wants the question repeated but, as Fournies (2000) observes, let the person know by your body language (e.g. sitting back comfortably in the chair) that *you* are not going to answer it.

3 **A protective response**. The coach's questions might be inching towards issues that the coachee finds distressing to discuss (e.g. not getting the promotion she so wanted or being treated badly by her boss). Signs that this might be the case are a lowering of her mood, avoiding eye contact, changes in body posture, voice tone and longer silences between questions. The coach can suggest conducting an in-session experiment whereby the coachee talks about the issue for five minutes to test her prediction that she will be 'overwhelmed and lose control'. At the end of five minutes – it is very important not to go beyond the agreed time limit – the accuracy of the prediction can be assessed and the coachee can decide whether or not to continue (in

my experience, most do). If the coachee decides to terminate discussion of that particular issue, it can always be reactivated at a later date when she feels more psychologically able to deal with it.

4 **As a punishment**. The coachee does know the answers to the coach's questions but is deliberately withholding the information because of, for example, his belief that she has slighted him. The relationship will suffer and it is the coach's responsibility to investigate the reasons for this rupture and initiate its repair:

Coach: Have I said or done anything to annoy you?
Coachee: Yes! You've talked over me on several occasions. I find it rude and disrespectful when you do that. Why should I answer your questions when you behave like that?
Coach: I apologise for my behaviour and it won't happen again. Is my apology sufficient to refocus attention on your concerns or are there more comments you would like to make about my behaviour?
Coachee: Yes, it is sufficient. I just hope you mean what you say.

The coach will need to monitor closely her behaviour in order to fulfil her assurance and also probe the reasons for her 'talking over' tendencies: 'What stops me from letting him finish what he has to say? Because I want to jump in and impress him with my sharp mind!'

5 **A sarcastic response**, followed by 'You seem to have all the answers'. The coach has been behaving like a wiseacre: he sees the coachee as an audience who will appreciate his 'wisdom' but she is unimpressed. Maybe the coach's supervisor, listening to the session's audio-recording, might say: 'Listen very carefully to her replies: do you think she is responding positively to all the wisdom you're offering?'

The sound of silence

To the best of my knowledge, no coaching book or trainer criticises silence in coaching, yet many people who have attended my training courses over the years have informed me that they are uncomfortable with silence and avoid it as much as possible. Verbal 'noise' is preferable to silence:

Trainer: What's the difficulty with silence in the session?

Trainee: It feels awkward, you should be doing something.

Trainer: Can silence be doing something like allowing the client time to respond to your question?

Trainee: I'm sure that's right but silence feels like you're not helping the person. You've got to justify your fee by moving things along, trying to find solutions.

Trainer: So the meaning of silence for you is . . .?

Trainee: Incompetence.

Trainer: In order to establish your competence or incompetence from your clients' perspective, have you asked them whether they prefer quiet time in order to reply or are helped by your interruptions while they are thinking?

Trainee: (Sheepishly) No, I haven't done that. I could ask them.

Trainer: Could or will?

Trainee: Will.

Silence itself is not the problem, but the negative meaning you apply to it is, which then makes it imperative for you to intervene whenever silence occurs. Another problem with trying to expunge silence from the session is a fundamental one: Socratic questioning requires the person to *think* about his answers; in fact, it might be an issue that he has not thought through before and therefore he may take some time before he replies. To 'start talking to fill the pause and to rescue the client from the discomfort of this awkward . . . situation . . . would be a mistake . . . as it interrupts the client's thought processes and disrupts the purpose of the Socratic question' (DiGiuseppe, 1991: 184).

Instead of filling pauses with emollient chatter, the coach might ask further questions hoping to 'nudge' the person into giving an answer but, again, this tactic subverts the Socratic process – each new question undermines the purpose of the previous one and the person's thinking time is 'crowded out' with several questions competing for her attention. Also, the person might be experiencing discomfort from the cognitive dissonance (i.e. psychological tension arises when a person's beliefs contradict each other or her behaviour) triggered by the coach's question (e.g. 'You say you'll do whatever it takes to deal with this issue yet you don't carry out the tasks you've agreed to do. So what stops intent and action from keeping in step?'). The person's struggle to answer this question might reveal his block(s) to change (e.g. 'My head wants the change but my heart is not so sure'). As DiGiuseppe (1991: 184) comments: 'It is wise to let the client feel the discomfort. Thirty seconds or so of silence in a . . . session may seem like an eternity, but it may be time well spent.' The person can then seek ways of mending this schism between head and heart.

Not listening

The Channel 4 news presenter, Jon Snow, once remarked that sometimes he is so busy preparing his next 'penetrating' question that he misses important information his interviewee (e.g. a politician) has just disclosed that could have led to a more substantial or revealing interview. A common belief I have heard among coaches is: 'I've got to keep one step ahead in coaching.' This prompts the question: 'One step ahead of what?' Usual replies include 'anticipating the person's next move', 'not being caught out when she stops talking' or 'being ready to deal with anything he throws at me'. Unfortunately, these replies demonstrate that the coach is not really listening because his attention is on his own thinking in his determination not to be 'caught out' as an 'incompetent coach' (a recurring theme in my training and supervision of coaches). This self-talk only allows an intermittent focus on what the person is saying, instead of the non-distractible focus that is required. This kind of focus depends on the coach keeping in step with the client's thinking and feeling and not trying to predict its destination, thereby mentally racing ahead to have an answer ready and waiting when the client 'arrives'. Not listening can lead to stark incongruities between the person's concerns and the coach's response:

Coachee: (Concluding remarks) So I felt utterly destroyed by his comments when I had worked so damn hard on the project, when I had put everything I had into it.

Coach: (Matter-of-factly) So what's your next step then?

'Utterly destroyed' needs to be explored before steps are taken! As so many coaching books keep emphasising that coaching is forward-looking, some coaches might think that all their questions should have this forward focus to them and thereby neglect here-and-now reflection, which is equally important – it is unwise to advance with ignorance guiding the way. As Downey (2003: 62) observes: 'Many of us listen not with the intention to understand but with the intention to respond.' I think it takes considerable mental discipline to stay in the moment with the person in order to understand the full import of what she is saying and resist that almost compulsive urge to move ahead and have a response, any response, ready the moment she stops talking.

Insight is not enough

A moment of insight in the session ('The penny has just dropped. I can see so clearly now why I keep going around in circles on this issue') can seem as if the person is now on the cusp of change: insight will be quickly followed by sustained action. Unfortunately, as Haidt (2006: 26) points out: 'Epiphanies can be life-altering, but most fade in days or weeks.' Why they 'fade' is because there is no follow-through with a sustained action plan – cognition without ignition (Dryden, 1985). Some of my coachees have shown an initial enthusiastic surge of activity flowing from their insights, but these activity levels have dropped or stopped as surge turns into struggle in coping with the vicissitudes of change. Why insight is insufficient to promote change can start with the coach asking: 'Will simply acknowledging that you're a poor golfer turn you into a good one?' Once goals are attained, another question to ask is: 'Is achieving your goal the same thing as maintaining it, for example, is getting fit the same as staying fit?'

Creativity

Creativity is applying new thinking to old problems. Socratic questioning can be used in the service of divergent thinking to 'shake up' the person's familiar problem-solving attempts:

> Divergent thinking involves taking risks with your thinking in ways that defy logic, appear absurd and seem foolish to other people. As such, creative thinking frequently involves the temporary suspension of critical thinking to enable new ideas to develop, new associations to form and new perspectives to emerge in your mind.
>
> (Neenan and Dryden, 2002: 131)

I once saw a busy executive who kept on insisting how important exercise was to him but never took any. Instead of him spending the session telling me why he could not find the time for exercise or me trying to convince him of its importance, I asked him how he could start exercising *right now* (I had ascertained earlier that he had no health problems that would preclude exercise). He was initially flustered by the directness of the question but suggested 'maybe going for a brisk walk', which we did for thirty minutes. He said that my question had 'jumped over every excuse I could think of and forced me to put up or shut up'. He agreed to go out for brisk thirty-minute walks at least three times per week as part of his action plan for change. Some coaches might be wary about using divergent thinking in case they appear 'foolish' (i.e. not rational) in their coachees' eyes or because they must be certain of a successful outcome, which undermines its purpose.

Experiments

Experiments are a very effective way of gathering information, testing hypotheses, re-evaluating previous conclusions, responding to 'I don't know' – in other words, moving coachees into new territory. A manager said she overreacted to every criticism of her but was puzzled as to why she behaved like that until she carried out an experiment where she held her tongue when being criticised. What she discovered surprised her: in her mind, not responding put her in a subordinate position because the other person had won the exchange and therefore 'had something over me'; consequently, she might be viewed as 'weak' by senior managers and thereby jeopardise her chances of promotion. Also, she made the connection between being bullied at school and criticised at work: 'I'm not going to be pushed around.' So the costs for her of staying silent were high.

She was very keen on 'impression management' – that is, displaying a range of positive personae to colleagues and superiors, depending on the context. I asked her:

Coach: Might your overreaction be seen as being out of control or lacking a proportionate response to the circumstances?

Coachee: I worry about that too. I'm sure the impression I'm creating is not the right one, bit of a loose cannon, that sort of thing. I want to find some way of reacting constructively to criticism only when it's important to do so and not see it as being bullied.

Coach: Any ideas how to do that?

Coachee: Maybe develop some rule about when to respond.

Which is what she did. The new rule was based on present, not past, experiences and focused on the criterion: 'Does the criticism help me to improve my performance?' She carried out further experiments to determine not only if she could distinguish between helpful and unhelpful criticism and not react to the latter kind, but also if she was implementing the helpful sort. Although it was a struggle at times to keep her old impulses in check, she felt much more in control and found that so much mental energy that had previously gone into defending herself to others or brooding was now redirected to improving her performance and 'creating a more favourable impression'. The disadvantages of impression management were discussed, such as others becoming wary of trusting you as they cannot be sure which persona is the real person (Sperry, 2004). The coachee had not considered this and went away to ponder the pros and cons of behavioural consistency versus attempting to create a series of 'dazzling impressions'.

Making suggestions

Asking nothing but Socratic questions can be a form of mental torture – a remorseless extraction of every last ounce of cognitive data to identify and deal with the person's presenting issues. Asking questions is the major but not the only role of a coach; other activities include teaching skills, explaining concepts, giving feedback, offering advice and making suggestions. When considering offering a suggestion, gain the coachee's permission first. If he finds it helpful ('I like that idea a lot'), you can return to a Socratic mode and ask in what specific ways your suggestion is helpful to him in tackling his concerns. Then I suggest a closed question to concentrate his mind on the reply: 'Are you willing to take ownership of my suggestion?' This is an important step to take in case he says at the next session: 'Your suggestion didn't work!' Remind him of his ownership of the suggestion and then ask pointedly, 'How did *you* not make *your* suggestion work?' (Hauck, 1980).

Conclusion

Socratic questioning is as useful in coaching as it is in CBT. Through my experience as a cognitive behavioural therapist, coach and trainer/supervisor of coaches, I have explained what I believe to be good Socratic questions and have shown this questioning style in action in coach–coachee dialogues. To reach and maintain a high standard of Socratic questioning, deliberate practice is required, such as reviewing audio-recordings of sessions to provide a logical basis for the sequencing of the questions. Experienced or expert coaches may rely too much on intuition in 'just knowing' what to ask, avoid deliberate practice and, consequently, suffer erosion in their coaching competence, although it may take some time before this becomes apparent to them. Asking good Socratic questions is an essential skill for all coaches to have because it encourages your coachees to reflect on their thinking and actions in order to develop new problem-solving perspectives, improve performance, achieve goals and take their lives in often unanticipated directions.

Discussion issues

- What would be the indications that you are attempting to change minds rather than guide discovery?
- In what ways could guided discovery become too exploratory, thereby interfering with goal achievement?
- If you do not make a written record or audio-recording of your coaching sessions in order to review them, how would you know how much of the session is devoted to Socratic questioning or even if your questions actually are Socratic?
- What are your thoughts and feelings about silence in the session and how do you deal with them?

References

Auerbach, J. E. (2006) Cognitive coaching. In D. R. Stober and A. M. Grant (Eds.), *Evidence Based Coaching Handbook*. Hoboken, NJ: Wiley.

Bennett-Levy, J. (2006) Therapist skills: A cognitive model of their acquisition and refinement. *Behavioural and Cognitive Psychotherapy*, *34*(1): 57–78.

DiGiuseppe, R. (1991) Comprehensive cognitive disputing in RET. In M. E. Bernard (Ed.), *Using Rational-Emotive Therapy Effectively: A Practitioner's Guide*. New York: Plenum Press.

Downey, M. (2003) *Effective Coaching*, 2nd edn. London: Thomson-Texere.

Dryden, W. (1985) Cognition without ignition. *Contemporary Psychology*, *30*(10): 788–789.

Ericsson, K. A., Prietula, M. J. and Cokely, E. T. (2007) The making of an expert. *Harvard Business Review*, *85*(7/8): 115–121.

Fournies, F. F. (2000) *Coaching for Improved Work Performance*, rev. edn. New York: McGraw-Hill.

Haidt, J. (2006) *The Happiness Hypothesis*. London: Arrow Books.

Hanna, F. J. (2002) *Therapy with Difficult Clients*. Washington, DC: American Psychological Association.

Hauck, P. (1980) *Brief Counseling with RET*. Philadelphia, PA: Westminster Press.

James, I. A. and Morse, R. (2007) The use of questions in cognitive behaviour therapy: Identification of question type, function and structure. *Behavioural and Cognitive Psychotherapy*, *35*(4): 507–511.

Luecke, R. (2004) *Coaching and Mentoring*. Boston, MA: Harvard Business School Press.

Megginson, D. and Clutterbuck, D. (2005) *Techniques for Coaching and Mentoring*. Oxford: Elsevier.

Myers, D. G. (2004) *Intuition: Its Powers and Perils*. New Haven, CT: Yale Nota Bene Books.

Neenan, M. (2006) Cognitive behavioural coaching. In J. Passmore (Ed.), *Excellence in Coaching: The Industry Guide*. London: Kogan Page.

Neenan, M. and Dryden, W. (2002) *Life Coaching: A Cognitive-Behavioural Approach*. Hove, UK: Brunner-Routledge.

Padesky, C. A. (1993, September 24) Socratic questioning: Changing minds or guiding discovery? Paper presented at the *European Congress of Behavioural and Cognitive Therapies*, London.

Padesky, C. A. and Greenberger, D. (1995) *Clinician's Guide to Mind Over Mood*. New York: Guilford Press.

Sperry, L. (2004) *Executive Coaching*. Hove, UK: Brunner-Routledge.

Westbrook, D., Kennerley, H. and Kirk, J. (2007) *An Introduction to Cognitive Behaviour Therapy: Skills and Applications*. London: Sage.

Recommended reading

Neenan, M. (2006) Cognitive behavioural coaching. In J. Passmore (Ed.), *Excellence in Coaching: The Industry Guide*. London: Kogan Page.

5

Struggles with low self-esteem: Teaching self-acceptance

Stephen Palmer and Helen Williams

Introduction

This chapter discusses the concept of self-esteem and the challenges faced by the coach and coachee as they tackle low self-esteem and related issues such as fear of failure, worthlessness and perfectionism. The alternative concept of self-acceptance is presented and its potential role in the reduction or elimination of self-esteem induced stress explored. A range of techniques and interventions based on cognitive behavioural (Neenan and Palmer, 2001), rational (Palmer, 2009) and multimodal coaching (Palmer, 2008) are described for use with coachees needing to tackle self-esteem related problems and increase greater self-acceptance. Coaching dialogue is used throughout to bring the interventions to life.

Self-esteem

The concept of self-esteem is both colloquially familiar and commonplace as a topic of academic research. In 1890 William James first referred to self-esteem as 'an elementary endowment of human nature' (James, 1890). Cooley (1902) described how a person identifies the self through subjective feelings and seeks to see themselves as others do, coining the phrase 'the looking-glass self'. In the Cambridge Dictionary self-esteem is defined as '*the belief and confidence in your own ability and value*'.

In Western society it is very common for people to build their self-esteem on the basis of external factors, examples of which can include (see Palmer, 1997):

- Achievement (e.g. passing exams, obtaining professional qualifications).
- Good relationships with significant others.
- A satisfactory job.
- Effective performance or competence in personally significant areas.
- Material possessions.
- Being attractive.
- Being a good parent/grandparent.
- Being loved by significant others.
- Being approved of by significant others.
- Being a good lover or partner.
- Practising a religious faith.

It follows that if the person does not obtain the personally significant possession or other aspect, or does not retain it or live up to their expectation about themselves, then they are likely to become self-critical, thus re-affirming 'self-downing' beliefs (Dryden, 1995, 2011) and reducing their sense of self-esteem. Ellis (1996) described how many clients report 'ego-disturbance' whereby they have dis-esteemed themselves due to a perceived failure or avoidance of a problem. In extreme cases the loss of the significant external factor or factors, and the loss of self-esteem with it, can result in stress, anxiety and depression. Considering that each of these personal aspects or external factors may well be unattainable, or lost at some point in time, the person has arguably set themselves up to fail. This has been referred to as the 'self-esteem trap' (Palmer and Cooper, 2010).

Self-esteem and perfectionism

Self-downing and self-depreciating beliefs may also be derived as a consequence of dogmatic and demanding beliefs such as 'I *must* achieve my targets' (see Ellis, 1994, 1996, 2005). As such, low self-esteem is often accompanied by perfectionist tendencies; the individual becomes highly demanding of themselves, and of others, in order to demonstrate their worthiness and value as a person. Neenan and Dryden define perfectionism as '*the uncompromising pursuit of exceptionally high standards*' (Neenan and Dryden, 2002: 57). For example, the coachee may state: 'I must perform well otherwise I'm a total failure.' The cognitive behavioural coach will typically challenge the validity of the premise 'I must perform well' and also the subsequent derivative 'otherwise I'm a total failure'. It is easy to see how the two types of beliefs reinforce and sustain each other; if a person really thinks they are a 'total failure' then understandably they would insist they 'must' perform well. In our experience, if the derivative 'otherwise I'm a totally failure' is successfully disputed and modified, then the coachee is less likely to maintain the demand 'I must perform well'.

Acquisition and maintenance

Self-downing and self-depreciating beliefs are typically imbibed over a lifetime, with roots in childhood experiences and with parents, siblings and teachers playing influential roles. Palmer (1997) observes how when a child makes a mistake a significant other such as a parent or teacher might say, 'You stupid boy/girl for making a mistake', and when they do well at a task they may say, 'You good boy/girl for doing well in your exams'. Over a period of time the child can gradually infer that they are equivalent to their actions (Palmer, 1997). Ellis (1976b) has suggested that humans have a biological tendency to think both rationally and irrationally. Once self-downing beliefs are in place, they are likely to be continually re-enforced and maintained as the individual reminds themselves 'I'm useless' or 'I'm worthless'. Alfred Korzybski (1933), who originated the philosophy of General Semantics, suggested that the imprecise use of language often leads to distorted thinking, which in turn sustains and perpetuates irrational and unhelpful beliefs. In this respect it is not an easy task to dislodge these beliefs.

The difficulties with developing self-esteem

Conventional wisdom suggests that enhancing self-esteem is a desirable goal of coaching. However, self-esteem has its drawbacks and can often set up a cycle of avoidance and procrastination, especially if the person is a rigid perfectionist. With self-esteem, the person often feels good about themselves when life is going well but bad when life is not going well (see Palmer and Cooper, 2010; Wilding and Palmer, 2006, 2010). Coaching the coachee to acknowledge their strengths and achievements is likely to enhance self-esteem in the immediate to short term. However, the coachee may also dis-esteem themselves when they do not succeed at valued tasks, exhibit negative traits, act in an unacceptable manner or if they receive disapproval from others (Dryden, 1991; Palmer, 1997).

Self-acceptance

A typical aim of cognitive behavioural coaching is in facilitating psychological robustness, in other words assisting the coachee to develop the tendency not to disturb themselves and thereby enhance their performance in both work and social domains. As discussed, the concept of self-esteem has limitations in achieving this aim. An alternative concept to overcome self-rating is that of unconditional self-acceptance, where '*the individual fully and unconditionally accepts him or herself whether or not he behaves intelligently, correctly, or competently and whether or not other people approve, respect, or love him*' (adapted from Ellis, 1977a: 101). In self-help books self-acceptance has been described as '[*accepting myself*], *warts and all, with a strong preference to improve myself, even though realistically I don't have to*' (Palmer and Cooper, 2010: 83). Wilding and Palmer observe how '*The secret of true self-acceptance is to stop seeing ourselves as a single entity. We are made up of hundreds of component parts – our skills, abilities, physique, sporting or artistic leanings, levels of competitiveness, intelligence, emotional maturity, personal qualities . . . and many more*' (Wilding and Palmer, 2011: 48). Surprisingly, only limited research has been undertaken to focus on the intellectual and conceptual mutation from self-esteem to self-acceptance (Chamberlain and Haaga, 2001a, 2001b), and clearly more is needed.

In cognitive behavioural coaching the concept of self-acceptance is explained to the coachee, emphasising that there is overwhelming evidence that humans are by nature fallible and imperfect. By accepting themselves, warts and all, and by viewing the goal of personal improvement as strongly desirable but not imperative, the person is empowered to reduce perfectionist demands and the accompanying self-induced stress, and to experience a new sense of personal freedom (Palmer and Cooper, 2010). Other commentators such as Carl Rogers (1957, 1961) and Paul Tillich (1953) have also emphasised the value of individuals unconditionally accepting others and themselves.

Developing greater self-acceptance

To self-accept is to recognise specific weaknesses and skills deficits and to work on improving these, without disputing the value and worth of the self. Therefore, instead of global ratings such as 'failure', 'incompetent', 'worthless', the coachee is encouraged to accept themselves as fallible, complex, ever-changing human beings (Ellis, 1976a; Palmer and Dryden, 1995) and to only rate specific aspects of themselves (acts, deeds, thoughts, feelings and other behaviours) (Dryden, 1991; Lazarus, 1977). In so doing, they reduce their risk of experiencing unhealthy negative emotions such as depression, anxiety, guilt or shame (Ellis, 1994). If unconditional self-acceptance seems too big a step, then the coach may work with the coachee towards the goal of 'greater self-acceptance' (Neenan, 1997).

Dryden (1994: 118) recommends that coaches '*vary the medium, but not the message*'. The core message of self-acceptance can be communicated through a number of different coaching interventions. These are described in the remainder of this chapter and demonstrated through coaching dialogue, grouped into eight themes as follows:

1 Tackling self-downing and perfectionist thoughts.
2 Teaching self-acceptance.
3 Avoiding over-generalisations of specific weaknesses.
4 Humorous interventions.
5 Conditional self-acceptance.
6 Performance-enhancing forms.
7 Homework assignments.
8 Shame attacking.

1. Tackling self-downing and perfectionist thoughts

Having explained the contrasting concepts of self-esteem and self-acceptance to the coachee, and with the goal of developing greater self-acceptance in mind, it is useful to first create some cognitive dissonance as to whether it is helpful or unhelpful to hold self-downing and/or perfectionist beliefs. The following techniques may be used to this end.

Questioning

Didactic questions or statements are used to educate the coachee about their unhelpful self- or other-downing beliefs. The three major arguments used to dispute unhelpful, irrational beliefs are empirical (consistent with reality), logical (based on logic) and pragmatic (functional/helpful). For example:

- Empirical: *There is no evidence that if you fail at a task, therefore you are a total failure.*
- Logical: *It is not logical to conclude that if you fail at a task, therefore you are a total failure.*
- Pragmatic: *If you carry on believing that when you fail at a task you are a total failure, you will stay stressed, anxious and depressed.*

However, Socratic disputing of self/other-downing beliefs uses open questions to put the onus on the coachee to think and answer the questions. This is illustrated as follows:

- Empirical: *Where is the evidence that you are a total failure just because you did not complete this task perfectly?*
- Logical: *Is it logical to conclude that as you failed at one task, therefore you are a total failure?*
- Pragmatic: *Where is it going to get you if you carry on believing that as you do not do everything absolutely perfectly, you are therefore a total failure?*

Often coachees have a preference for either didactic or Socratic questioning. In addition, they may have a preference for the empirical, logical or pragmatic question. The coach usually needs to experiment to discover which works best for a particular coachee. If in doubt, ask the coachee for their preference.

Inference chaining

Inference chaining is an assessment technique that uses a series of questions to help the coachee identify the most critical or relevant aspect of the activating event that is inducing stress (Palmer and Cooper, 2010). This in turn enables the coach to identify the key stress-inducing thoughts or beliefs, such as those associated with low self-esteem and perfectionism. See the following example adapted from Palmer (2009: 11–12):

Coach: What is anxiety provoking in your mind about not giving a good presentation?
[The coach facilitates discussion of the Activating event, A, and starts inference chaining.]

Coachee: My colleagues may laugh.

Coach: Let's assume for the moment that they do laugh, what is anxiety provoking about that?

Coachee: I'll be discredited. They might think I'm stupid.

Coach: For the moment let's assume you are discredited and are seen as stupid, what's anxiety provoking about that?

Coachee: My boss may get to hear about it and I could lose my job.

Coach: If you did lose your job, what would you be anxious about?

Coachee: Well, I suppose I might lose my flat and end up on the street.
[Coach now reviews the four inferences.]

Coach: I'd just like to review what we've covered. You are possibly anxious about a number of issues: 1. your colleagues laughing; 2. being discredited and being seen as stupid; 3. you could lose your job; 4. you could lose your flat and end up on the street. When you are getting anxious, what do you think you are most anxious about?

Coachee: I very much doubt I'll lose my flat and end up on the street. But my job means so much to me. I wouldn't want to lose it. It's what I've always wanted.

Coach: Are you saying that it's not so much the presentation you're anxious about but losing the job you treasure is the real fear?

[The coach has derived the hypothesised Critical 'A' or most relevant aspect of the Activating event.]

Coachee: Yeah.

Coach: I want you to really imagine you have lost your job . . . the job you've always wanted. Remember, you've spent years striving to get this job and you've lost it. Can you imagine this in your mind's eye?

[The coach begins the process of eliciting stress-inducing, performance-interfering or resilience-reducing thoughts and beliefs.]

Coachee: I can.

Coach: What are you telling yourself at this very moment?

Coachee: I must not lose this job.

[NB: A rigid, absolutist, demanding belief.]

Coach: And if you did lose it?

[Question is asked to help the coachee to make conscious his or her feared event.]

Coachee: I couldn't stand it. Life would be awful.

[NB: Low frustration tolerance and awfulising beliefs.]

Coach: How would you see yourself as a person?

[Coach checks out if the coachee might lower self-acceptance if the job is lost.]

Coachee: A total failure!

[Low self-acceptance.]

In this case example the coach then focused on challenging and restructuring the self-downing belief, 'a total failure'. Note that the other unhelpful beliefs elicited may also need attention.

Thinking errors and skills

A number of common thinking errors have been identified (see Neenan and Dryden, 2002; Palmer and Cooper, 2010).

The coach can help the coachee to become aware of these thinking errors, to monitor their presence and to choose instead to engage in alternative realistic thinking skills. One or more of the thinking errors may be involved for an individual with perfectionism and underlying low self-esteem. Table 5.1 summarises the thinking errors and

Table 5.1 Thinking errors and skills

Tackle common thinking errors with effective thinking skills	
Errors	**Skills**
All or nothing thinking (e.g. I'll never get it right)	See the shades of grey
Labelling (e.g. globally rating ourselves a failure or incompetent)	Avoid labelling oneself or others; rate the behaviour not the person
Focusing on the negative (e.g. I've made a number of mistakes)	Befriend yourself; be supportive!
Discounting the positive (e.g. I was lucky when I passed the exam)	Focus on the positive
Under-playing or discounting strengths	Write a list of personal strengths
Mind-reading what others are thinking (e.g. they think I'm incompetent)	Seek evidence; avoid assumptions about other people's opinions or the future
Predicting the worst-case scenario (e.g. I'm going to screw up)	Keep things in perspective
Making mountains out of molehills	De-awfulise; keep things in perspective
Unfairly blaming oneself or others	Avoid the blame game; broaden the picture
Making unrealistic demands of oneself or others (e.g. I must perform well)	Avoid 'shoulds' and 'musts'; consider what is good enough
Thinking 'I can't stand it'; avoiding or delaying starting the task	Remind self that 'I can stand it'; avoid procrastinating (the longer we put it off, the worse it is)
Phoneyism or imposter syndrome (e.g. 'even if I perform well, one day my colleagues may find out I'm incompetent, a phoney')	Self-acceptance training

provides the thinking skills that may be useful alternatives for the coachee.

It is worth noting that, generally, once a perfectionist becomes experienced with undertaking a particular performance related task such as giving a lecture, their stress and performance anxiety usually are reduced as their fear of failure diminishes. However, if a person still reports high levels of performance anxiety even though they perform well, then they may be suffering from phoneyism (sometimes known as imposter syndrome), which will need to be addressed.

Zig-Zag/Two-chair

Dryden (1995, 2001) developed the Zig-Zag dialogue to encourage coachees to forcefully dispute their irrational beliefs. The first step is for the coachee to sit in their usual chair, and to write down a rational belief such as 'I'm a fallible person'. The coachee then rates their degree of conviction in the rational belief, from zero (no conviction) to one hundred (total conviction). The coachee is then asked to sit in another chair before forcefully disputing the rational belief, noting down the objections. The coachee then returns to their usual chair and forcefully answers each of the irrational disputes in turn. Finally, the coachee re-rates his or her level of conviction in the rational belief.

2. Teaching self-acceptance

The self is too complex to be globally rated

Big I, little i

The Big I, little i technique was developed by Arnold Lazarus (1977), based on the concept of the 'egoless self', and can be used for both life and executive coaching. Ellis, Gordon, Neenan and Palmer (adapted 1997: 112–114) describe through dialogue how the technique is used. The coach draws a 'Big I' on a whiteboard or sheet of paper (see Figure 5.1):

Figure 5.1 Big I, little i

Coach: Now, this Big 'I' represents you, your totality. And I'm going to fill it up in a minute with little 'i's, which stand for various things about you, such as the way you smile, the kind of TV programme you like, and so on.

Coachee: I get you.

Coach: OK. Now let's fill in this Big I with a few things about you. What would your family or friends say were some of your good points?

[Focuses on positive aspects first.]

Coachee: Oh, well, I've got a good sense of humour, and let me see, I am kindhearted, good to my children, I keep the house clean, I see that they're looked after properly . . . will that do?

[As the coachee was speaking the coach drew small 'i's inside the Big I to represent different aspects about the coachee.]

Coach: Each of these little 'i's stands for some aspect of you; this one (pointing to a little 'i') stands for your good sense of humour, this other one stands for your kind-heartedness, and these other little 'i's represent all those other good points you mentioned you had.

Coachee: I understand.

Coach: Now, these are some of the positive things. I'd imagine your friends and family may know you reasonably well.

Coachee: Yes.

Coach: What negative things would they say about you? [Now focuses on negative aspects.]

Coachee: I easily get angry, I drive too fast . . . and I'm too trusting.

Coach: (Writing more little 'i's inside the Big I) . . . Gets angry, drives too fast, too trusting. Now what about any neutral or indifferent things about yourself?

[To avoid 'all or nothing' perspective regarding the self, neutral aspects are now included.]

Coachee: Oh well, my dress sense isn't too bad, I can do alterations to the children's clothes and my house decorating ability is about average.

Coach: (Adding more little 'i's to represent the coachee's neutral points) If we spent all day on this and considered all the things you have done, including every thought or idea you've had since you were born, how many little 'i's do you think we would have?

Coachee: Loads! We'd easily fill up the Big I.

Coach: Yes, millions of different aspects of yourself, good, bad and neutral. Now let's return to your problem. When you fail at something, like picking your ex-boyfriend and then finding you've made a bad choice [coach now circles one little 'i' to denote this], you say, 'Because I picked this partner and I made a poor choice yet again, that proves I'm weak and an inadequate person'. Bearing in mind what we've been discussing in the last five minutes, are you actually being accurate?

[Asking the coachee to reflect on the exercise and linking it to the presenting problem.]

Coachee: Well, I did make a big mistake when I picked him, and that's the fourth time I've been dumped after picking the wrong guy! Once again I failed to pick somebody who was right for me.

Coach: (Pointing to the little 'i' he had circled inside the Big I) Agreed; you did fail to pick the right person. But how does that – this little 'i' – make you (drawing a circle around the entire Big I) a total failure, and a totally weak and inadequate person?

Coachee: I suppose it doesn't.

Coach: Granted that you may have some skills deficits when it comes to choosing the right partner and you may sometimes act in a weak and inadequate manner but, as we can see from the diagram, this doesn't make you a total failure. When would we have all the facts in, so we could really decide if you were a total failure and a totally weak and inadequate person?

[Taking a bigger perspective.]

Coachee: . . . When I die I suppose!

Coach: You're absolutely right. On your deathbed, when you could have your own day of judgement. You could open up the big book (coach opens his hands as if opening up a large book) and count up the number of times you had been a failure in your entire life. 'Yes, I was a failure on 23 February in 1978; in 1983 I got a low grade in that exam; on four occasions I exhibited poor decision making skills when I picked the wrong partners; my children weren't happy every day of their childhood; in 1985 I acted weakly; I lost my job, twice!'

[Using a humorous didactic style.]

Coachee: (Laughing) Stop! Don't go on. It's ridiculous – to be a total failure I would have to be a failure all of my life, which is blatantly absurd.

Coach: Could you summarise what point you think I'm attempting to make?

[Checking the coachee's understanding of the exercise.]

Coachee: I'm too complex to be rated as a total failure although you can rate the things I do, such as acting weakly or picking the wrong partner four times.

Coach: You're right. You can rate your traits, deeds, appearance, actions, skills or skills deficits but you are too complex to rate your entire self.

> To be fair to yourself, the only time you may wish to rate yourself globally is when you have all the facts in, on your deathbed. And even then, if we discover that you have failed at some or even many things in your life it would still be an impossible task to rate yourself as a total failure! In fact one of the aspects of being human is dying, and I can guarantee that you won't fail at that.
> [Summarising the self-acceptance concept.]

Coachee: (Laughs) You're not joking.

With this technique, it is important to avoid just taking a didactic approach. By asking Socratic questions and appropriate humour, coachees usually become actively involved in the method and then provide ample ammunition to dispute their self-downing beliefs (Palmer, 1997).

Tissue box technique

Mitchell Robin (1993) described how he used the technique with a client attending a performance anxiety workshop. Although she was a trained singer she had never been to an audition and was depressed about her lack of attainment. Although this is an example taken from therapy it is equally applicable to the coaching context:

> The specific client mentioned above presented with a full tissue box and was asked to list her strengths and weaknesses. As she listed each positive and negative trait, I asked her to pull one tissue from the tissue box. (This occasionally leaves a small number of tissues remaining in the box and a larger number of tissues scattered around the room. The remaining tissues can also be used to remind clients that they can probably never fully know all of their positive and negative traits.) When the client was satisfied that we had 'seen the worst', I asked her to tell me which tissue was the box: that is, which trait is the person. I asked her, 'Does the container change value even if the contents are lousy?' Some clients will then remind me of the cliché

that 'a rotten apple ruins the bunch', but I point out the basket isn't ruined, and the rotten apple can be removed without changing the basket or the rest of the apples. This particular client was able to see that, by globally rating herself based on her lack of accomplishment at either getting to auditions or actually auditioning once she got there, she was trading one problem for two: she was still not auditioning and now she was feeling both anxious and guilty. She also saw that, by tenaciously focusing on this one particular negative trait, she was ignoring many of her other valuable traits. Such a 'battle of the metaphors' aids the client in coming to grips with the central value in rational emotive therapy: What people do is not what people are.

(adapted from Robin, 1993: 175)

Circles of perfect, bad, fallible person

Three circles are drawn onto an A4 page or flipchart. The first circle drawn represents what most perfectionists strive for, the 'perfect person' (sometimes described as 'Superwoman' or 'Superman'). The coachee is asked to insert a tick for each of their good aspects. The second circle drawn represents an 'imperfect' or 'bad person'. The coachee is asked to insert a cross for each of their imperfect or bad aspects. Finally, a third circle is drawn that realistically represents a fallible person, with ticks and crosses inserted and small circles that represent neutral aspects dependent upon the person, such as brown hair, average sense of humour, and so on (see Figure 5.2).

This technique can illustrate very quickly the illogicality of the 'good versus bad person' concept that a coachee may hold, in contrast to the fallible person.

Sticky-notes

'Sticky-notes' is a further alternative for demonstrating that the self is too complex to be given a single global rating. The coach provides the coachee with a pen and a batch of

Perfect person (alias Superwoman or Superman)

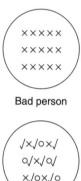

Bad person

Fallible person

Figure 5.2 **The Fallible Self**

sticky-notes. The coachee is asked to think about how they and others would describe themselves, as in the techniques described previously, and to write the first description on a sticky-note. The coachee is asked to stick the sticky-note somewhere on their person: on their face, arms, body, legs. The coachee is then asked to write out another description on another sticky-note, and to stick this note somewhere on their person. This process is repeated as many times as possible, allowing twenty minutes or more for the completion of the task. The coach encourages the coachee to include perceived positive, neutral and negative aspects or traits, and then finally include a description that represents the current presenting problems or concerns. The coach then asks the coachee: 'Which one of these sticky-notes represents you, the whole you?' The coachee typically answers that no single sticky-note represents them, that the process has demonstrated in a rather humorous way that they are made up of a number of different aspects and traits. Some may realise that they are too complex to be rated by any one trait or deed. The coach then returns to the presenting problem and may challenge the coachee about the extent to which they are defined by the sticky-note(s) representing the problem or concern.

A key benefit of using visual techniques is that the coachee usually finds them easier to recall than just dialogue when they become stressed about a particular event. For example, a number of coachees have recounted how they saw in their mind's eye a picture of the 'Big I, little i' diagram when attempting to counter negative thoughts, sometimes years later.

3. Avoiding over-generalisations of specific weaknesses

Bowl of fruit

This well-known intervention temporarily focuses the attention of the coachee away from their presenting problem and provides an interesting analogy:

Coach: I just want to ensure that I've understood you correctly. You're saying that if you fail to reach your deadline, in your eyes, you are a 'failure' and a 'complete right-off'.

[Linking task with global self-rating.]

Coachee: Yep. That's correct – a failure and complete right-off.

Coach: I would like to return to this in a few minutes but in the meantime consider an analogy that may help you to see the situation differently. Is that OK?

[Explaining reason for discussing the analogy.]

Coachee: Fine.

Coach: Just for the moment, imagine you have a bowl of fruit in front of you. In fact, what are your favourite fruits?

Coachee: Pears, apples, oranges. Perhaps grapes.

Coach: In your mind's eye, really imagine the pears . . . apples . . . oranges . . . and grapes . . . in the fruit bowl. Can you see them?

[Building up the picture in the coachee's mind in order to make the analogy more vivid.]

Coachee: Yes, easily.

Coach: Now look at the grapes. Imagine finding one bad grape in the bowl. What would you do?

Coachee: I'd throw the grape away, of course.

Coach: Isn't it interesting. If you have just a bowl of fruit with one bad grape, you would throw away the bad grape and keep the rest of the fruit. Yet if you fail to reach a deadline, you consider yourself as a 'failure' and a 'complete right-off', and effectively would throw yourself away! [Highlighting how the coachee is choosing a different approach in a similar situation.] Do you agree that you are more complex than a bowl of fruit?

Coachee: Of course!

Coach: Then something doesn't quite add up.

Coachee: I see what you're saying. It doesn't add up.

Coach: Do you think it would be useful if we continue examining your belief, 'I'm a failure and a complete right-off'?

Flat tyre

Young (1988) describes a technique for illustrating the illogic of over-generalising. Similar to the bowl of fruit example, in the 'flat tyre' technique the coach asks the coachee whether s/he would 'junk the whole car because it has a flat'. Most coachees would say that would be silly, because the whole car is not ruined on account of a tyre. The coach then points out that this is exactly what they have been doing: 'junking themselves because of a particular fault' (adapted from Young, 1988: 138).

4. Humorous interventions

Ellis (1977a, 1996) recommends the use of humour in therapy to help clients 'take things seriously, but not too seriously'.

Green frog method

A useful humorous technique which can be used in individual or group coaching is that of the 'green frog' method. Coachees often believe that they do not possess the skills to change their global self-rating; the 'green frog' method demonstrates that they do already possess the skills (adapted from Palmer, 1997: 14):

Coach: So you are saying that if your boss thinks you're stupid for making mistakes then he must be right? [Links behaviour to global rating of the self.]

Coachee: Yes.

Coach: If I said, 'You are a green frog', would you believe it?

Coachee: (Laughs) Of course not!
[Note that most coachees usually do not agree with the coach's suggestion as it sounds too ridiculous.]

Coach: Okay. Let's extend this argument. What if all eight of us in this room looked at you and said, 'You really are a green frog'. Would you believe it?

Coachee: Of course not!

Coach: What happens if you went to a football match and a whole stadium of people, perhaps 10,000 people, all turned to you and sang 'Jayne is a green frog, do da, do da, Jayne is a green frog, do da do da day', would you believe it?

Coachee: (Laughs) I might start to doubt myself.

Coach: If you then went and looked in a mirror and just saw yourself as you are now, what then?

Coachee: Assuming I didn't look the same as a green frog, I would think that everybody else had lost their minds (laughs)!!
[Coachee demonstrates that she can discriminate between reality and other people's beliefs if they are incorrect.]

Coach: What if I or we all in this room said 'you've made one mistake, therefore you are stupid', would you believe us?

[Linking the example back to the presenting problem.]

Coachee: Probably.

Coach: Isn't this interesting. When 10,000 people in a stadium say you are a 'green frog', you retain great powers of discrimination. Yet after making a mistake, if you mind-read your boss, or we tell you that you are stupid, you lose all your powers of discrimination and agree with our crazy thinking.

Coachee: I haven't thought of it like that before.

Coach: All I'm suggesting is that you could also choose to use your mental powers of discrimination in situations where you make mistakes and upset yourself.

The coach then continues the discussion until the coachee gains more insight into how she does not have to believe or agree with the self-downing beliefs that she either mind-reads or is told by her boss.

As complex as an amoeba

Dryden (adapted 1987: 107–108) details below an example intervention that helps to promote intellectual rational insight for therapy clients who 'feel worthless'. The intervention can also be used in coaching as this problem may arise in life and executive coaching.

Practitioner: OK, so you say that you're worthless for cheating on your wife, is that right?

[Linking global rating of self to behaviour.]

Client: Yes, that's what I believe.

Practitioner: OK, but let's test that out. Are you saying that you are worthless, or what you've done is worthless?

[Separating out the behaviour from the self-rating.]

Client:	I'm saying that I'm worthless, not just what I did.
Practitioner:	OK, but let's see if that is logical. You know when you say 'I'm worthless' you are giving you, your personhood or your essence a single rating. Can you see that? [Logical challenge.]
Client:	Yes.
Practitioner:	But let's see if you warrant that. You're 35. How many thoughts have you had from the day you were born till now?
Client:	Countless, I guess.
Practitioner:	Add to that all your actions and throw in all your traits for good measure. From that time till now how many aspects of you are there?
Client:	Millions, I guess.
Practitioner:	At least now when you say that Y-O-U ARE WORTHLESS you can see that you're implying that you are about as complex as a single-cell amoeba, and that this cell is worthless. Now is that true from what we've just been discussing?
Client:	No, of course not.
Practitioner:	So do you, in all your complexity, merit a single rating? [Demonstrating that the self is too complex to be rated.]
Client:	No, but I did do a pretty worthless thing and it was serious.
Practitioner:	Agreed, but what has greater validity, the belief 'I'm worthless in all my essence' or the belief 'I am too complex to be rated, but I did do something lousy that I regret'? [Note that the coach does not challenge the belief that what he did behaviourally was a pretty worthless thing to do.]
Client:	The second.

Note how Dryden focuses on challenging the global rating of the self as 'worthless' and does not get side-tracked into discussing whether or not the behaviour (i.e. 'cheating on his wife') was a worthless or lousy thing to have done because this would not address the key self-rating issue.

Tennis

A humorous method of communicating the principle of self-acceptance is that of Dryden's (1994: 119) 'rational and irrational tennis'. Irrational tennis is defined as: 'I hit a bad shot, therefore I am a bad person – I hit a good shot, therefore I am a good person.' Rational tennis is defined as: 'I hit a bad shot, therefore I am a fallible person – I hit a good shot, therefore I am a fallible person.'

The coach demonstrates 'stupid' behaviour

Dryden also outlines a more direct role that the practitioner may take in the use of humour to communicate the principles of self-acceptance. The coach throws a glass of water over him/herself and then asks the practitioner (Dryden, 1994: 119) 'Was that a silly thing to do?', to which the coachee frequently replies 'Yes'. The coach then asks the coachee 'Does that therefore make me a silly person?', to which hopefully the coachee responds 'No'! An alternative humorous action the coach may take, perhaps more suitable for group settings, is to bark like a dog.

5. Conditional self-acceptance

If the coachee has great difficulty in accepting the concept of unconditional self-acceptance, then the coach may suggest the concept of conditional self-acceptance (Palmer, 1997). Sometimes this is the only successful concept to teach when working with coachees with strong religious convictions, whereby conditional self-acceptance focuses on acceptance of the person by their God or prophet. It is more appropriate in personal and life coaching settings.

An example of a typical dialogue with a Christian is detailed below (adapted from Palmer, 1997: 23–25). Note how the coach uses the approach often employed by the television police detective, Colombo – going back to first principles and then asking the coachee to explain anomalies that do not make any apparent sense.

Coachee: I am a worthless person for my marriage break-down. I really can't forgive myself for what I've done.

Coach: You said last week that you are religious.

Coachee: Yes. I'm a practising Christian.

Coach: So you believe in God and that his son was Jesus Christ.

Coachee: Of course.

Coach: I have found it really useful with other clients if I spend a few moments discussing their religious beliefs as often they have a bearing on how they feel. Is that okay?

Coachee: That's fine.

Coach: Good ... Weren't there really two parts to the Bible? In the Old Testament God was not very forgiving.

Coachee: Yes. That's right.

Coach: But you're a Christian. Now let me think about this. ... This means that you believe in Christ's message. I apologise if I'm not very good at this. What do you think were his important messages?

Coachee: He came to save us from our sins.

Coach: So unlike the previous message in the Old Testament, Christ, the Son of God, was into forgiveness. Would you say that it is important for you to listen to his message?

Coachee: Yes. You've hit the nail on the head and that is one of the reasons that I'm so upset. I've caused the breakdown of my marriage and this goes against my Christian values. What will the friends in my congregation think?

Coach: I'm not convinced that you were totally respon-sible for the breakdown of your marriage. Perhaps we could come back to that issue later. [Coach avoiding being side-tracked from dealing with low self-acceptance.] I just don't quite understand something. Can you explain how you believe in Christ's message, but, please correct me if I'm wrong, you don't appear to practise it yourself?

Coachee: What do you mean? I've always done my best to be a good Christian.

Coach: If I've misunderstood things please correct me. Christ gave up his life to save our souls and preached forgiveness. Is that right?

Coachee: Yes.

Coach: You are a practising Christian?

Coachee: Yes.

Coach: Yet you don't practise forgiveness. . . . You don't forgive yourself for what's happened to your marriage.

Coachee: Well, that's different.

Coach: In what way?

Coachee: I just can't forgive myself for what I've done. The family is so important to me.

Coach: Tell me; are you more important than Jesus Christ?

Coachee: No, not in the overall picture.

Coach: Have I got this right? If I could resurrect Jesus and he was here in this room he would forgive you your sins – in this case possibly causing the break-up of your marriage?

Coachee: Well, I suppose so.

Coach: So exactly what makes you so special that your God or his Son can forgive you but you can't forgive yourself?

Coachee: I don't know.

Coach: (Looking serious and very intent) Please help me on this point as I'm having great difficulty understanding this issue. When it comes to forgiveness, one of the most important messages Jesus preached about, are you saying that you are above your God or his Son?

Coachee: Put that way, I suppose I am! That's not right, is it?

Coach: I don't know. But am I right in thinking that Jesus Christ would forgive you your sins and not consider you as a totally 'worthless' individual?

Coachee: I suppose so.

Coach: Even if the congregation disapproved of your behaviour could you still accept yourself on the understanding that Jesus would forgive you and accept you, and this is probably far more important than the congregation's views?

Coachee: Put that way, of course.

Coach: Remind me. Doesn't it say somewhere in the Bible, 'Forgive the sinner but not the sins'?

Coachee: You're right.

Whenever possible, coaching for self-acceptance is generally the preferred intervention when dealing with issues of low self-esteem. However, teaching conditional self-acceptance in some circumstances is more acceptable to the coachee. It goes beyond the remit of a coach to challenge religious beliefs but it is acceptable to explore their beliefs if it assists the coachee to view themselves in a more helpful way.

6. Performance-enhancing forms

Performance-enhancing forms can be used to help the coachee note down their performance-inhibiting thinking (PIT) and then develop performance-enhancing thinking (PET). Figure 5.3 provides an example of a completed form that tackles rules, self-depreciation/self-downing thoughts and low frustration tolerance.

Appendix 1 is a blank of the form that can be enlarged and used for coaching.

7. Homework assignments

A variety of in-between coaching session assignments may be suggested to coachees to help them strive towards unconditional self-acceptance, or greater self-acceptance, such as the following:

- Reading self-help literature or books on increasing self-acceptance (e.g. Dryden and Gordon, 1990a, 1990b, 1992; Ellis, 1977b, 1988, 2005; Ellis and Harper, 1997; Lazarus, Lazarus and Fay, 1993; Palmer and Burton, 1996; Palmer and Cooper, 2010; Wilding and Palmer, 2006, 2010, 2011).

Target problem	Performance-interfering thinking (PIT)	Emotional/behavioural reaction	Performance-enhancing thinking (PET)	Effective and new approach to problem
(A)	(B)	(C)	(D)	(E)
Undertaking a difficult task	I should do a perfect job (Demand)	Performance anxiety Procrastination Butterflies in stomach	It's strongly preferable to do a good job but realistically I don't have to	Stay focused on immediate task to achieve goals
	If I do not do a perfect job then I'm totally useless (Self-depreciation)		I can learn to accept myself if I don't do a perfect job	Start the 'boring bits' earlier and reward self with a large latte coffee and favourite cake once a 'boring bit' has been finished
	I can't stand doing boring tasks (Low frustration tolerance)		Although I don't like doing boring tasks, I'm living proof that I can stand doing them	

Figure 5.3 Completed Performance-Enhancing Form (© Centre for Coaching, 2011)

- Listening to audio-recordings (e.g. Ellis, 1977c) or watching audiovisual recordings such as videos, DVDs or YouTube clips.
- Listening to recordings of the coaching sessions.
- Reading rational coping statements.
- Daily reading or referring to lists (Ellis et al., 1997).

8. Shame attacking

To help a coachee learn that he or she does not have to globally rate him/herself by their behaviour, a 'shame attacking' exercise may be suggested. The coach agrees with the coachee a safe although shame/embarrassing-provoking act that they will undertake in full view of members of the public, colleagues, family or friends. Before undertaking the exercise, the coach cognitively prepares the coachee for the task by disputing the self-downing belief and devising a rational coping statement (Palmer, 1997). For example, the coachee may decide to ask members of the public directions to the nearest train station whilst standing outside a station. If the coachee believes 'If I act stupidly, therefore I am a totally stupid and worthless person', the rational coping statement might be: 'However stupidly I behave it never makes me a totally stupid and worthless person. If other people think I'm stupid then I don't have to agree with them.' This exercise can help a coachee to become more resilient and less concerned about acting stupidly or making mistakes in public.

Conclusion

It is commonplace for coaches to bring self-esteem problems to the coaching conversation. Often it is associated with performance anxiety, fear of failure and holding themselves back from promotion or responsibility. It is recommended that the concept of unconditional and/or greater self-acceptance be introduced and a number of techniques and interventions used to repeatedly communicate this message. We agree with Neenan (1997) that the concept of greater self-acceptance is more easily attainable and probably more realistic for most coachees (and coaches) to achieve.

Last, but not least, coaches may also have self-esteem issues that they bring into the coaching arena, such as ego related performance anxiety or approval seeking, which may hinder the coaching relationship and/or the effectiveness of the coach. Fortunately coaches can self-coach using the techniques in this chapter.

Discussion issues

- Are the concepts of self-esteem and self-acceptance radically different?
- Is achieving unconditional self-acceptance realistic or should the focus be the goal of achieving greater self-acceptance?
- Many of the self-acceptance training techniques and interventions were developed originally for the therapeutic field. Are they suitable for coaching?
- Is it important for the coach to work on increasing their own self-acceptance in order to become more effective coaches?

References

Chamberlain, J. M. and Haaga, D. A. F. (2001a) Unconditional self-acceptance and psychological health. *Journal of Rational-Emotive and Cognitive-Behavior Therapy*, *19*: 163–176.

Chamberlain, J. M. and Haaga, D. A. F. (2001b) Unconditional self-acceptance and reaction to negative feedback. *Journal of Rational-Emotive and Cognitive-Behavior Therapy*, *19*: 177–189.

Cooley, C. H. (1902) *Human Nature and the Social Order*. New York: Scribner's.

Dryden, W. (1987) *Counselling Individuals: The Rational-Emotive Approach*. London: Whurr.

Dryden, W. (1991) *Reason and Therapeutic Change*. London: Whurr.

Dryden, W. (1994) *Progress in Rational Emotive Behaviour Therapy*. London: Whurr.

Dryden, W. (1995) *Brief Rational Emotive Behaviour Therapy*. Chichester, UK: Wiley.

Dryden, W. (2001) *Reason to Change: A Rational Emotive Behaviour Therapy (REBT) Workbook*. Hove, UK: Brunner-Routledge.

Dryden, W. (2011) *Dealing with Clients' Emotional Problems in Life Coaching*. London: Routledge.

Dryden, W. and Gordon, J. (1990a) *Think Your Way to Happiness*. London: Sheldon.

Dryden, W. and Gordon, J. (1990b) *What is Rational-Emotive Therapy? A Personal and Practical Guide*. Loughton: Gale Publications.

Dryden, W. and Gordon, J. (1992) *Think Rationally: A Brief Guide to Overcoming your Emotional Problems*. London: Centre for Rational Emotive Behaviour Therapy.

Ellis, A. (1976a) RET abolishes most of the human ego. *Psychotherapy, 13*: 343–348.

Ellis, A. (1976b) The biological basis of human irrationality. *Journal of Individual Psychology, 32*: 145–168.

Ellis, A. (1977a) Psychotherapy and the value of a human being. In A. Ellis and R. Grieger (Eds.), *Handbook of Rational-Emotive Therapy*. New York: Springer.

Ellis, A. (1977b) Fun as psychotherapy. *Rational Living, 12*(1): 26.

Ellis, A. (1977c) *A Garland of Rational Humorous Songs* (cassette recording and songbook). New York: Institute for Rational Emotive Therapy.

Ellis, A. (1988) *How to Stubbornly Refuse to Make Yourself Miserable about Anything – Yes, Anything!* Secaucus, NJ: Lyle Stuart.

Ellis, A. (1994) *Reason and Emotion in Psychotherapy* (revised and updated edn). New York: Birch Lane Press.

Ellis, A. (1996) *Better, Deeper and More Enduring Brief Therapy: The Rational Emotive Behavior Therapy Approach*. New York: Brunner/Mazel.

Ellis, A. (2005) *The Myth of Self-Esteem: How Rational Emotive Behaviour Therapy can Change your Life Forever*. New York: Prometheus Books.

Ellis, A. and Harper, R. A. (1997) *A Guide to Rational Living* (revised and updated edn). North Hollywood, CA: Wilshire.

Ellis, A., Gordon, J., Neenan, M. and Palmer, S. (1997) *Stress Counselling: A Rational Emotive Behaviour Approach*. London: Cassell (now Sage).

James, W. (1890) *Principles of Psychology*. New York: Dover.

Korzybski, A. (1933) *Science and Sanity*. San Francisco, CA: International Society of General Semantics.

Lazarus, A. A. (1977) Toward an egoless state of being. In A. Ellis and R. Grieger (Eds.), *Handbook of Rational-Emotive Therapy*. New York: McGraw-Hill.

Lazarus, A. A., Lazarus, C. and Fay, A. (1993) *Don't Believe it for a Minute: Forty Toxic Ideas that are Driving you Crazy*. San Luis Obispo, CA: Impact Publishers.

Neenan, M. (1997) Reflections on two major REBT concepts. *The Rational Emotive Behaviour Therapist, 4*(1): 31–33.

Neenan, M. and Dryden, W. (2002) *Life Coaching: A Cognitive Behavioural Perspective*. Hove, UK: Routledge.

Neenan, M. and Palmer, S. (2001) Cognitive behavioural coaching. *Stress News*, *13*(3): 15–18.

Palmer, S. (1997) Self-acceptance: concept, techniques and interventions. *The Rational Emotive Behaviour Therapist*, *4*(2): 4–30.

Palmer, S. (2008) Multimodal coaching and its application to workplace, life and health coaching. *The Coaching Psychologist*, *4*(1): 21–29.

Palmer, S. (2009) Rational coaching: A cognitive behavioural approach. *The Coaching Psychologist*, *5*(1): 12–18.

Palmer, S. and Burton, T. (1996) *Dealing with People Problems at Work*. Maidenhead, UK: McGraw-Hill.

Palmer, S. and Cooper, C. (2010) *How to Deal with Stress*. London: Kogan Page.

Palmer, S. and Dryden, W. (1995) *Counselling for Stress Problems*. London: Sage.

Robin, M. H. (1993) Overcoming performance anxiety: Using RET with actors, artists, and other 'performers'. In W. Dryden and L. K. Hill (Eds.), *Innovations in Rational-Emotive Therapy*. Newbury Park, CA: Sage.

Rogers, C. R. (1957) The necessary and sufficient conditions of therapeutic personality change. *Journal of Consulting Psychology*, *21*: 95–103.

Rogers, C. R. (1961) *On Becoming a Person*. Boston, MA: Houghton Mifflin.

Tillich, P. (1953) *The Courage to Be*. New York: Oxford.

Wilding, C. and Palmer, S. (2006) *Zero to Hero*. London: Hodder Arnold.

Wilding, C. and Palmer, S. (2010) *Beat Self-Esteem with CBT*. London: Teach Yourself.

Wilding, C. and Palmer, S. (2011) *Boost your Self-Esteem*. London: Flash.

Young, H. S. (1988) Teaching rational self-value concepts to tough customers. In W. Dryden and P. Trower (Eds.), *Developments in Rational-Emotive Therapy*. Milton Keynes, UK: Open University.

Recommended reading

Wilding, C. and Palmer, S. (2006) *Zero to Hero*. London: Hodder Arnold.

Wilding, C. and Palmer, S. (2010) *Beat Self-Esteem with CBT*. London: Teach Yourself.

Wilding, C. and Palmer, S. (2011) *Boost your Self-Esteem*. London: Flash.

6

Understanding and developing resilience

Michael Neenan and Windy Dryden

Introduction

Resilience is an intriguing yet elusive concept: intriguing because it provides some kind of answer to why one person crumbles in the face of turbulent times while another gains strength from them, but elusive in that the concept resists a definitive definition. Vaillant (1993: 287) calls resilience an 'ineffable quality' while Coutu (2003: 18) suggests 'that we will never completely understand it'. A starting point in attempting to understand resilience is to look for the meaning (attitude) that people attach to noxious events: 'There's got to be a way out of this mess and I'm going to find it' or 'What's the point? Nothing will ever change'. People react differently to the same event based upon how they view it, which underscores the point that there is *always* more than one way of seeing events: in other words, you choose your viewpoint even if, at times, it is difficult to discern any other viewpoint than the current one (Butler and Hope, 2007). So meaning is not static and therefore can change over time: in the above example, the first person falls into despair when his initial attempts at problem-solving fail, while the second person begins to see a glimmer of hope when she gets some unexpected help. This latter point shows that developing resilience is not solely intrinsically determined but is affected by a collection of factors, including access to social support and the severity and duration of the adversity (Bonanno, 2006; Rutter, 1993).

It is not always easy to say who is demonstrating resilient behaviour in times of misfortune: a snapshot of a particular moment in the struggle can give the wrong impression of who will make it in the longer term and who will not. What we think is unhelpful in discussing resilience is the popular idea of 'bouncing back' from adversity, which reminds me (MN) of a childhood toy I had: a blow-up, chest-high figure of Yogi Bear that, when punched, fell to the floor but sprang back immediately to the upright position. 'Bouncing back' suggests a rapid and effortless return from adversity with barely a hair out of place, an enviable sangfroid. This might be the ideal that some wish to aspire to and yet it seems more of a comic book view that may well trigger self-depreciation (seeing oneself as inadequate) if this ideal is not realised in times of crisis. If the person can spring back so effortlessly, was it a genuine adversity she actually experienced? Is staying late at work for several days in a row just as much of an adversity as being caught in a bomb blast?

Obviously adversity is subjectively determined but, as some writers point out, a resilient response to adversity engages the whole person, not just aspects of the self, in order to face, endure, overcome and perhaps be transformed by the struggle (Grotberg, 2001). To us, this suggests that coming or struggling back from adversity is the more realistic response than bouncing back (Neenan, 2009). Therefore, as Walsh (2006: 6) observes, 'We must be careful not to equate competent functioning with resilience' – that is, taking in our stride daily demands on our time and energy is not the same as attempting to deal with traumatic events such as sexual assault or losing a limb in a car crash.

Another unhelpful idea about resilience is that because you have been toughened by hard times you are now invulnerable – nothing can crush this veritable superman. No matter how robust you have become through your difficult experiences, you still remain vulnerable to coping poorly with future adverse events; no one has an absolute resistance to adversity. Resilience cannot be seen as a fixed attribute of the person – when circumstances change, resilience alters (Rutter, 1993). In his study of the psychological effects of war on soldiers, *The Anatomy of Courage* (1945/2007), Lord Moran (Charles Wilson) famously likened courage to capital, not continuing income: whatever the amount in any individual soldier's account, it will eventually be spent – 'When their capital was done, they were finished' (2007: 70).

With regard to the idea of indefatigable resilience, a tough and resourceful manager that I (MN) was coaching was involved in a car accident and suffered some cuts and bruises as well as shock, but the real shock for him was that he needed a week off work to recover. He had a normal human response to the accident but dismissed it contemptuously as 'being pathetic' and could not understand why he was not back at his desk the next day. He thought he was 'stress resistant' – no adverse event could weaken or undermine his hardiness. Initially, he made matters worse for himself by refusing to learn some important lessons from the discrepancy between his actual response to the accident and the ideal one he wanted; eventually, he reformulated his view of resilience in more realistic terms: 'Strong and capable, but still vulnerable at times.' He also provided more support to those of his colleagues he had previously dismissed as 'losers' when they complained about their heavy workloads or missed performance targets.

Another point to consider with the 'bouncing back' image is this: Does your life return to exactly the same state it was before the adversity? As new meaning has emerged from overcoming the adversity (the transformational component), some previous beliefs and behaviours will probably become obsolete, so it is very unlikely that your life would return unchanged to this pre-adversity state. And for this new meaning to emerge, considerable time may be needed to process emotionally charged material resulting from the adversity (e.g. the unexpected death of a family member). 'Bouncing back' suggests that little time would be allowed for this process.

The term 'survivor' has heroic connotations: the person is still standing strong and resolute when the storm has passed. A survivor and a person demonstrating resilience are not necessarily undergoing the same adaptive process of recovery. A survivor can be mired in bitterness and blame while the resilient person is displaying personal growth and pursuing important goals (Walsh, 2006). 'Unlike the term *survivor*, *resilient* emphasizes that people do more than merely get through difficult emotional experiences, hanging on to inner equilibrium by a thread' (O'Connell Higgins, 1994: 1; italics in original). So surviving per se may fall short of the requirements for a resilient response to tough times.

Finally, there is no prescriptive way for people to be resilient: they can assemble their own resilience-building strategies depending on their personality styles, ages, individual strengths, cultural differences (Newman, 2003) – customised resilience. The research shows that everyone has the capacity to become resilient; it is not the innate ability of a chosen few (Grotberg, 2001; Siebert, 2005).

So far, we have been talking about resilience in the context of adversity but the discussion of resilience has been expanded by some writers and researchers:

> to become a primary focus of each person's life, whether or not that person has experienced great adversity. All of us encounter some degree of stress and challenge in everyday life. No one can predict which of us will at some point face unimagined adversity.
>
> (Brooks and Goldstein, 2004: 3)

Reivich and Shatté (2002) suggest that resilience is not just struggling with setbacks but also includes reaching out to others to develop deeper friendships and create more opportunities for a richer life. Maddi and Khoshaba (2005: 5) founded the Hardiness Institute, a consulting and training organisation that is 'devoted to teaching people attitudes and skills that make them resilient under stress'. Resilience is a topic of interest for positive psychology. Launched in the late 1990s, this movement is based on identifying and building strengths and virtues (what is right with you) instead of the deficit and weakness model of traditional psychology (what is wrong with you). A key question for this vision of psychology is: What are the enabling conditions that make people flourish? (Seligman, 2003). It is this expanded discussion of resilience that will be the subject of this chapter because people who receive coaching are unlikely to be struggling with adversity at every turn in their working and personal lives.

Defining resilience

Vaillant (1993: 284) states that 'we all know perfectly well what resilience means until we listen to someone else trying to define it'. With some of the foregoing points in mind and distilling our own collective experience as therapists and coaches, here is our attempt to define resilience: responding adaptively and resolutely to tough times and emerging from them stronger, wiser and more capable. This definition emphasises that just getting through tough times is not enough: constructive personal change also should be evident.

Blocks to developing resilience

These are unhelpful ideas that keep people trapped in non-resilient ways of responding to life's vicissitudes.

1 **'It's not my fault. I'm a victim.'** This means feeling helpless in the face of events, continually blaming others for your misfortunes and not taking responsibility for effecting constructive change. Helplessness is a hypothesis, not a fact, because it is based on the view that there is nothing you can do to change. As Glover (1988: 108) observes: 'We are never, while alive and aware, *quite* deprived of all choice, and in most situations the range of choice is normally greatly in excess of that which we readily acknowledge' (emphasis in original). With regard to blame and responsibility, even if others did cause or contribute to your misfortunes, the problem is still yours to solve whether or not you get assistance from them. For example, if your car burst into flames after being hit by a lorry, would you refuse to rescue yourself because you did not cause the crash and insist that the lorry driver pull you out of the burning wreckage, or would you make a determined effort to save yourself irrespective of his behaviour? Wolin and Wolin (1993) caution that the

expectation of sympathy that comes with victim status is 'enticing bait'; however, to maintain the sympathy of others – which will probably diminish over time – means forever bewailing your lot in life.

2 **'I'll never get over it.'** The 'it' may be a traumatic event, unhappy childhood or any stressful episode the person believes destroyed her life and sense of security and identity. Can a shattered Humpty-Dumpty ever be put together again? Flach (2004) argues that 'falling apart' in the face of significant stress is part of the resilience response because during this period of disruption new ways of responding to life events can be developed so that the pieces of ourselves can be reassembled in a different and sturdier way. Individuals who have been burdened with disadvantages in childhood and where the predictions for a happy and stable life seem bleak can turn up trumps: 'We have much to learn from once-fragmented Humpty Dumpties who ten – or even forty – years later become whole', wrote Professor George Vaillant (1993: 284), director of a 60-year prospective longitudinal study of adult development at Harvard University of 456 men from socially disadvantaged backgrounds. These inner city men, born between 1925 and 1932, were one of three cohorts studied (Vaillant, 2002).

3 **'I'm a failure. There's no point in trying to change.'** Such self-devaluation keeps the person in a state of demoralised inertia as she acts in accordance with her self-image – 'this is how I am'. This self-image is not fixed in perpetuity: she can learn to develop a balanced (i.e. looking at oneself in the round) and compassionate view of herself and thereby refrain from harmful global judgements of the self; the label 'failure' can never capture the complexity of the self or the totality of one's life. Decoupling the behaviour from the self can lead to a new outlook – that one's behaviour may sometimes fail, but the person never does.

4 **'Experiencing discomfort is intolerable.'** Also known as low frustration tolerance (LFT; Ellis, 2001), discomfort avoidance keeps the person from embracing the hard work of goal-directed endeavour because he believes that

the struggle involved is too much to endure; so he looks for the path of least resistance, which in the short term seems the right choice but in the longer term opportunities for change and growth are missed. Ironically, in avoiding the discomfort of change, discomfort sets in about the stasis in his life ('My life is going nowhere'). In order for his life to go 'somewhere', it is important to choose productive discomfort or high frustration tolerance (HFT) – that unpleasant situations or tasks are endurable (experiments can test this assumption by, for example, carrying out previously avoided tasks) if stasis is to be replaced by opportunity. As Leahy (2006: 94) emphasises: 'Making discomfort a daily goal is the key to making progress.'

5 **'Why me?'** The answer is usually implicit in the question: 'It shouldn't have happened to me. I don't deserve this. I've done nothing wrong or bad.' Her assumption of a just world has been shattered by the traumatic experience (Lerner, 1980). 'Why me?' introspection is unlikely to yield any new or helpful information to tackle her distress. A radical change of perspective, however, might provide a different kind of answer. 'Why not me?' states an unpalatable truth: no one is immune from the possibility of experiencing tragedy or misfortune in life. The *just* world view gets in the way of internalising this perspective.

6 **'It shouldn't have happened!'** This viewpoint encompasses any situation the person feels frustrated about. Denying reality just prolongs and usually exacerbates his current difficulties and frustrations. Like 'Why not me?', 'It should have happened' offers an unexpected perspective: all the conditions were in place at the time for it to have happened – for example, the person was low on petrol and kept passing petrol stations because he was not prepared to queue in his eagerness to get home after a tiring day (his behaviour might have been different if he had been less tired). To his disbelief, he eventually ran out of petrol, several miles from home. As Edelman (2006: 74) observes: 'Everything that we say and do, including those things that turn out to have negative consequences, happens because all of the factors that were necessary for them to

occur were present at that time.' Therefore, he could not have acted other than he did based on his thinking at that time in that situation. So it is time-wasting and unproductive to demand that what happened should not have happened; instead, attention should be turned to learning from the incident in order not to repeat the mistakes.

7 **'You can't escape the past.'** The past maintains its unshakeable and malign grip on the person's present behaviour. It is not the past per se that maintains this grip but the person's present beliefs about past events – she continues to think in the same way she has always done: 'Being adopted made me realise how bad I must be for my real parents not to want me.' Breaking the grip of the past starts with changing one's beliefs about it; the past remains unalterable.

Attitude: The heart of resilience

We mentioned earlier in our discussion of resilience the central role that our attitudes play in determining how we respond to difficult or dark times in our lives. This viewpoint is supported by resilience researchers (e.g. Brooks and Goldstein, 2004; Reivich and Shatté, 2002; Walsh, 2006) and also some philosophers, ancient and modern: Epictetus (c. AD 55–135, a Stoic philosopher and, we might say, a founding father of resilience) said: 'What upsets people is not things themselves but their judgments about the things' (trans. White, 1983: 13); and Anthony Grayling (2005: 23) said: 'Attitude is very consequential stuff. It determines everything one does, from falling in love to voting for one candidate rather than another.' Many things happen in life that we have no control over but our attitudes and judgements are within our control and therefore can be changed if we so choose. Attitude in action can be seen in the following three examples of remarkable resilience in extreme circumstances.

The psychiatrist and psychotherapist Viktor Frankl (1905–1997) survived the horrors of Auschwitz and famously wrote that 'everything can be taken from a man but one thing: the last of the human freedoms – to choose one's attitude in any given set of circumstances, to choose one's own way' (1946/1985: 86). Frankl saw that those who gave meaning to their lives even in the most miserable of circumstances were the most likely to survive. Those prisoners who lost faith in the future were doomed, he observed. As a result of his experiences in the camps he developed an existentialist therapy called logotherapy, which helps people to find meaning in their lives when they might otherwise give up – 'meaning is the primary motivational force in man' (Frankl, 1985: 121). According to Coutu (2003), Frankl's theory underpins most resilience coaching in business.

A passionate devotee of Epictetus's doctrines was James Stockdale (1923–2005), a navy pilot shot down over North Vietnam in 1965, who endured more than seven years of imprisonment, including torture, as a POW. He went into captivity with a broken leg and even though it was crudely operated on he was in pain for several years. Stockdale frequently consoled himself with Epictetus's dictum (he had memorised many of his dicta):

> Lameness is an impediment to the leg but not to the will [Epictetus was lame]; and say this to yourself with regard to everything that happens. For you will find such things to be an impediment to something else, but not truly to yourself.
>
> (Stockdale, 1993: 11)

His Epictetan outlook informed his style of leadership as the senior commanding officer in the prison. He attributed his ability to endure captivity and return home psychologically intact, but physically debilitated, to Epictetus's teachings. Sherman (2005: 6) called his Epictetan experiment 'empowerment in enslavement'. He was much in demand as a speaker, his central theme being how to prevail when facing adversity, whether in war or peace. Bennis and Thomas's (2003: 39) research into leadership in business 'suggests that one of the most reliable indicators and predictors of true leadership is the ability to learn from even the most negative experiences'.

Helen Keller (1880–1968) lost her sight and hearing at an early age. She was helped to speak, read and write by a teacher, Annie Sullivan. Helen grew up to become an author, lecturer and educator of blind people as well as supporting other progressive causes. She was viewed by many people around the world as an inspiring role model in overcoming such seemingly insurmountable handicaps. Although the temptation to succumb to a life of pessimism was great, she resisted it:

> Sometimes, it is true, a sense of isolation enfolds me like a cold mist as I sit alone and wait at life's shut gate. Beyond there is light, and music, and sweet companionship; but I may not enter. Fate, silent, pitiless, bars the way . . . but my tongue will not utter the bitter, futile words that rise to my lips, and they fall back into my heart like unshed tears. Silence sits immense upon my soul. Then comes hope with a smile and whispers, "There is joy in self-forgetfulness." So I try to make the light in others' eyes my sun, the music in others' ears my symphony, the smile on others' lips my happiness.
>
> (Keller, 2007: 64–65)

These three extraordinary individuals have much to teach us that can be applied to our own lives: principally, that we have the ability to develop an inner freedom from despair and thereby face whatever confronts us in life with courage, determination and dignity.

Resilience is ordinary, not extraordinary

As we mentioned in the introduction to this chapter, everyone has the capacity to develop resilience in their own idiosyncratic fashion. The above examples are at the awe-inspiring end of the resilience continuum. Closer to the centre of the continuum is what we call the resilience of everyday life (e.g. taking the children to and from school, holding down a job, looking after pets, caring for an elderly relative). This view might be dismissed by most people as 'simply getting on with it' and they see nothing resilient about what they do. However, what would happen to the children, pets, jobs and elderly relatives without your persistence, dedication and problem-solving skills?

In analysing situations that people believe they coped poorly with (e.g. losing a valued job), it is important to point out to them that not immediately rising to the challenge of problem resolution does not indicate personal ineffectiveness: it often takes perseverance to find an effective response. And in our perseverance we can tap into strengths that we probably would not have uncovered or developed if we could take every setback in our stride. As Grayling (2002: 39) remarks: 'It is not what we get but what we become by our endeavours that makes them worthwhile.'

I (WD) demonstrated a resilient attitude when I took voluntary redundancy from my lecturing job at Aston University in Birmingham, thinking that it would not be too difficult finding a new job. In fact, I was wrong: it took me over two years and 54 job rejections to find my next post. People who hear this story think that I must have been depressed, but I was not. I kept going and did so, in retrospect, because I demonstrated the following resilient-like responses.

1 **A healthy attitude** based on:

- Self-acceptance: 'Job rejections do not devalue my worth as a person. My worth as a person stays constant whatever happens in my life.'
- Hope: 'If I keep going I will find a worthwhile job in the end.'

2 **Constructive behaviour** based on:

- Perseverance: I kept applying for jobs, filling out application forms and attending interviews.
- Involvement in personally meaningful activity: While going through the job-finding process I carried on writing and editing books, actions that are personally meaningful to me.
- Changing my behaviour in interviews: I found it difficult at that time to get feedback on my interview performance, but I eventually discovered that what I thought was self-confidence was being seen by the interviewers as arrogance. Consequently, I trained myself to demonstrate humility in the interview process and got a job soon after.

3 **Social support**. My friends and family, particularly my wife, gave me the encouragement that allowed me to proceed in my own way and demonstrated faith that I would achieve my goals in the end. What I learned from this job-hunting experience was the following:

- It is important to persevere in the face of adversity, in both behaviour and attitude.
- One's self is so much larger than the experiences that we face and thus to define one's worth at any point in time is detrimental to developing resilience.
- It is important to involve oneself in life beyond the adversity even if one's mind is preoccupied with it. If you do so, your mind will eventually follow your behaviour.
- Get feedback from others whenever you can, otherwise you may be repeating errors that can be corrected.
- Let others in and support you. Be with those who are supportive and disengage from those who are not.

Factors associated with resilience

Writers on resilience invariably offer their list of characteristics or factors underpinning it. This is our list of the key components of a resilient outlook:

- **High frustration tolerance** – the ability to endure in times of distress or upheaval without continually complaining how difficult the struggle is or lapsing into self-pity every time a new setback is encountered.
- **Keeping things in perspective** – not jumping to catastrophic or gloomy conclusions when difficulties are experienced but, instead, appraising events in a calm and measured way that enables you to see which aspects of the situation you can influence and which aspects you cannot.
- **Self-acceptance** – compassionate acceptance of yourself and others as fallible human beings and eschewing global evaluations of the self (e.g. 'I'm a failure) because these can never capture its complexity, changeability and uniqueness.
- **Adaptability** – the ability to think and act flexibly in the face of challenging and changing circumstances.

- **Support from others** – asking for or accepting support rather than believing you have to display compulsive self-reliance.
- **Self-discipline** – the ability to set and achieve realistic goals, avoid acting impulsively and maintain a balance between your short- and longer-term interests so neither is neglected.
- **Emotional regulation** – moderating your intense feelings in order to stay focused in stressful situations and displaying consistent behaviour across situations (so you do not appear unpredictable to others).
- **Curiosity** – taking an experimental approach to life by trying things out rather than always staying within the confines of the safe and predictable.
- **Self-belief** – within reason, you have the ability to take your life in the direction you want it to go.
- **Humour** – finding light moments in dark times and, more generally, not taking yourself or your ideas too seriously.
- **Problem-solving skills** – identifying and removing internal blocks to change (e.g. excessive self-doubt) and executing successfully goal-directed action plans.
- **Absorbing interests** – the pleasure of immersing yourself in such activities not only as an end in itself but also as time out from the mundane responsibilities of daily living.

These attributes are interdependent and therefore it is difficult to determine which are primary in order for the others to develop. For example, do problem-solving skills develop because you have the self-discipline to learn them or is self-discipline established once you have the self-belief that you are largely in control of your life and can achieve what you want? We would liken this discussion to the question of the chicken and egg: which one came first? Also, as Flach (2004) remarks, there is not a perfectly maintained balance amongst these qualities; rather, there is a changing emphasis on some qualities more than others at different times. For example, you may be admirably self-disciplined but inclined to let social support recede when it would be helpful to make use of it; you are very curious about trying new experiences but usually avoid those experiences where you might be criticised or rejected, thereby only half-heartedly attempting to internalise self-acceptance.

Keep on keeping on

A senior police officer I (MN) was coaching – he sought me out privately – was very angry that his new boss was making his working life difficult and interfering greatly with what he thought was going to be a pleasant winding-down process to retirement in a few years' time. He said he had dealt with many difficult and sometimes very unpleasant situations in his career, but this present one did not appear to have a solution that he could see (retiring early was out of the question because he wanted to collect his full pension). However, he was determined to find one.

Coachee: I don't want to fall at the last hurdle, so to speak, but why does he behave like that? I wouldn't behave like that. He really is an ill-tempered bastard, always finding fault. My wife gets fed up with me moaning about him all the time.

Coach: Well, we could speculate about his motives or explore some ideas on how to manage yourself better in your relationship with him. Which one might be more productive at this stage?
[Analysing his boss's possible motives is likely to distract the coachee from learning to adapt to this difficult situation if he wants to make his last few years at work more tolerable.]

Coachee: I'm tempted to say him.

Coach: Whose behaviour is within your control to change – yours or his?
[If the coach does not move in early to make this crucial distinction, the coachee is likely to continue to see his boss as the source of *all* his difficulties.]

Coachee: Well, obviously mine. Why does my behaviour need to change? I'm not the problem.

Coach: You are to some extent. Shall I explain? (Client nods)

[The coach thus gains the coachee's permission for some didactic input to raise his awareness about his internal blocks to change.]

Coach: People who are angry about others' behaviour are usually demanding that these others shouldn't be the way they undoubtedly are. It's like constructing an internal brick wall (taps his head) which you keep on banging your head against every day – 'He shouldn't be like that!' – without any corresponding change in your boss's behaviour to show that your strategy is working. So you've got two problems for the price of one: his difficult behaviour and you making yourself angry about it.

[The 'internal brick wall' has proved to be a useful metaphor for other coachees to show them that their anger is both self-created and futile.]

Coachee: I probably have got my own brick wall but it sounds like you are supporting his behaviour.

Coach: I'm not doing that – just pointing out, however unpalatable it might be to you, that *his* behaviour flows from *his* values and viewpoint, not yours. If he shared your viewpoint, then this problem presumably would not have arisen.

[This is a common response from coachees (and clients in therapy) when this point is made, so the coach is trying to help the coachee stand back from his relentless focus on his boss's behaviour in order to gain some objectivity.]

Coachee: Okay, so if I accept it . . .

Coach: Without liking it.

[This is to pre-empt the usual comeback that acceptance means giving in to the other person or giving up trying to effect change in some way.]

Coachee: . . . without liking it, that he is the way he is and I stop being angry every day, then what?

Coach: Can you imagine in what ways your life at work might be different if you dismantled this internal brick wall?

[Attempting to flesh out what change might look like.]

Coachee: Not really. I can't see past the anger, but I want to.

Coach: Okay. Maybe we're jumping ahead too soon. As an experiment, don't take your anger to work with you and observe – make notes if you wish – any changes in yourself and in your relationship with him.

Coachee: What if nothing happens?

Coach: Let's just see what happens, whatever it is. That's the purpose of an experiment.

[Trying to determine the outcome of an experiment before it is carried out undermines its purpose.]

Coachee: Okay. I've got nothing to lose but my anger. I'm sure if I tell my wife about my brick wall, she'll agree with you!

Coach: Your wife might have some good ideas you're not listening to. Something else to consider is this: if you think your anger is justified because of his behaviour, he probably thinks his anger is justified because of yours.

[This is to disabuse the coachee of any unique or righteous justification for his anger.]

Coachee: Hmm. I hadn't thought of that. I'm sure he does as he finds fault with me quite frequently. You know, I came to the session today thinking the focus would be on him yet it's all about me. Interesting, but unsettling.

A rule of thumb in attempting to influence (not control) someone else's behaviour is to manage yourself first: 'Getting angrily upset over a frustration does not usually remove the frustration and always adds to your discomfort. In fact, most of the time the greatest distress comes not from what others do to us but from what we let our upsets do' (Hauck, 1980: 122). Once the coachee accepted and acted upon the idea that he made himself angry about his boss's behaviour, then the stage was set for a marked change in his own behaviour. He now saw work as a laboratory where he could try out new beliefs and behaviours. One new response he experimented with, as advocated by Ellis (1977), was to be nice when his boss displayed obnoxious behaviour.

Coachee: I thought you were crazy when you suggested it. He doesn't know how to handle it. He's baffled by my behaviour but he's much less obnoxious now. It's as if he's wilting in the face of my niceness and calmness, though I still have days when the old angry impulses return, but not for long. You know, I previously thought that fighting back would be asking him to step outside for a bout of fisticuffs (laughs).

Coach: You are fighting back in a low-key, non-violent but determined way. The key question to ask: Is it working?

Coachee: It is, but I had to clear away the red mist before I could see that the range of options to deal with this problem was wider than I ever thought. I still don't like him, and I even feel sorry for him at times because he's such a lousy manager, but I now feel that these last few years before I retire are controlled by me, not him, even though he's my boss. That is a most welcome change.

Conclusion

In this chapter, we have explored the concept of resilience in order to move beyond the popular but unenlightened view of it as 'bouncing back' from adversity. Any genuine adversity would probably preclude much 'bounce'. On the other hand, your attitude to adversity will help you to understand if you are 'struggling well' (O'Connell Higgins, 1994) to find an adaptive response to misfortune or floundering in despair because you believe nothing good can ever come from anything bad. We welcome the extension in the study of resilience to include handling better the stresses and strains of daily living. As many resilience researchers point out, developing resilience is a universal capacity. It is a shame not to make the best use of this capacity even if, in the meantime, our understanding of resilience remains incomplete.

Discussion issues

- How would you define resilience?
- Do you think it is possible to 'bounce back' from every adversity in life?
- What lessons can be learnt from studying people who have demonstrated extraordinary resilience in extreme circumstances?
- What resilience strengths do you possess and can you think of some recent or past examples of your resilience in action?

References

Bennis, W. G. and Thomas, R. J. (2003) Crucibles of leadership. In *Harvard Business Review on Building Personal and Organizational Resilience*. Boston, MA: Harvard Business School Press.

Bonanno, G. A. (2006) Grief, trauma, and resilience. In E. K. Rynearson (Ed.), *Violent Death: Resilience and Intervention Beyond the Crisis*. New York: Routledge.

Brooks, R. and Goldstein, S. (2004) *The Power of Resilience: Achieving Balance, Confidence, and Personal Strength in Your Life*. New York: McGraw-Hill.

Butler, G. and Hope, T. (2007) *Manage Your Mind: The Mental Fitness Guide*, 2nd edn. Oxford: Oxford University Press.

Coutu, D. (2003) How resilience works. In *Harvard Business Review on Building Personal and Organizational Resilience*. Boston, MA: Harvard Business School Press.

Edelman, S. (2006) *Change Your Thinking*. London: Vermilion.

Ellis, A. (1977) *Anger: How to Live With and Without It*. Secaucus, NJ: Citadel Press.

Ellis, A. (2001) *Feeling Better, Getting Better, Staying Better*. Atascadero, CA: Impact Publishers.

Flach, F. (2004) *Resilience: Discovering a New Strength at Times of Stress*, 2nd edn. New York: Hatherleigh Press.

Frankl, V. E. (1985) *Man's Search for Meaning*. New York: Washington Square Press. (Original work published 1946)

Glover, M. (1988) Responsibility and therapy. In W. Dryden and P. Trower (Eds.), *Developments in Cognitive Psychotherapy*. London: Sage.

Grayling, A. C. (2002) *The Meaning of Things: Applying Philosophy to Life*. London: Phoenix.

Grayling, A. C. (2005) *The Heart of Things: Applying Philosophy to the 21st Century*. London: Weidenfeld & Nicholson.

Grotberg, E. H. (2001) *Tapping Your Inner Strength: How to Find the Resilience to Deal with Anything*. New Delhi, India: New Age Books.

Hauck, P. (1980) *Calm Down*. London: Sheldon Press.

Keller, H. (1903/2007) *The Story of My Life*. Teddington, UK: Echo Library.

Leahy, R. L. (2006) *The Worry Cure: Stop Worrying and Start Living*. London: Piatkus.

Lerner, M. J. (1980) *The Belief in a Just World: A Fundamental Delusion*. New York: Plenum Press.

Maddi, S. R. and Khoshaba, D. M. (2005) *Resilience at Work: How to Succeed No Matter What Life Throws at You*. New York: Amacom.

Moran, Lord (2007) *The Anatomy of Courage*. London: Robinson. (Original work published 1945)

Neenan, M. (2009) *Developing Resilience: A Cognitive Behavioural Approach*. Hove, UK: Routledge.

Newman, R. (2003) In the wake of disaster: Building the resilience initiative of APA's public education campaign. In E. H. Grotberg (Ed.), *Resilience for Today: Gaining Strength from Adversity*. Westport, CT: Praeger.

O'Connell Higgins, G. (1994) *Resilient Adults: Overcoming a Cruel Past*. San Francisco, CA: Jossey-Bass.

Reivich, K. and Shatté, A. (2002) *The Resilience Factor: 7 Keys to Finding Your Inner Strength and Overcoming Life's Hurdles*. New York: Broadway Books.

Rutter, M. (1993) Resilience: Some conceptual considerations. *Journal of Adolescent Health, 14*: 626–631.

Seligman, M. E. P. (2003) *Authentic Happiness: Using the New Positive Psychology to Realize Your Potential for Lasting Fulfillment*. London: Nicholas Brealey.

Sherman, N. (2005) *Stoic Warriors: The Ancient Philosophy Behind the Military Mind*. New York: Oxford University Press.

Siebert, A. (2005) *The Resiliency Advantage*. San Francisco, CA: Berrett-Koehler.

Stockdale, J. B. (1993) *Courage Under Fire: Testing Epictetus's Doctrines in a Laboratory of Human Behavior* (Hoover Essays). Stanford, CA: Hoover Institution Press.

Vaillant, G. E. (1993) *The Wisdom of the Ego*. Cambridge, MA: Harvard University Press.

Vaillant, G. E. (2002) *Aging Well.* New York: Little, Brown & Co.

Walsh, F. (2006) *Strengthening Family Resilience*, 2nd edn. New York: Guilford Press.

White, N. P. (1983) (trans.) *The Encheiridion [Handbook] of Epictetus.* Indianapolis, IN: Hackett Publishing.

Wolin, S. J. and Wolin, S. (1993) *The Resilient Self.* New York: Villard Books.

Recommended reading

Neenan, M. (2009) *Developing Resilience: A Cognitive Behavioural Approach.* Hove, UK: Routledge.

Seligman, M. E. P. (2003) *Authentic Happiness: Using the New Positive Psychology to Realize Your Potential for Lasting Fulfillment.* London: Nicholas Brealey.

7

Stress and performance coaching

Kristina Gyllensten and Stephen Palmer

Workplace stress is a serious problem that is causing great concern and has been gaining attention from both academic journals and the press for some years (Arthur, 2004; Palmer and Laungani, 2003). Indeed, it is related to a number of negative psychological, physiological and economical outcomes (Palmer and Cooper, 2010). It is important that action is taken to tackle stress and organisations employ many different interventions in order to prevent and manage stress. An intervention that is not commonly associated with stress reduction is coaching (Gyllensten and Palmer, 2006; Palmer and Gyllensten, 2008). Nevertheless, it was suggested a decade ago that coaching could be useful in tackling stress by helping to identify causes of stress, developing new effective strategies and maintaining the changes (Hearn, 2001).

According to Peltier (2001) coaching carries less of a stigma compared to counselling or therapy. This suggestion was supported by a qualitative study by the authors investigating the perceptions of counselling for workplace stress. It was found that coaching was perceived more positively than counselling (Gyllensten, Palmer and Farrants, 2005). Thus, it is useful for coaches to have knowledge of workplace stress and to be aware of various techniques that can be used for dealing with workplace stress. This chapter will provide information regarding workplace stress, present a cognitive behavioural model for understanding stress, discuss a number of cognitive, behavioural and physiological techniques and present a summary of the relevant research (Palmer, 2003).

What is stress?

Stress is a term that is used in different ways depending on the person and the environment. As a cognitive behavioural coach it is very important to ask a client what they mean when they say that they are stressed. Indeed, a common mistake is that the coach assumes that they understand what the client means when they talk about common terms like stress or self-confidence. The coach may know what this term would mean for them, but needs to ask the client to explain further. Socratic questions described in Chapter 4 by Michael Neenan are very useful for exploring individual meaning. It is always very interesting to find out how a coachee defines stress because it is highly individual. Someone may describe stress as 'I have too many thoughts in my head' whereas someone else will say 'My mind is just blank when I am stressed'.

There are a number of definitions of workplace stress and it could be useful for the cognitive behavioural coach to be aware of some of these. According to the UK's Health and Safety Executive (HSE) (2001: 1) stress is defined as: 'the adverse reaction people have to excessive pressures or other types of demand placed on them'. The American National Institute for Occupational Safety and Health (1999: 6) defines work stress as: 'the harmful physical and emotional responses that occur when the requirements of the job do not match the capabilities, resources or needs of the worker'. These two definitions are similar because they emphasise that stress is the individual's reaction to external pressure. A longer definition of stress that originates from the Occupational Safety and Health Service in New Zealand is:

> Workplace stress is the result of the interaction between a person and their work environment. For the person it is the awareness of not being able to cope with the demands of their work environment, with an associated negative emotional response.
>
> (Occupational Safety and Health Service, 2003: 4)

The perception of the individual is very important within a multimodal cognitive behavioural framework. Palmer, Cooper and Thomas (2003: 2) propose the following cognitive definition: 'stress occurs when the perceived pressure exceeds your perceived ability to cope'.

In many studies the terms stressors and strain are used. Stressors are the external factors that may cause stress whereas strain is the individual's reaction to the stressors (Cooper, Dewe and O'Driscoll, 2001). Overall, it is useful to be aware of the definitions and terms but the most important aspect is to explore the client's own experience of stress.

Why is stress a problem?

For the period 2008–2009 the HSE (2009, 2010) estimated that 415,000 people in Great Britain, who worked in the last 12-month period surveyed, reported that they were suffering from stress, depression or anxiety that was either caused or made worse by their past or current work – in other words, 1400 per 100,000 people (1.4%). Stress, depression and anxiety are the second most common type of work related health problem. It is estimated that 11.4 million working days or equivalent are lost, with the average person taking 27.5 days off, and an annual loss of 0.48 days per worker in a 12-month period costs society £4 billion. The occupational groups that reported higher than average *prevalence* rates for stress, depression or anxiety were: health and social welfare associate professionals; teaching and research professionals; corporate managers; business and public service associate professionals.

Similarly, Cartwright and Cooper (2005) reported that work related stress has a negative impact upon organisational productivity as well as individuals' health. Melchior, Caspi, Milne, Danese, Poulton and Moffitt (2007) reported that high psychological job demands increase the risk of developing depression and generalised anxiety disorder to a great extent. These studies highlight that workplace stress is a serious problem that is damaging to the individual, the organisation and the society as a whole.

What is causing stress?

The experience of stress is individual and a situation that may be stressful for one person may be positively challenging for another person. Nevertheless, research on working conditions has identified a number of risk factors within the workplace, also called stressors, that have been associated with higher levels of stress among employees (Cousins, Makay, Clarke, Kelly, Kelly and McCaig, 2004). These risk factors can be divided into six categories:

1 **Demands** – refers to workload, for example the employee may have too much to do during a short period of time or may not have the capacity to deal with the demands.
2 **Control** – refers to the level of control the employee has over their work.
3 **Support** – refers to the support and encouragement the employee is receiving from management and colleagues.
4 **Relationships** – refers to how relationships are handled in the workplace, for example how unacceptable behaviour is dealt with.
5 **Role** – refers to whether the employee experiences conflicting roles or if they have problems understanding their job role.
6 **Change** – refers to how change is dealt with within the organisation, with emphasis on how it is communicated.

The HSE has developed guidelines for standards to be achieved for each risk factor and recommends that organisations should conduct risk assessments. The exact nature of how to carry out an assessment will not be described here (for a free downloadable questionnaire based on this approach and more information, see: www.HSE.gov.uk), but a coach could examine the factors with the coachee in order to identify environmental factors affecting the coachee's level of stress. The 'model of workplace stress' (Palmer, Cooper and Thomas, 2001) in Figure 7.1 highlights how these stressors can be related to symptoms of stress and negative outcomes.

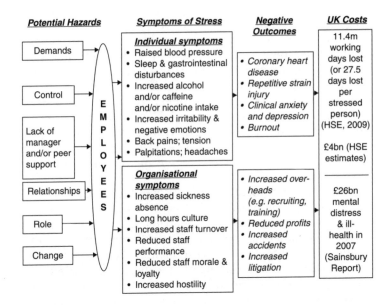

Figure 7.1 **Model of Work Stress (adapted from Palmer, Cooper and Thomas, 2001)**

Why would cognitive behavioural coaching be useful to tackle stress?

Cognitive behavioural coaching (CBC) could be useful to tackle stress by helping to identify stressors and developing strategies for change and lasting solutions (Hearn, 2001). It could also help to reduce stress indirectly by helping coachees to attain their goals (e.g. improve presentation skills or dealing with procrastination), thereby decreasing the stress caused by presentation or procrastination. 'CBC enables clients to identify and subsequently modify the cognitive, behavioural and emotive blocks that impede the execution of their goal-directed activities. It can improve performance, enhance well-being and prevent stress' (Palmer and Neenan, 2005). CBC is a particularly useful approach for dealing with stress as it focuses on what is stopping the client from reaching their goals, is transparent and aims for the coaching client to increase their self-awareness, learn skills to deal with their problems and ultimately become their own coach. As stated in the introduction, coaching appears to have a more positive image compared to counselling, which is a common intervention for stress. Thus, there may be less of a stigma in seeking help from a coach at an earlier stage of the problem compared to seeking help from a general practitioner (GP) or therapist once the problem is more serious. Dealing with stress in coaching may be a way of preventing the problem from getting worse.

CBC can be a useful intervention in tackling stress and can sometimes be more useful than counselling or other more clinical interventions. Nevertheless, when discussing stress it is important to consider the fact that coaching should not deal directly with mental health problems, although 25–30% of coaching clients do suffer from mental health problems (Cavanagh, n.d.). Grant's (2001a) model highlighted the difference and the overlap between the coaching and clinical population. Stress is an issue that may or may not be a mental health problem. An individual could experience a high level of stress because they get very nervous when they have to do presentations at work. The stress is only related to this issue and the individual does not feel nervous talking with people in other situations and otherwise functions well in life. This could be a problem that is ideal to work with in CBC. On the other hand an individual with the same problem may also have problems talking to people in other situations and may find that social situations are so anxiety-provoking that they are avoiding many social activities, which could have a very negative impact upon the client's overall life. This individual may be suffering from an anxiety disorder and may need help from a GP or a therapist and not from a coach. It is very important that a cognitive behavioural coach is trained to recognise when a coachee is suffering from a mental health problem and needs to be referred to another professional such as a GP, psychologist or therapist. Once again this highlights the importance of finding out the coachee's personal experience of stress.

Understanding stress according to the CBC model

The cognitive behavioural model: A way of understanding stress

Within CBC it is important to identify what is happening to the coachee in the situations they are finding stressful. There are many different models and questionnaires that can be useful in assessing a stressful situation. One cognitive model that can be used in the coaching is Padesky's rings (Greenberger and Padesky, 1995). This model (see Figure 7.2) helps to identify the coachee's cognitions, behaviour, emotions and physiological responses and helps to identify how these influence each other. Moreover, the model also takes into account situational factors and relationships that may be influencing the coachee.

The model can be used to identify what is happening in one specific situation, and the client and the coach can write the relevant information in the model. One example of what this can look like is illustrated in Figure 7.3. The situation in this example happened to one of the authors (KG) when she was lecturing. The first time she was going to give a lecture she was very nervous and she had managed to button

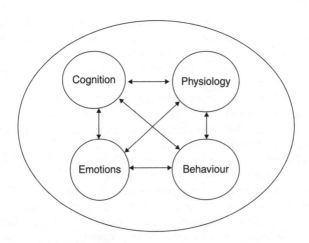

Figure 7.2 **Padesky's Rings**

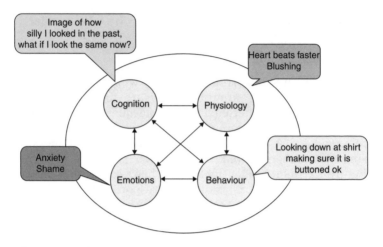

Figure 7.3 Padesky's Rings: An Example

her shirt incorrectly. During the first break one of the students kindly told her about the mistake. The situation presented in Figure 7.3 refers to when she was going to lecture for the second time and became stressed as she thought of the embarrassing mistake she made during the first lecture. In fact this was a mistake she only made once, but this is an example of how a memory was activated by a similar situation although there were no specific triggers in the actual situation. If this situation was discussed in coaching it would be important for the coachee to recognise what happened and understand that the anxiety and shame originated from the mental image from the previous lecture. Such knowledge could help her to distance herself from the previous situation causing the anxiety and shame, and instead focus on the here and now.

The model can also be used to illustrate that when a person is stressed there is an imbalance in the system and some modalities may be more powerful than others. When people are stressed they are often very active, they work long hours and they may work instead of taking breaks. Thus, the behavioural modality is proportionately large in the model. They are often thinking a lot about work, even when they are at home, and they are also telling themselves that they need to work this hard because of reasons such as high demands or fear of not getting the promotion or losing their position within the company. Consequently, the cognitive modality is also proportionately large in the model. However, the emotional and physiological signals in stress are often ignored. People may have problems sleeping and may feel tired, dizzy and anxious without doing anything about it. The physiological and emotional modalities are thus proportionately small in the model. Figure 7.4 illustrates what the model can look like for a stressed client or coachee.

Once the coachee and the coach have analysed the stressful situation and have completed the model it is useful if the coachee gets a copy of the model as it is easy to forget what has been discussed during the session. A homework task may be to identify other stressful situations using the model, this would provide more information about the coachee's stress. Some coachees may be better at identifying some aspects of the model compared to others, and some may not experience problems in all modalities. If the coachee never reports any problems in one modality it is important

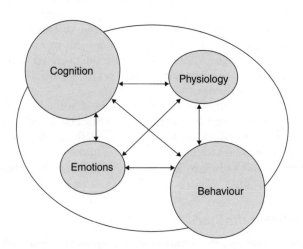

Figure 7.4 **Padesky's Rings and Stress**

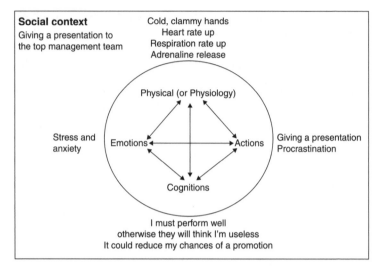

Figure 7.5 **A SPACE Diagram Illustrating Performance Related Stress and Anxiety (adapted from Palmer and Szymanska, 2007)**

to find out if this is because they do not have any symptoms or if they have difficulty in identifying symptoms. For example, some coachees may not be used to talking about emotions and may need to receive some information about our basic emotions. The model can be used in different creative ways and coachees may want to do it on the computer or use images instead of words.

A similar framework, although used somewhat differently, was developed by Edgerton (see Edgerton and Palmer, 2005; Williams, Edgerton and Palmer, 2010) and this uses an easy to remember acronym, SPACE. Figure 7.5 provides an example of a coachee with a stress and performance related anxiety problem.

Cognitive techniques

In CBC coachees are encouraged to increase their awareness of their thinking in stressful situations. The next step is to examine if the thoughts are helpful or if they are causing the coachee to feel worse and are goal-blocking. If the coachee identifies that their thinking is unhelpful they are encouraged to develop more helpful alternatives. Palmer and Neenan (cited in Palmer et al., 2003) use the terms stress-inducing thinking (SIT) and stress-alleviating thinking (SAT). They suggest that coachees should keep track of their SIT and SAT in a Stress Thought Record, an example of which can be seen in Figure 7.6 (see Appendix 3 for a blank form).

A very similar record can be used in order to identify performance-interfering thinking (PIT) and develop performance-enhancing thinking (PET) (see Figure 7.7 and Appendix 2 for a blank form). This is used when the coachee wants to improve performance in an area of their work or home life (Palmer et al., 2003). Also note that five-column forms can be used to tackle performance related issues (see Figure 5.3 on p.128).

When the coach helps the coachee to identify unhelpful thinking and to develop new helpful thinking, one common trap for the coach to fall into is to suggest how the coachee should think. This could have a negative effect on the alliance because the coachee may feel that the coach underestimates

Problem: Call a manager to ask for help with a new task	
Stress-inducing thinking (SIT)	**Stress-alleviating thinking (SAT)**
I should know how to do this, I should not have to ask for help	I don't have to know everything within my job and my manager is there to help me if I need it

Figure 7.6 Stress Thought Record (© Centre for Coaching, 2011)

Problem: Not proofreading reports	
Performance-interfering thinking (PIT)	**Performance-enhancing thinking (PET)**
I can't be bothered, there is no point, I can't spell anyway	I am bothered, the report will probably be improved if I proofread it

Figure 7.7 Enhancing Performance Form (© Centre for Coaching, 2011)

their capacity. Moreover, a new cognition developed by the coach is often less effective than the coachee's own suggestions. In some cases the coach may end up in a scenario where they make many suggestions and the coachee replies with 'yes but'. It is much more effective if the coach, with the help of Socratic questions, invites the coachee to develop their own SAT or PET. Below is an example of a dialogue where the coach is having this problem.

Coach: Okay, so the problem you would like to work with is that you get stressed and anxious when you have to call your manager to ask for help.

Coachee: Yes, I don't like that situation at all.

Coach: And what goes through your mind in that situation?
[Assessing SIT.]

Coachee: Well, I am thinking that I should know how to do this task.

Coach: Okay, so you tell yourself that you should know how to do the task.

Coachee: Yes, and that I should not have to ask for help.
[SIT is elicited.]

Coach: And where is the evidence for this thought?

Coachee: I think that the manager expects me to know what I am doing by now, I have been working with the company for three years.

Coach: Is this a task that you have been doing before or is it new?

Coachee: It is new for me as I was recently given new responsibilities.

Coach: Okay, so perhaps you should not be so hard on yourself and remember that it is not realistic to know how to do new things in the beginning.
[Coach suggests SAT.]

Coachee: Yes but you don't understand, I have always been a quick learner and I should know how to do this task.

This is an example of a conversation where the coach and the coachee have identified the relevant SIT. However, the problem is that the coach wants to be constructive and therefore suggests that SAT may be very helpful but this is not accepted by the coachee. It would have been more useful to find out more information about the SIT and then ask the coachee to develop SAT. Perhaps they had been in similar situations previously and already have SAT that has been effective in the past, or they may be able to come up with helpful SAT with relevant Socratic questions from the coach. Building on existing strengths can be very useful, as highlighted in positive psychology research, and this approach is used with strengths and solution focused coaching to good effect.

For some coachees it may be helpful to use a framework that obtains more information about the stressful situation than the SIT/SAT and PIT/PET two-column records. Dr Albert Ellis (Ellis et al., 1997) developed the ABC model, which can be very useful for analysing the sequence of events that leads to stress (Palmer and Cooper, 2010):

A = Activating event.

B = Beliefs about the event or others triggered by the event.

C = Consequences (emotional, behavioural and/or physiological).

An example of how to use this model can be illustrated by the following scenario. A coachee is asked to have a meeting with their manager. The coachee immediately thinks that they have done something wrong and becomes anxious. Using the model the situation looked like this:

A = Manager asks to have a meeting.

B = 'I have done something wrong'.

C = Anxiety and shame.

In order to help the coachee to find more helpful ways of thinking in the situation, Ellis added two more stages of the model (Palmer and Dryden, 1995):

D = Disputation of the belief at 'B'.

E = Effective new approach to deal with the problem at 'A'.

Other practitioners have included another state (e.g. Palmer and Cooper, 2010):

F = Future focus – What have I learnt from this process that I can use in future if the need arises again?

In order to dispute unhelpful thoughts at 'D' there are a number of questions that can be used (for more information, see Chapter 5). The following are examples of challenging questions (Palmer and Cooper, 2010):

- Is my thought logical?
- Where is the evidence for my thought?
- Is my thought realistic?
- What would my colleagues or friends say about this thought?
- What is the best, worst, most likely that could happen?
- Am I mind-reading?
- Am I fortune-telling?
- Am I expecting too much from myself?
- How important will my problem seem in 1, 3, 6 or 12 months?
- Is this thought helping me to reach my goals?

For the coachee above, continuation of the model looked like this:

D = Where is the evidence for my thought? Is this thought helpful for me? I'm fortune-telling and I'm mind-reading my manager again!

E = There is no evidence that I have done something wrong. I'll prepare for the meeting and take it as it comes.

F = Future focus – In future if the manager asks to have a meeting with me then it may not be about me doing something wrong.

Note that often the behavioural strategy goes into the 'E' section, which in this case is preparing for the meeting.

The more the coachee practises, the better they are going to become at identifying unhelpful thoughts and developing more helpful effective alternatives in stressful situations. The coach's key role is to facilitate the process and educate the coachee about the ABCDEF model. Thought Record Forms focusing on stress or performance can be completed in the coaching session to help facilitate the ABCDE process. Figure 7.8 is a five-column Stress Management Form (see Appendix 4 for a blank form). It illustrates an example where a coachee regularly is stressed about arriving late to meetings. A goal is negotiated and noted down in the 'Target problem' (or 'A' for activating event or awareness of an issue) column. The coach encourages the coachee to think about and imagine the next time it could happen in order to elicit the key stress-inducing thoughts, which are noted down in the SIT (or 'B' for beliefs) column. It is useful to demonstrate the link between thoughts in the SIT column and the subsequent 'Emotional/behavioural reaction' (or 'C' for consequences) column. Then the

Target problem (A)	Stress-including thinking (SIT) (B)	Emotional/ behavioural reaction (C)	Stress-alleviating thinking (SAT) (D)	Effective and new approach to problem (E)
Anticipation of arriving late for an important meeting	I must arrive on time	Stressed and anxious	Although I say I 'MUST' arrive on time, realistically, I cannot control the world!!!	Decide which items to leave out of the meeting and attempt to arrive feeling relatively calm
Goal: Stay relatively calm and develop a strategy if I arrive late.	This is going to look terrible!!	Anxiety	I may be late but it's not the end of the world	Remind myself to stay focused on the task
	I've blown my chances of a bonus	Depressed Angry at self	It's unlikely that I'll be judged by one event	FUTURE FOCUS (F)
	I'm going to appear so nervous	High anxiety	Doubt they will notice. I can take this opportunity to use my relaxation skills	In future, if I'm likely to arrive late, needlessly winding myself up does not help me tackle the impending situation. Just stay focused on the task and not get side-tracked by my concerns
		Driving fast and not concentrating	If I carry on like this, I could crash the car! Slow down!	
		Palpitations		

Figure 7.8 **Stress Management Form Illustrating an Example of Arriving Late (adapted: © Centre for Stress Management, 2000)**

coach facilitates the coachee in developing stress-alleviating thoughts in the SAT (or 'D' for disputation) column. The 'Effective and new approach' is developed in the last column. At the bottom of this column the coachee can also note down anything they may have learnt that they can apply in the future. Outside of the coaching session the coachee can use the forms to self-coach.

Behavioural techniques

For many coachees experiencing stress may not be enough to change their thinking; they need to change their behaviours as well. Common problem behaviours and useful interventions are presented below (Palmer and Cooper, 2010; Palmer and Dryden, 1995; Palmer et al., 2003):

- Avoidance – examples include avoiding doing presentations or making difficult phone calls. The most useful intervention for this problem is exposure to the situation that the coachee avoids. When planning the exposure the coachee and the coach make a hierarchy of the anxiety-provoking situations, starting with the least anxiety-provoking situation and building up to the most anxiety-provoking situation. The exposure can be in real life ('in vivo') or imaginary.
- Non-assertive behaviour – examples include problems saying 'no' to people, not expressing one's opinions and not being able to give constructive feedback or complain. In the coaching session the coachee can identify and practise assertive behaviour in a discussion or in a role-play. Palmer and Puri (2006) present a three-step model of assertion:

  Step 1. Carefully listen to the other person and demonstrate that you have heard and understood.
  Step 2. Express your thoughts and feelings.
  Step 3. Express what you would like to happen.

- Not asking for support – seeing support as a weakness and therefore never asking for help. The coach could help the coachee to identify the support available for different situations and this could help to decrease the stress.

- Procrastination – examples include putting the task off until the last minute and doing less important tasks instead. The coachee and the coach can identify the thoughts that lead to procrastination, the behaviours the coachee tends to do while procrastinating and the negative feelings that initially decrease when putting things off but return after some time (Neenan and Dryden, 2002).

Imagery techniques

Imagery and visualisation techniques are established methods used within the field of sports to enhance performance (see McMorriss and Hale, 2006; Sheilch and Korn, 1994). The well-known international golfer Jack Nicklaus (2010) has previously mentioned his use of imagery and visualisation:

I never hit a shot, not even in practice, without having a very sharp, in-focus picture of it in my head. First I see the ball where I want it to finish, nice and white and sitting up high on the bright green grass. Then the scene quickly changes, and I see the ball going there: its path, trajectory, and shape, even its behavior on landing. Then there is a sort of fade-out, and the next scene shows me making the kind of swing that will turn the previous images into reality.

This short case study demonstrates how an expert golfer can use end-goal imagery, then mastery imagery and finally rehearsal imagery to focus and develop a strategy to hitting the golf ball in a manner that will hopefully achieve the desired result. It can also illustrate to coachees how useful these techniques are, because sometimes coachees are reluctant to use imagery or visualisation techniques.

Imagery and visualisation techniques are also used within executive and life coaching to help coachees to prepare for future stress-triggering events, such as giving important presentations at work or in getting over perceived failures such as failing a professional exam. Coping imagery is a key technique that is regularly used within cognitive behavioural coaching to address these problems.

In coping imagery the coachee visualises him- or herself coping in a difficult, stressful or challenging situation (see Palmer, 2008; Palmer and Cooper, 2010). The visualisation is realistic because coachees see themselves dealing adequately but not perfectly with the challenging situation or problem. It is important that the imagery developed is within their perceived capabilities. Coping imagery can reduce stress and increase confidence and performance before challenging situations. Within the coaching session, the coach and coachee can develop a realistic approach to dealing with the future problem and then the coachee visualises tackling the problem using the strategies devised.

The technique can be broken down into discrete steps that the coach facilitates as follows (adapted from Palmer and Cooper, 2010: 92–93):

1 Think about the situation you are stressed about.
2 Let us note down the aspects of the situation that you are most stressed about. (NB: Coach notes down the items in chronological order.)
3 Let us discuss and develop ways to deal with these difficulties you envisage possibly happening. (NB: Sometimes the coachee may be able to develop solutions to each difficulty. However, some coachees will need ideas from the coach.)
4 You may wish to close your eyes, which will help you to imagine or picture the scenario.
5 Now visualise yourself just prior to the start of your feared situation. Remembering to use, in your mind's eye, the helpful strategies we have just previously discussed, slowly picture yourself coping with each anticipated difficulty as it arises. (NB: Coach may need to talk the coachee through this part of the activity. However, some coachees do not need assistance at this stage and find the coach talking a major distraction.)
6 The coach needs to obtain feedback at this stage and can ask a variety of questions, such as: How did you find this exercise? What did you find useful? What did you find unhelpful? Before you practise it again, do you need to change one of your coping strategies?

7 Let us have another go at the coping imagery exercise in the session.
8 After the exercise, the coachee is encouraged to practise coping imagery daily.

Although the coach is focusing on tackling the issues that the coachee is anxious about, listening out for strengths in the coaching conversation is also important because these can be incorporated within the coping imagery if appropriate.

Other imagery techniques that cognitive behavioural coaches use are: anger-reducing imagery (Palmer and Puri, 2006), motivation imagery (Palmer and Neenan, 1998; Palmer and Cooper, 2010), staying focused (or goal) imagery (Palmer and Puri, 2006), step-up imagery (Palmer, 2010), time projection imagery (Lazarus, 1984) and relaxation imagery (see Palmer and Cooper, 2010; Palmer et al., 2003).

Physiological techniques

There are a number of physiological symptoms of stress, including sleep disturbance, fatigue, tense muscles, headache and increased blood pressure. Physiological interventions can therefore be effective at decreasing stress and tension.

Interventions include:

- **Relaxation exercises**. There are many different forms of relaxation, such as learning to relax different parts of the body, yoga, massage, taking a hot bath and simple breathing exercises. (For more information, see Palmer and Cooper, 2010.)
- **Exercise**. Exercise is really useful for decreasing both physiological and psychological symptoms of stress. Focusing on getting started with a suitable form of exercise can be a good goal for coaching.
- **Nutrition, smoking and alcohol**. These aspects can be important to discuss with a stressed client who may be using food, smoking or alcohol as a way of dealing with stress. The coach can always encourage the coachee to discuss these aspects with their GP if it is not relevant to deal with it in coaching.

Research on CBC for stress and related areas

Although a decade ago there was a lack of research investigating coaching in general (Grant, 2001a) and also the impact of coaching on stress specifically, since then the research base has been increasing, with a gradual increase in research investigating whether coaching can prevent or reduce stress. The overall findings from the existing studies are mixed, with some finding that coaching helped to reduce stress and others finding that it had no significant effect (for a brief summary, see Gyllensten and Palmer, 2005). Most of the CBC related studies did not investigate coaching and stress/mental health exclusively and the coaching did not usually target stress. However, the studies included measures of stress, anxiety or depression as part of the study. A study by Grant (2001b) investigated the effects of cognitive, behavioural and cognitive behavioural coaching approaches in a sample of students. It was found that all three coaching approaches significantly reduced test anxiety. Non-study related mental health (depression, anxiety and stress) was also measured in the study and only cognitive coaching was found to significantly reduce levels of depression and anxiety. The behavioural and cognitive behavioural coaching did not significantly reduce depression, anxiety or stress. In another study by Grant (2003) it was found that a life coaching group programme with 10 sessions based on cognitive behavioural and solution focused principles reduced participants' levels of depression, anxiety and stress post-coaching. The coaching did not target mental health specifically. Similarly, Green, Oades and Grant (2006) investigated the effects of a 10-week cognitive behavioural, solution focused life coaching group programme. Both a coaching group and a control group participated in the study. It was found that participation in the life coaching group programme was associated with significant increases in goal striving, well-being and hope.

Grbcic and Palmer (2006, 2007) investigated a novel stress self-help manual based on a cognitive behavioural self-coaching approach developed for middle managers. Participants were randomly assigned into the coaching or control group. Significant results were obtained on the BSI (Brief Symptom Inventory) at post-coaching, as well as on the SA45 (symptom assessment), indicating that levels of psychological problems and symptoms had decreased. Interestingly the intervention appeared effective regardless of the fact that frequency of work stressors and lack of organisational support remained unchanged. In another randomised controlled design, students were randomly allocated to an individual life coach, using a cognitive behavioural and solution focused approach, or to a wait-list control group (Green, Grant and Rysaardt, 2007). The participants received 10 sessions and it was found that the coaching was associated with significant increases in levels of cognitive hardiness and hope, and significant decreases in levels of depression. Grant (2008) conducted a study investigating the effect of cognitive behavioural and solution focused coaching on student coaches. It was found that participation in coaching reduced anxiety, increased goal attainment and enhanced cognitive hardiness. Grant, Curtayne and Burton (2009) in a randomised controlled study found that executive coaching enhanced goal attainment, resilience and workplace well-being. Gyllensten, Palmer, Nilsson, Regnér and Frodi (2010) used a qualitative design based on interpretative phenomenological analysis and found that cognitive coaching helped participants to change unhelpful thinking and regulate difficult emotions.

Summary

This chapter has outlined research and theories on workplace stress that can inform a cognitive behavioural coach's practice. It has also presented a cognitive behavioural model that can be helpful in identifying thoughts, feelings, behaviours and physiological sensations in stressful situations. A number of cognitive, behavioural and physiological techniques have been presented and it is important to highlight that their application needs both practice and supervision. Finally, a brief summary of the research on CBC has been outlined.

Discussion issues

- Why is stress a problem?
- In what way does the cognitive behavioural approach help to explain the causes of stress?
- Is there less of a stigma in seeking help from a coach compared to seeking help from a counsellor or therapist.
- How important is the use of imagery techniques within coaching and do you use them?

References

Arthur, A. R. (2004) Work-related stress, the blind men and the elephant. *British Journal of Guidance & Counselling, 32*(2): 157–169.

Cartwright, S. and Cooper, C. (2005) Individually targeted interventions. In J. Barling, E. K. Kelloway and M. R. Frone (Eds.), *Handbook of Work Stress*. London: Sage.

Cavanagh, M. (n.d.) Mental-health issues and challenging clients in executive coaching. Retrieved on 7 January 2009, from www.groups.psychology.org.au/Assets/Files/article_cavanagh.pdf

Cooper, C. L., Dewe, P. J. and O'Driscoll, M. P. (2001) *Organizational Stress: A review and Critique of Theory, Research and Applications*. Thousand Oaks, CA: Sage.

Cousins, R., Makay, C. J., Clarke, S. D., Kelly, C., Kelly, P. J. and McCaig, R. H. (2004) Management standards and work–related stress in the UK: Practical development. *Work and Stress, 18*: 113–136.

Edgerton, N. and Palmer, S. (2005) SPACE: A psychological model for use within cognitive behavioural coaching, therapy and stress management. *The Coaching Psychologist, 1*(2): 25–31.

Ellis, A., Gordon, J., Neenan, M. and Palmer, S. (1997) *Stress Counselling: A Rational Emotive Behaviour Approach*. London: Cassell (now Sage).

Grant, A. M. (2001a) *Towards a psychology of coaching*. Retrieved on 12 May 2003, from www.psych.usyd.edu.au

Grant, A. M. (2001b) Coaching for enhanced performance: Comparing cognitive and behavioural approaches to coaching. Paper presented at *3rd International Spearman Seminar: Extending Intelligence: Enhancing and New Constructs*, Sydney. Retrieved on 30 December 2007, from: www.psych.usyd.edu.au

Grant, A. M. (2003) The impact of life coaching on goal attainment, metacognition and mental health. *Social Behaviour and Personality*, *31*(3): 253–264.

Grant, A. M. (2008) Personal life coaching for coaches-in-training enhances goal attainment and insight, and deepens learning. *Coaching: An International Journal of Research, Theory and Practice*, *1*(1): 47–52.

Grant, A.M., Curtayne, L. and Burton, G. (2009) Executive coaching enhances goal attainment, resilience and workplace well-being: A randomised controlled study. *Journal of Positive Psychology*, *4*(5): 396–407.

Grbcic, S. and Palmer, S. (2006, December 18) A cognitive-behavioural manualised self-coaching approach to stress management and prevention at work: A randomised controlled trial. Research paper presented at *1st International Coaching Psychology Conference*, City University, London.

Grbcic, S. and Palmer, S. (2007) A cognitive-behavioural self-help approach to stress management and prevention at work: A randomized controlled trial. *The Rational Emotive Behaviour Therapist*, *12*(1): 41–43.

Green, L. S., Oades, L. G. and Grant, A. M. (2006) Cognitive-behavioural, solution-focused life coaching: Enhancing goal striving, well-being and hope. *Journal of Positive Psychology*, *1*(3): 142–149.

Green, S., Grant, A. and Rysaardt, J. (2007) Evidence-based life coaching for senior high school students: Building hardiness and hope. *International Coaching Psychology Review*, *2*(1): 24–32.

Greenberger, D. and Padesky, C. (1995) *Mind over Mood*. New York: Guilford Press.

Gyllensten, K. and Palmer, S. (2005) Can coaching reduce workplace stress? *The Coaching Psychologist*, *1*: 15–17.

Gyllensten, K. and Palmer, S. (2006) Experiences of coaching and stress in the workplace: An interpretative phenomenological analysis. *International Coaching Psychology Review*, *1*(1): 86–98.

Gyllensten, K., Palmer, S. and Farrants, J. (2005) Perception of stress and stress interventions in finance organisations: Overcoming resistance towards counselling. *Counselling Psychology Quarterly*, *18*: 19–29.

Gyllensten, K., Palmer, S., Nilsson, E.-K., Regnér, A. M. and Frodi, A. (2010) Experiences of cognitive coaching: A qualitative study. *International Coaching Psychology Review*, *5*(2): 98–108.

Health and Safety Executive (2001) *Tackling Work-Related Stress: A Manager's Guide to Improving and Maintaining Employee Health and Well-Being*. Sudbury, UK: HSE Books.

Health and Safety Executive (2009) *Health and Safety Statistics 2008/09*. Sudbury, UK: HSE Books.

Health and Safety Executive (2010) *Self-Reported Work-Related Illness in 2003/2004: Results from the Labour Force Survey.* Sudbury, UK: HSE Books.

Hearn, W. (2001) The role of coaching in stress management. *Stress News, 13*(2): 15–17.

Lazarus, A. A. (1984) *In the Mind's Eye.* New York: Guilford Press.

McMorriss, T. and Hale, T. (2006) *Coaching Science: Theory into Practice.* Chichester, UK: Wiley.

Melchior, M., Caspi, A., Milne, B., Danese, A., Poulton, R. and Moffitt, T. (2007) Work stress precipitates depression and anxiety in young, working women and men. *Psychological Medicine, 37*: 1119–1129.

National Institute for Occupational Safety and Health (1999) *Stress.* Retrieved on 11 April 2003, from www.cdc.gov/niosh

Neenan, M. and Dryden, W. (2002) *Life coaching: A cognitive-behavioural approach.* Hove, UK: Brunner-Routledge.

Nicklaus, J. (2010) '*I never hit a shot . . .*', extended quote from Thinkexist.com. Retrieved on 28 November 2010, from http://thinkexist.com/quotes/jack_nicklaus/

Occupational Safety and Health Service (2003) *Healthy work: Managing stress in the workplace.* Retrieved on 1 September 2005, from www.osh.dol.govt.nz/order/catalogue/3.shtml

Palmer, S. (2003) Whistle-stop tour of the theory and practice of stress management and prevention: Its possible role in postgraduate health promotion. *Health Education Journal, 62*(2): 133–142.

Palmer, S. (2008) Coping imagery. *The Coaching Psychologist, 4*(1): 39–40.

Palmer, S. (2010) Step-up imagery technique. *The Coaching Psychologist, 6*(1): 42.

Palmer, S. and Cooper, C. (2010) *How to Deal with Stress.* London: Kogan Page.

Palmer, S. and Dryden, W. (1995) *Counselling for Stress Problems.* London: Sage.

Palmer, S. and Gyllensten, K. (2008) Stress management for employees: An evidence based approach. In A. Kinder, R. Hughes and C. Cooper (Eds.), *Employee Well Being Support: A Workplace Resource.* Chichester, UK: Wiley.

Palmer, S. and Laungani, P. (2003) Special symposium issues: Stress – Part 1. *International Journal of Health Promotion and Education, 41*: 99.

Palmer, S. and Neenan, M. (1998) Double imagery procedure. *The Rational Emotive Behaviour Therapist, 6*(2): 89–92.

Palmer, S. and Neenan, M. (2005, October 12) Cognitive-behavioural coaching. Paper presented at *Cognitive Therapy Conference,* Gotenburg, Sweden.

Palmer, S. and Puri, A. (2006) *Coping with Stress at University: A Survival Guide*. London: Sage.

Palmer, S. and Szymanska, K. (2007) Cognitive behavioural coaching: An integrative approach. In S. Palmer and A. Whybrow (Eds.), *Handbook of Coaching Psychology: A Guide for Practitioners*. Hove, UK: Routledge.

Palmer, S., Cooper, C. and Thomas, K. (2001) Model of organisational stress for use within an occupational health education/ promotion or wellbeing programme: A short communication. *Health Education Journal, 60*: 378–380.

Palmer, S., Cooper, C. and Thomas, K. (2003) *Creating a Balance: Managing Stress*. London: British Library.

Peltier, B. (2001) *The Psychology of Executive Coaching: Theory and Application*. New York: Brunner-Routledge.

Sheilch, A. A. and Korn, E. R. (1994) *Imagery in Sports and Physical Performance*. Amityville, NY: Baywood Publishing.

Williams, H., Edgerton, N. and Palmer, S. (2010) Cognitive behavioural coaching. In E. Cox, T. Bachkirova and D. Clutterbuck (Eds.), *The Complete Handbook of Coaching*. London: Sage.

Recommended reading

Palmer, S. and Cooper, C. (2010) *How to Deal with Stress*. London: Kogan Page.

Palmer, S., Cooper, C. and Thomas, K. (2003) *Creating a Balance: Managing Stress*. London: British Library.

Williams, H., Edgerton, N. and Palmer, S. (2010) Cognitive behavioural coaching. In E. Cox, T. Bachkirova and D. Clutterbuck (Eds.), *The Complete Handbook of Coaching*. London: Sage.

8

Mindfulness based cognitive behavioural coaching

Patrizia Collard and
Gladeana McMahon

In recent years many people have become increasingly inter-ested in mindfulness based approaches. Mindfulness based stress reduction (MBSR) and mindfulness based cognitive therapy (MBCT) are therapeutic interventions used in medical and mental health settings to treat clients with a variety of psychological and mental health problems (Baer, 2005). Examples of such problems include pain management (Kabat-Zinn, Lipworth, Burnet and Sellers, 1987), allevi-ating physical symptoms associated with stress (Astin, 1997) and the treatment of conditions such as depression (Segal, Williams and Teasdale, 2001) and anxiety (Kabat-Zinn, Massion, Kristeller and Peterson, 1992).

The phenomenon of wanting to remain well in a culture that rarely permits enough free time to recuperate from long working hours, commuting and often having to put up with less than healthy living environments is in itself a paradoxical desire. On the one hand individuals seek well-being but on the other hand the impact of, and employee adherence to, longer working hours and a poor environment have all been linked with an increase in stress related difficulties (Palmer and Dryden, 1995; Rose, 1994). Nevertheless, it is human nature to want to live to a ripe old age, while experiencing good health and a sense of meaning and purpose. The concepts of meaning and purpose have been identified as key factors for increasing psychological as well as physical resilience, which is equally important whether related to work or to life in general (Morris, 2008) – for example, interest in the meaning of life as a way of increasing personal satisfaction (Seligman, 2002). Meaning and purpose have also been linked to a sense of engagement in the workplace and those who experience this tend to be healthier, happier and more fulfilled (Giacalone and Jurkiewicz, 2003). In turn, these individuals also add to the profitability of organisations (Stairs, Galpin, Page and Linley, 2006).

Mindfulness based cognitive coaching (MBCC) is the latest development that draws upon the strategies of mindfulness based therapies and the skills and methodology of cognitive behavioural coaching (CBC). MBCC is applied to client groups who do not fall within the medical or therapeutic client arenas.

This chapter endeavours to introduce the reader to the main principles of MBCC and will briefly consider some of the historic roots of mindfulness. Case studies and applications as well as research evidence are intended to show how mindfulness based interventions can be used within the coaching arena with groups as well as in one-to-one coaching sessions. Jon Kabat-Zinn (2001), who is considered to be one of the founding fathers of MBSR, has defined mindfulness as an intentional focused awareness and a way of non-judgmental attention on purpose and being in the present moment.

Mindfulness is seen as the ability to engage in the experience of life on a daily basis with deliberate intention and alert awareness. For example, when walking to work how often does an individual take time to experience the full sensory awareness of their environment and their own physical, emotional and psychological responses to this? This awareness could include anything from noticing the way the pavement is uneven or the differing shades of colour of the paving stones that have been weathered over time to recognising an emotional experience of pleasure at seeing a stone carving on a building that the individual perceives as beautiful. At this point in time the individual is focused solely on and engaged in each moment of the activity taking place.

Being mindful differs significantly from how the 24/7 life-style has tended to shape 21st-century living. It is now possible to undertake personal chores such as banking anytime during the day or night, take-away food can be delivered to your door at almost any time and some supermarkets are open 24/7. Technology does not sleep and so communicating with anyone, anywhere, is possible at any time of the day or night. Many gyms are open from 5am and do not close until midnight, and about a fifth of the UK workforce work more than 45 hours a week (Office for National Statistics, 2009). In addition, it is rare for individuals to be emotionally or psychologically present (Brown and Ryan, 2003), but rather more prevalent is the way that individuals engage with the thoughts and feelings related to the past or the hopes, fears and desires associated with the future. When an individual is fully present in the moment, he or she is focused solely on the task in hand, recognising and being aware of all the emotional, psychological and physical responses that this engenders. Examples of being engaged in activities that take the individual away from the present would include worrying about a negative comment received at a past event or over a difficult meeting to come, rather than focusing on what is happening in the moment.

It is perfectly reasonable to reflect on the past and, indeed, much can be learned from historical experiences to ensure that past mistakes are not repeated or alternatively that pleasant nostalgic memories are enjoyed. In addition, reflecting on the future can also be helpful, for example, if an individual is thinking about how to shape his or her own career progression. However, what makes reflecting on the past or the future an appropriate activity is whether the individual makes a conscious and purposeful choice to engage in such an activity rather than experiencing intrusive and unhelpful thoughts about the past and/or the future.

The ability to connect with what is going on in the moment stimulates a completely different physiological response as different parts of the nervous system become activated, allowing the experience to take on new meaning

(Collard and Walsh, 2008). In the centre of the human brain is an emotional area, the limbic brain, which is made of different neural tissue than that of the cognitive brain. Limbic structures are responsible for emotions and contain natural mechanisms for self-healing (having innate abilities to find balance and well-being) and it would appear that over time the structures of the brain can be altered through the process of mindfulness based approaches (Ryback, 2006). This is particularly helpful in assisting those whose emotional responses are distressing or unhelpful to create a greater sense of calm and control, which then leads to minimising the risk of unwanted stress related reactions, aids clearer thinking and improved decision-making and provides a greater sense of satisfaction with life (Siegel, 2007).

There is significant evidence that learning to experience life from 'moment to moment' can create a sense of calm and well-being. The repeated experience of engaging in mindfulness based activities can in turn change the emotional response of the brain, assisting the individual to create the ability to respond to daily events in a calmer manner, whereas over-planning, ruminating and fretting can trigger the so-called 'stress response'. The stress response is the term given to the way the body reacts when a threat is perceived. Many individuals may be more familiar with the more commonly used term of 'fight or flight'. This response is the body's way of attempting to deal with stressful situations by promoting the release of stress hormones aimed at increasing alertness and physical stamina to deal with the perceived threat in question. If the stress response is experienced over a prolonged period of time it can bring with it a host of self-defeating physical, emotional, psychological and behavioural aspects that can ultimately culminate in physical and mental illness (Palmer and Cooper, 2010).

History of mindfulness approaches

The origins of mindfulness can be found by going back to the Sutras, written around 2500 BC, as well as Taoist and Yogic writings. All of these approaches in one way or another emphasise the benefits of staying focused in the present by either the use of meditation or the need to be aware of one's own physical, psychological and emotional state of being. One of the first texts of importance published in English in the 20th century is *The Miracle of Mindfulness* by the Vietnamese monk Thich Nhat Hanh (1975). It was originally written as a letter from Hanh's exile in France to one of the monks who had remained in Vietnam during the war years.

The school that Hanh had founded in Vietnam in the 1960s was intended to help rebuild bombed villages, teach children and set up medical stations for both sides engaged in the conflict. Hanh was then exiled for what was perceived by the government of the day as a criticism of the ruling party. His intention was to support the work he had started in a spirit of love, compassion and understanding. Its aim was to remind the monks still working in Vietnam of the essential discipline of mindfulness, even in the midst of very difficult circumstances.

Hanh used the services of an American volunteer to translate his letter. The translator was instructed to undertake the task slowly, steadily and in a mindful manner that befitted the task and only two pages a day were translated. Hanh encouraged the translator to be aware of the feel of the pen and paper, the position of his body and of his breath in order to maintain the essence of mindfulness while undertaking this task. When the translation was completed, 100 copies were printed.

The *Miracle of Mindfulness* has been translated into many languages and has been distributed on every continent in the world. Prisoners, refugees, health care workers, psychotherapists, educators and artists are among those whose lives have been touched by it. Denied permission to return to Vietnam, Hanh still spends most of the year living in Plum Village, a community he helped found in France. It is open to visitors from around the world who wish to spend a mindfulness retreat there. The proceeds from the sale of the fruit from the hundreds of plum trees that are grown at Plum Village are used to feed hungry children in Vietnam.

Mindfulness also found its way into the medical sector through the work of Jon Kabat-Zinn, a molecular biologist with an interest in the mind–body link in relation to healing. Kabat-Zinn had a personal interest in meditation, which led to him bringing together both his personal and scientific interests in exploring the concept of whether mindful meditation could have healing benefits.

Kabat-Zinn and his colleagues went on to develop the first MBSR programme in 1979 at the University of Massachusetts Medical Centre. Bill Moyers, a famous American television presenter, featured the Stress Reduction Clinic in his 1993 series, 'Healing and the Mind'. Following the broadcast of this programme, many health care professionals became interested in offering similar programmes (Kabat-Zinn and Santorelli, 2002). The MBSR group-based programme developed by Kabat-Zinn and colleagues is aimed at populations with a wide range of physical and mental health problems and has been studied extensively since the late 1970s. The Centre for Mindfulness has been continually delivering MBSR to patients within a large traditional American hospital for over 25 years. By 1999 over 10,000 patients had completed the programme. Kabat-Zinn and his colleagues extended the teaching of MBSR into prisons, poor inner-city areas, corporate settings and to medical students. MBSR has become part of a newly recognised field of integrative medicine within behavioural medicine and general health care.

Mindfulness based cognitive therapy (MBCT) was developed by Zindel Segal, Mark Williams and John Teasdale based on Jon Kabat-Zinn's MBSR programme. The MBCT programme was originally designed specifically to help people who suffered from repeated bouts of depression (Williams, Teasdale, Segal and Kabat-Zinn, 2007). Whilst there are no data available as to why such an approach was used initially with repeated bouts of depression rather than with single episodes, one might assume that in the same way that MBCT came into being from the desire to assist individuals to manage pain when all other approaches had failed, the same rationale may be true of individuals where traditional approaches to treating depression seemed to be less successful. MBCT is an integration of MBSR with cognitive behavioural therapy (CBT) developed and initially researched through a three-site randomised controlled trial. It was developed to teach recovered but recurrently depressed participants to disengage from habitual 'automatic' unhelpful cognitive patterns. The core skill that MBCT teaches is to intentionally bring awareness to unhelpful thoughts. The focus is on a systematic training to be more aware, moment by moment, of physical sensations, cognitions and emotions. This facilitates a 'decentred' relationship to thoughts and feelings. When an individual experiences such a way of being, it is possible to experience the emotions and thoughts associated with the event, in the same way that a bystander may watch an event unfold in front of their eyes. The individual experiences the emotions and thoughts associated with the event but is not overtaken by them. The evidence base of MBCT shows that it can halve the relapse rate in recovered patients with three or more episodes of depression. Other targeted versions of MBCT have now been developed, including for chronic fatigue syndrome (Surawy, Roberts and Silver, 2005) and oncology patients (Matchim and Armer, 2007) and presently a study on suicide is being conducted at the Oxford Centre for Cognitive Therapy.

The research evidence

There is an increasing evidence base regarding the effectiveness of mindfulness based approaches. These research studies include those by: Rosenzweig, Reibel, Greeson and Brainard (2003), who demonstrated the lowering of psychological distress amongst medical students; McCraty (2003), who demonstrated a reduction in blood pressure and an increase in emotional health, including an improvement in job satisfaction, for hypertensive employees; Davidson et al. (2004), who highlighted improved changes in brain and immune function brought about through mindfulness meditation; and Collard and Walsh (2008), who saw an improvement in the well-being of participants in all areas of their life.

These studies highlight how mindfulness based interventions can significantly improve the quality of subjective well-being on a psychological and physiological level for individuals by incorporating mindful awareness training into daily life.

Mindfulness based cognitive coaching

Teaching clients to become more *mindful* helps them to reconnect to the experience of 'being' rather than of 'doing'. In turn, this increases individual effectiveness and, as a by-product, personal productivity (Linley and Joseph, 2004). The experience of being is one where the individual experiences the full range of physical, emotional and psychological experiences associated with the event in question. Whilst taking action is important and linked to the sense of 'doing', being able to fully experience what is happening at a given moment allows the individual to stay focused in the present and is associated with what is termed 'being'. This may be seen in areas such as interviewing new members of staff, where being more present during the process enables the interviewer to home in on more details during the interview. The interviewer is then able to collect more data on which to base his or her decision. At the other end of the spectrum, when an employee needs to leave the organisation due to downsizing, this process can be conducted with more compassion, thereby becoming a less stressful experience for both parties.

At the same time as being mindful, the skills associated with CBC are interwoven with those of mindfulness based awareness training. Examples of this interweaving process would be helping clients to identify self-defeating core beliefs, underlying assumptions and surface thoughts that lead to unhelpful emotional and behavioural consequences (McMahon and Leimon, 2008). For example, if an individual discovered that he or she had been made redundant, the person might initially engage in a surface thought such as 'What have I done wrong?', and this thought might be linked to the individual's underlying assumption of 'If I work hard then I will be rewarded', which in turn might be based on a core belief of 'I am a hard worker and hard workers are successful'.

Cognitive behavioural coaching focuses on the thoughts, feelings and behaviours that a client engages in and the effect that these have on an individual's physiology. There is some dispute as to whether CBC focuses solely on thoughts and beliefs or if it takes in feelings, behaviours and physiology. However, the more holistic approach to CBC considers the role of all of these aspects, believing that whilst thoughts based on beliefs play a key role, feelings, behaviours and physiology are also important (McMahon and Leimon, 2008). In many ways this more holistic approach can be linked back more to the origins of multimodal therapy developed by Arnold Lazarus (Lazarus, 1989) than perhaps to the traditional CBT approach developed by Aaron Beck (Scott, Williams and Beck, 1989). Clients are encouraged to develop more effective and self-enhancing ways of thinking, feeling and behaving (McMahon, 2007).

The synthesis between mindfulness based awareness training and CBC, which led to the birth of MBCC, provides the individual with the skills and strategies to devise new and healthier beliefs about self, others and the world (i.e. those beliefs that assist the individual to deal with situations and personal emotional challenges more effectively) together with the ability to connect to the present. This has links with the realm of positive psychology, which also places emphasis on the need to learn to live effectively in the present by minimising the negative impact of placing too great an emphasis on the past and future (Boniwell, 2008; Leimon and McMahon, 2009). Positive psychology is one of the latest developments in the world of psychology. Traditional approaches have tended to focus on what goes wrong and how to put it right (e.g. in treating mental illness and the causes of anxiety, depression etc.) whereas positive psychology places the emphasis on identifying what works and why.

MBCC can be used with individuals as well as with groups. The coaching programme involves initially introducing clients to the background, research and skills associated with mindfulness and its benefits. In this respect, the coach engages in the same psycho-educative approach used in traditional CBC (Neenan and Dryden, 2002). The coachee needs to understand how this approach works and be an active participant in his or her own coaching programme. The relevance and benefits of using a mindful approach are explored in relation to the coachee's presenting issue(s). The coach and client decide on the best way of engaging in the MBCC process. Commitment is an essential requirement to ensure the best possible outcome and the client is made aware of this right from the start.

The coachee may opt for the complete MBCC programme or have some of the concepts of MBCC introduced into an already existing coaching programme. For example, if a CBC programme is under way, the mindfulness component can be positioned at the point in the programme where the coach believes this will be of greatest value. Alternatively, if an MBCC group is being set up, a client may opt to be part of this and will therefore have received materials and information regarding the aims of the MBCC programme prior to joining.

During the coaching programme, either with an individual or as part of a group, clients are asked to engage in mindfulness based meditative exercises. Individuals may believe that the meditative part of the process requires engagement in complex meditative sittings on a daily basis and this belief may initially make the person less inclined to participate in this approach. Although meditation is encouraged because it teaches clients how to locate sensations, emotions and thoughts, some coachees may be uncomfortable at such a prospect. This discomfort may be based on the belief that this type of meditation takes more time than the individual is prepared to allocate or that it has some type of religious connotation. Many coachees are surprised to discover that the skills of mindfulness can be applied to mundane daily tasks that take little time and that can be engaged in easily without any references to a religious or spiritual belief (see Box 8.1). These mindfulness exercises may only take a few minutes but, as Collard and Walsh (2008) found, coachees can still reap the benefits even from such short periods of practice. The learning of what is termed 'mindful awareness' increases with each and every application.

Box 8.1 Daily mindfulness based exercises

1 Take five minutes in the morning to be quiet and meditate, listen to the sounds of nature, gaze out of the window, take a quiet walk, drink a cup of tea and really taste it.
2 When you sit down in your car, become aware of the quality of your breathing and how your body feels. While you are driving, notice any tension in your body. Are your hands gripping the wheel? Is your stomach tight? Do you feel you have to be tense to drive effectively?
3 When you stop at a red light, or are stuck in traffic, bring awareness to your breathing or the sky, or the sights around you.
4 While sitting at your desk, bring attention on a regular basis to your bodily sensations and your breathing. Some people use the top of the hour as a time to check on their breathing, making sure it is slow and comfortable, taking a few minutes to **'Just be'**.

Whilst there are a number of longer meditative exercises, such as the body scan (where an individual takes time to focus slowly on each part of his or her body for approximately 45 minutes), benefits can accrue from much shorter exercises (Kabat-Zinn, 1994).

The insights and challenges that the client experiences when participating in the mindfulness part of the programme become the focus for discussion between the coach and the coachee. It is here that the more traditional elements of CBC come into play. For example, if a coachee finds it hard to concentrate on being focused in the present, due to constant thoughts about what others might think or of work needing to be done, the coach encourages the client to explore the meaning and impact of this intrusive thinking. Table 8.1 outlines the types of changes that the cognitive behavioural part of the MBCC programme would be seeking to achieve

Table 8.1 **Perfectionist thinking versus healthy achiever thinking**

Client's thoughts associated with self-defeating perfectionist thinking	Healthy achiever thinking based on CBC methodology
If I make a mistake then it is awful and I have done a bad job.	If I make a mistake it is not the end of the world, I can always learn from it and do better next time.
If I make an error then people will think badly of me and I will seem incompetent.	Everyone makes mistakes and there is nothing to be ashamed of. I did my best.
No one wins any prizes for coming second.	I am pleased I did so well.

in helping a coachee develop a more self-enhancing thinking style when dealing with perfectionist thinking.

The coachee is encouraged to consider how a more realistic and compassionate way of perceiving the world increases personal effectiveness and decreases negative emotional outcomes for everyone concerned. Someone in a heightened emotional state such as anxiety may manifest this by becoming overly emotional with those around them or by becoming irritable, and these emotional reactions have an adverse impact not only on the person experiencing them but also on those who come into contact with him or her. This process is used to assist the creation of the behavioural changes required to produce a more beneficial way of being (McMahon and Rosen, 2008).

Cognitive behavioural coaching places emphasis on the identification of self-defeating thinking. Thoughts are identified by using tools such as Thought Record Forms, where the individual is taught how to identify his or her personal thinking style. In executive coaching this is often called a 'PIT and PET' Form – performance-inhibiting thinking and performance-enhancing thinking (Neenan and Palmer, 2001; see also Table 8.2).

In summary, MBCC brings together two approaches into a model that provides the client with more control over, and enjoyment of, his or her daily life.

Table 8.2 **Example of performance-inhibiting thinking (PIT) and performance-enhancing thinking (PET)**

PIT	PET
I can't ask my boss for help as he will think I am stupid.	I have not been asked to undertake a task like this before and it would be unreasonable for me to know what to do if I have never been trained. My boss will be able to assist me and once he has shown me what to do or suggested someone I can speak to I will have all the information I need and will know what to do in the future.
My colleague must think I am an idiot because she keeps on making comments when it is obvious what I mean.	Just because I think something is obvious does not mean other people think that too. Maybe my colleague does not understand and perhaps I need to speak further with her about what I am doing and explain how I am approaching this task.

Mindfulness programmes for groups or individuals

The traditional way of engaging with MBCC is either by participating in an eight-week group programme or by the coach teaching all or most of the important aspects of the eight-week course to an individual client on a one-to-one basis.

The advantage of participating in a group is the learning that is gained not only by looking at the client's individual story but also by hearing the stories of others and receiving feedback and questions from them. The advantage of one-to-one MBCC coaching lies in the fact that the programme can be adapted to the client's personal timetable and learning style.

The eight-week programme (and its adaptation for individuals) incorporates topics such as:

- recognising the automatic pilot mode and learning how to *be* rather than to *do* (Baer, 2006);
- dealing with the barriers that the client experiences when trying to implement the home-practice exercises (Kazantzis, L'Abate and Gerard, 2007);

- working with the concepts of breathing, bringing attention to sounds and thoughts and engaging in daily activities in a truly 'mindful' manner (Bhikkhu, 1997).

Other skills that are taught include:

- walking meditation and mindful movement (Vriezen and Hanh, 2008);
- recognising automatic thoughts and their effects (Beck, 1976);
- acceptance of and allowing thoughts to be as they present themselves, as a way of learning to respond to life's challenges rather than merely reacting automatically (Hayes, Follette and Linehan, 2004);
- basic teaching on the physiology of stress and providing neuropsychological insights (Siegel, 2007);
- ways of learning how to manage aspects of an individual's daily life, such as self-care, using time management, exercise, diet, relaxation, etc. (Chödrön, 1994).

Each session focuses on one particular meditation and includes time for feedback (inquiry) and also the appropriate positioning of the relevant cognitive intervention(s) related to the needs of the individual. For example, following a full body scan exercise where an individual is guided to experience the sensations felt in each part of his or her body, starting at the feet and working up to the head, the person may report back that their mind kept on thinking about other things, which made it difficult to be fully present while undertaking the exercise. When asked about these thoughts the person might state that he or she was thinking about a forthcoming meeting, who would be there and his or her fears about an item the individual has to present. The coach then explores whether such intrusive thoughts are a common experience for the client in other situations, together with any associated negative outcomes. Following this, the coach helps the coachee to identify the type of cognitive distortion(s) being engaged in and the ways in which the individual could counter these to develop a more effective way of thinking. The eight-week course is also supported by a range of handouts, such as a home practice diary, and a number of CDs containing meditations.

The programme is extremely effective provided that participants are prepared to engage in regular practice in order to reach the desired outcome. The programme recommends that clients undertake a daily 40-minute meditative practice, five to six times a week, and they are encouraged to make a pro-active investment in individual well-being.

Case study

Sarah was a banker who had recently moved to London. She found commuting difficult and exhausting, as were her working hours. In addition, she had moved into a flat with noisy neighbours above and below her.

By the time she started her MBCC programme she was suffering from a number of stress related symptoms. She stated that, in the first instance, she wanted to deal with the situation herself rather than seek medical advice. Her symptoms included outbursts of anger, withdrawal from friends, higher levels of anxiety and restless and insufficient sleep.

Sarah came for two individual sessions where MBCC training was introduced to her. Within four weeks of engaging in the programme her sleep improved significantly, because whenever she found it difficult to sleep she engaged in mindfulness practice. She also learnt to apply mindfulness practices during her daily commuting, which in turn made the experience less stressful and even, on occasions, enjoyable. She also noticed that she had started to enjoy meeting friends again and was now striking up conversations with fellow commuters.

Sarah still practises her mindful meditations on a regularly basis and has opted to attend a bi-monthly one-day mindfulness retreat.

The following provides an example of some dialogue from one of Sarah's sessions:

Coach: So Sarah, you've mentioned that since you started your Mindfulness Based Coaching Programme you already feel a difference in many areas of life which you previously found challenging and difficult to deal with.

[Summarising the previous statement about the client's improvement, which is aimed at strengthening the new neuro-pathways that are being laid down in the client's brain together with reinforcing the benefits of the changes the client is experiencing in her behaviour.]

Sarah: Yes, it's almost like a miracle – I never thought that just 'being', chilling out so to speak and challenging my thinking style, could make that much difference.

Coach: What has happened recently that you attribute to your mindfulness based interventions?

[Seeking specific examples about the choices the coachee has made in selecting and using both the mindfulness based interventions she has been introduced to together with which of these practices she has found most helpful. As the programme combines mindfulness based interventions with CBC the coach is looking out for those aspects that belong to each of these ways of working. Focusing on a specific situation and the intervention(s) engaged in, this provides material for discussion and allows the coach to evaluate the coachee's understanding and progress. It also provides the coach with information regarding future areas to develop or focus on during the coaching programme.]

Sarah: Funny you should ask, because last night there was a situation that could have stressed me out, but I did not let it. When I got home my neighbours were having a party and playing really loud music. I noticed my anger levels rising and instead of simply sitting there getting angrier and angrier and feeling sorry for myself I decided to use the 'three-minute breathing step' exercise. As I felt myself calming down and coming more into the present I noticed how I was feeling but did not allow those feelings to take control of me as they would have previously. I then thought about the 'compassionate language' exercise we had been discussing and started to think about the language I was using and what I could say to my neighbours. I then took some time to identify those thoughts that were unhelpful and more likely to fuel my anger and challenged these. This took about twenty minutes and when I was in the right frame of mind I went over and rang their door-bell. By then I was much calmer and much more focused on how to handle the situation without blaming my neighbours. I asked them whether it was possible to turn the sound down by eleven as I had to work the next day. They immediately apologised and asked me whether I had eaten and invited me in to join them. I hesitated but they said I didn't need to stay long. They had a huge buffet laid out in the kitchen and I was quite hungry. It was a real treat not to have to cook for myself and the food was lovely. They turned out to be very vivacious folks, he is Greek I think. They looked after me, involving me in the conversation and somehow I didn't notice the music any longer. When I left at around eleven I was relaxed and went to bed. By the time I had started my 'body scan' exercise in bed they had turned down the music and I slept really well.

Then this morning on the tube I found myself smiling and didn't stress about the crowded train. I took out my I-pod and listened to your guided 'breathing meditation' standing up and focused on my breathing and got to work feeling quite chilled. One of my team members actually mentioned how I seemed cheerful and said it was probably a 'thank God it's Friday' state of mind. But I actually thought my weekend had already started on Thursday.

Coach: You are really using the tools you have learnt from your coaching programme very effectively. Firstly, you recognised your anger and instead of allowing this to build as you would have done previously with all the negative consequences we have spoken about, you used the 'three-step breathing' exercise to calm your heightened physiological state. Once you were calmer, you then thought about how to be in the moment, recognising your feelings but not allowing them to take over and you used the compassionate language exercise to plan what you would say, being kind to yourself but also thinking about how to position what you wanted to say. Lastly, you identified and challenged those thoughts you identified as being unhelpful. It sounds like you were able to focus on your own needs and how best to get these met by keeping calm and approaching your neighbours from a thought out and less physiologically aroused position. By allowing yourself to engage with your neighbours you also got an unexpected pay-off and were able to begin to create a more rewarding relationship. Then, this morning, even though you had to stand up during your commute to work, you were able to turn this normally unpleasant and draining experience into one that actually refreshed you and set the tone for your mood for the day.

[Outlining the steps in the process the client had undertaken and the benefits of these so as to reinforce how each part of the process builds on the previous one. Such explanations allow the coach to strengthen the client's motivation by feeding back the positive consequences from each action while ensuring the client understands the purpose of each intervention and how to use it to best effect together with the resultant positive outcomes associated with using it.]

The challenges faced when using MBCC

There are a number of challenges that a coach wishing to incorporate MBCC into his or her coaching repertoire faces. These challenges are:

- The need for the coach to be trained to a competent level in the application of mindfulness techniques. It is unlikely that someone with little or no understanding of 'mindful ways of being' will effectively assist the client to make sense of his or her experience. There is no need for the coach to be an 'expert' trainer in mindfulness application, but a minimum degree of proficiency is required. We find that those who practise mindfulness regularly themselves have better outcomes with coachees (Kabat-Zinn and Santorelli, 2002).
- The coach also needs a basic proficiency in CBC to facilitate the coachee's understanding of the way that he or she perceives the world (Leimon, Moscovici and McMahon, 2005).
- Helping coachees understand that MBCC is not a religious or mystical way of seeing the world, but rather a synthesis of the skills of mindfulness based meditation that has stood the test of time (2500 years) integrated within the more scientific framework of CBC (Baer, 2003).
- Encouraging clients to become an active participant in their own coaching programme, especially when it comes to undertaking home-practice exercises, whether they refer to the mindful or the more traditional CBC part of the training (McMahon and Leimon, 2008).

MBCC brings together two approaches in one model that provides the coachee with more control over and enjoyment of his or her daily life.

MBCC is a relatively new approach still in the process of being developed which requires to be evaluated more fully. However, anecdotal comments and the positive outcome of coachee application together with the findings from an increasing research base suggest that this way of working holds much promise in assisting coachees to develop a more realistic and healthier cognitive ability in relation to the outlook the person has on the world as well as on individual problem solving ability. These factors increase personal satisfaction with life together with locating individual meaning and purpose.

Perhaps the last word should be given to a coachee (a chief executive from the financial services sector) who, at the end of a CBC programme that introduced MBCC halfway through the process, stated:

> I practised mindfulness for a few weeks, there seemed a shift in attitude, all I needed to do was 'nothing deliberately'. My application was not consistent but its effects were significant. I have had a sense of being less at war with myself. What's more I have just achieved a significant promotion and am about to head up a much larger organisation. The changes in personal behaviour have translated into business success. There is not one area of life that has not been positively affected.

Discussion issues

- Mindfulness is seen as the ability to engage in the experience of life on a daily basis with deliberate intention and alert awareness. Do we need training to learn this ability?
- Do you agree that it is important for the coach to practise mindfulness if he or she is going to encourage coachees to use it?
- When might you, if at all, introduce some of the concepts of MBCC into a coaching programme?
- What do you see as the main challenges as a coach wishing to incorporate MBCC into his or her coaching repertoire?

References

Astin, J. A. (1997) Stress reduction through mindfulness meditation: Effects on psychological symptomatology, sense of control, and spiritual experiences. *Psychotherapy and Psychosomatics*, *66*(2): 97–106.

Baer, R. A. (2003) Mindfulness training as a clinical intervention: A conceptual and empirical review. *Clinical Psychology: Science and Practice*, *19*: 125–143.

Baer, R. E. (2005) *Mindfulness-Based Treatment Approaches: Clinician's Guide to Evidence Base and Applications*. Maryland Heights, MO: Academic Press.

Baer, R. (2006) Meditation, mindfulness, and psychological functioning in a sample of experienced meditators. *4th Annual International Conference on Mindfulness in Medicine, Health Care and Society*, Worcester, MA.

Beck, A. (1976) *Cognitive Therapy and the Emotional Disorders*. New York: International Universities Press.

Bhikkhu, B. (1997) *Mindfulness with Breathing: A Manual for Serious Beginners*. Boston: Wisdom Publications.

Boniwell, I. (2008) *Positive Psychology in a Nutshell*. London: Personal Well-Being Centre.

Brown, K. and Ryan, R. (2003) The benefits of being present: Mindfulness and its role in psychological well-being. *Journal of Personality and Social Psychology, 84*: 822–848.

Chödrön, P. (1994) *Start Where You Are: A Guide to Compassionate Living*. Boston: Shambhala Press.

Collard, P. and Walsh, J. (2008) Sensory awareness mindfulness training in coaching: Accepting life's challenges. *Journal of Rational-Emotive and Cognitive-Behavior Therapy, 26*(1): 30–37.

Davidson, R. J., Kabat-Zinn, J., Schumacher, J., Rosenkranz, M., Muller, D., Santorelli, S., et al. (2003) Alterations in brain and immune function produced by mindfulness meditation. *Psychosomatic Medicine, 66*: 148–152.

Giacalone, R. A. and Jurkiewicz, C. L. (2003) *The Handbook of Workplace Spirituality and Organizational Performance*. Armonk, NY: M. E. Sharpe.

Hanh, T. N. (1975) *The Miracle of Mindfulness*. New York: Random House.

Hayes, S., Follette, V. and Linehan, M. (2004) *Mindfulness and Acceptance*. London: Guilford Press.

Kabat-Zinn, J. (1994) *Wherever You Go, There You Are*. New York: Hyperion.

Kabat-Zinn, J. (2001) *Full Catastrophe Living: How to Cope with Stress, Pain and Illness Using Mindfulness Meditation*. London: Piatkus Books.

Kabat-Zinn, J. and Santorelli, D. (2002) *Mindfulness-Based Stress Reduction Professional Training – MBSR Curriculum Guide and Supporting Materials*. Worcester, MA: Center for Mindfulness in Medicine, Health Care, and Society.

Kabat-Zinn, J., Lipworth, L., Burnet, R. and Sellers, W. (1987) Four-year follow-up of a meditation-based program for the self-regulation of chronic pain: Treatment outcomes and compliance. *Clinical Journal of Pain, 2*: 159–173.

Kabat-Zinn, J., Massion, A., Kristeller, J. and Peterson, L. (1992) Effectiveness of a meditation based stress reduction program in the treatment of anxiety disorders. *American Journal of Psychiatry, 149*: 936–943.

Kazantzis, N., L'Abate, L. and Gerard, F. (2007) *Handbook of Homework Assignments in Psychotherapy*. New York: Springer.

Lazarus, A. (1989) *The Practice of Multimodal Therapy: Systematic, Comprehensive, and Effective Psychotherapy*. Baltimore, MD: Johns Hopkins University Press.

Leimon, A. and McMahon, G. (2009) *Positive Psychology for Dummies*. Chichester, UK: John Wiley & Sons.

Leimon, A., Moscovici, F. and McMahon, G. (2005) *Essential Business Coaching*. Hove, UK: Brunner-Routledge.

Linley, P. A. and Joseph, S. (2004) *Positive Psychology in Practice*. Chichester: Wiley.

McCraty, R. M. (2003) Impact of a workplace stress reduction programme on blood pressure and emotional health in hypertensive employees. *Journal of Alternative and Complementary Medicine, 9*(3): 355–369.

McMahon, G. (2007) Understanding cognitive behavioural coaching. *Training Journal*, January: 53–57.

McMahon, G. and Leimon, A. (2008) *Performance Coaching for Dummies*. Chichester, UK: Wiley.

McMahon, G. and Rosen, A. (2008) Why perfectionism at work does not pay. *Training Journal*, May: 60–63.

Matchim, Y. and Armer, J. M. (2007) Measuring the psychological impact of mindfulness meditation on health among patients with cancer: A literature review. *Oncology Nursing Forum, 34*(5): 1059–1066.

Morris, T. (2008) *What Do Buddhists Believe: Meaning and Mindfulness in Buddhist Philosophy*. New York: Walker & Company.

Neenan, M. and Dryden, W. (2002) *Life Coaching: A Cognitive Behavioural Approach*. Hove, UK: Brunner-Routledge.

Neenan, M. and Palmer, S. (2001) Cognitive behavioural coaching. *Stress News, 13*(3): 15–18.

Office for National Statistics (2009) *Labour Force Survey*. London: ONS. Retrieved from www.statistics.gov.uk/downloads/theme_labour/LMS_FR_HS/WebTable08.xls

Palmer, S. and Cooper, C. (2010) *How to Deal with Stress*. London: Kogan Page.

Palmer, S. and Dryden, W. (1995) *Counselling for Stress Problems*. London: Sage.

Rose, A. H. (1994) *Human Stress and the Environment*. London: Taylor & Francis.

Rosenzweig, S., Reibel, D. K., Greeson, J. M. and Brainard, G. C. (2003) Mindfulness-based stress reduction lowers psychological distress in medical students. *Teaching and Learning in Medicine*, *15*(2): 88–92.

Ryback, D. (2006) Self-determination and the neurology of mindfulness. *Journal of Humanistic Psychology*, *46*(4): 474–493.

Scott, J., Williams, J. R. and Beck, A. T. (1989) *Cognitive Therapy in Clinical Practice: An Illustrative Casebook*. New York: Routledge.

Segal, Z. V., Williams, M. G. and Teasdale, J. D. (2001) *Mindfulness-Based Cognitive Therapy for Depression*. New York: Guilford Press.

Seligman, M. E. P. (2002) *Authentic Happiness*. New York: Free Press.

Siegel, D. (2007) *The Mindful Brain: Reflection and Attunement in the Cultivation of Well-Being*. New York: W.W. Norton.

Stairs, M., Galpin, M., Page, N. and Linley, A. (2006) Retention on a knife edge: The role of employee engagement in talent management. *Selection and Development Review*, *22*(5): 19–23.

Surawy, C., Roberts, J. and Silver, A. (2005) The effect of mindfulness training on mood and measures of fatigue, activity, and quality of life in patients with chronic fatigue syndrome on a hospital waiting list: A series of exploratory studies. *Behavioural and Cognitive Psychotherapy*, *33*(1): 103–109.

Vriezen, W. and Hanh, T. N. (2008) *Mindful Movements*. Berkeley, CA: Parallax Press.

Williams, M., Teasdale, J., Segal, Z. and Kabat-Zinn, J. (2007) *The Mindful Way Through Depression: Freeing Yourself from Chronic Unhappiness*. New York: Guilford Press.

Recommended reading

Hayes, S., Follette, V. and Linehan, M. (2004) *Mindfulness and Acceptance*. London: Guilford Press.

Williams, M., Teasdale, J., Segal, Z. and Kabat-Zinn, J. (2007) *The Mindful Way Through Depression: Freeing Yourself from Chronic Unhappiness*. New York: Guilford Press.

9

Developing a coaching culture at work

Alison Whybrow and Siobhain O'Riordan

Overview

Organisations today are characterised by flexibility, hyper-complexity and chaos (Caldwell, 2006). At this time in particular, they face deeper levels of uncertainty as markets and businesses experience stringent economic and social challenges. In this context, coaching may be part of a survival strategy for some, whereas at the other end of that continuum, coaching may be seen as a means of optimising individual and organisational performance and innovation, creating a human capital advantage over competitors.

The growth of coaching in organisations is a reflection of our continuing belief in its potential benefits. This trend is evidenced by recent Chartered Institute of Personnel and Development (CIPD) surveys indicating the use of coaching (including mentoring) in organisations having shifted from 63% in 2007 to 90% in 2009 (CIPD, 2007, 2009). Increased attention is also being paid to developing a coaching culture in organisations to enhance performance.

Developing a coaching culture as part of a change agenda brings to the fore the complexities facing any change initiative. There are multiple drivers and multiple outcomes, with some expected and others more surprising. The view of change as an emergent process, where multiple dialogues exist, systems are self-organising, leadership is distributed and individuals have little rational or intentional control, is becoming more predominant (Caldwell, 2006). The unbounded optimistic belief in rational, planned change processes with a clear agenda, with 'intentional agency' at the core and where strategic action can be taken is moving from centre stage as we appreciate that rational, process driven methodologies are not effective on their own.

How then do organisations develop along intentional pathways to deliver their performance agenda? How do organisations develop a coaching culture when it is a lot easier to get things started than it is to bring enduring change into being (Senge, Kleiner, Roberts, Ross and Smith, 1994)? Certainly, if change is viewed as more emergent than planned it would be unhelpful to 'push' a rigid perspective and unrealistic to expect coaching to unfold in predictable ways, as coaching in organisations is certainly not a standard development (Whybrow and Henderson, 2007).

There are strong parallels between emergent change at the organisational level and the language of coaching at the individual level. It seems relevant then to build from the principles of coaching as they might be applied at the individual level as a starting point.

What do we mean by coaching?

Two definitions of coaching are offered here as a way of describing the essence and principles of coaching. Whitmore (1992: 8) states: 'Coaching is unlocking a person's potential to maximise their own performance. It is helping them to learn rather than teaching them.' The second definition is that of Van Oudtshoorn (2002), for whom coaching is 'reflective conversations for the construction and reconstruction of personally significant, relevant and viable meaning through negotiation and exchange'.

To us, these definitions highlight the essence of coaching as:

- fundamentally supporting learning in others and, through that learning, raising performance;

- a conversation that emerges as the context changes – the construction and rethinking of what is important, salient and feasible at any one point in time;
- content free – not teaching what we know, but helping people to discover their own resources and their own knowledge.

In order to be better 'learners', individuals need to become more self-aware (including awareness of beliefs and ideas that underpin behaviours and outcomes) and responsible (taking responsibility for the choices and the consequences of those choices). The process of enabling performance through increased self-awareness and responsibility is articulated by Whitmore (1992). In order for change to occur, individuals need to have control over that change, it has to be relevant to the context and performance agenda and individuals need to be interested in delivering the change.

In coaching then, rational and intentional principles of purpose and performance sit alongside self-organisation, emergence and construction. Drawing out these core principles makes it clearer that 'coaching' is a useful methodology to apply to individual and small group change, and change at the organisational or system level.

A cognitive behavioural framework?

Within the context of this book, we are curious to explore how an underpinning cognitive behavioural framework perspective can support the development of coaching conversations, perhaps supporting effective dialogue by raising awareness and acceptance of the reality of situations, as well as raising individual responsibility for the choices they make. Cognitive behavioural frameworks focus on raising awareness of the thinking habits a person holds and on shifting those habits to bring about change. In particular, a core technique is to make explicit unhelpful, unrealistic and illogical thinking in a situation and work with individuals to develop new ways of thinking (that are realistic, rational, logical and helpful), creating new perspectives from which to view and, more importantly, act from. A key premise is that we can become skilled thinkers, developing 'in the moment' awareness of how our beliefs and assumptions are limiting our perspective or choices. We can draw a link between the benefits of a flexible thinking approach and the challenge of working to deliver goals within an emergent, shifting context.

A practitioner working from a cognitive behavioural perspective pays particular attention to the language patterns that others and they themselves use and raises awareness of the consequences of particular actions or strategies. There is no right or wrong way to do things when working from this perspective; there are only effective and ineffective approaches. A common insight for people is to find that they can control their responses to a situation, even when they are unable to 'control' the situation. By changing their responses, a wider choice of resources (actions, behaviours and new thoughts) is opened up to individuals. Cognitive behavioural frameworks are essentially client or coachee centred.

During the course of this chapter, we will overlay this particular approach at the individual and system level, to explore the potential value of cognitive behavioural principles and concepts in supporting organisations to effectively deliver a coaching culture.

Our approach to enquiry

In this chapter, we draw on two sets of in-depth exploratory interviews. One set included five internal organisational stakeholders sharing their experiences, learning and stories of their journey as they work to develop coaching. The second set of interviews included three seasoned consultants with particular expertise and experience in the field of coaching. We interweave many narratives in this chapter, including:

- the conceptual and theoretical narrative;
- the organisational development story;
- the individual stories about what it is to drive the coaching agenda;
- the stories about coaching experienced in organisations.

Story-telling is a way of handling complexity, ambiguity, uncertainty and rapid change (Allan, Fairtlough and Heinzen, 2002). These stories build an emerging picture of what it is to develop a coaching culture in organisations and we recognise that there is insufficient space to do justice to the fullness of these stories in one chapter alone.

Our interviews provide a rich source, covering:

- The meaning and purpose of coaching in organisations.
- Who is involved in driving the coaching agenda.
- How is the development of coaching being approached.
- What coaching interventions have been introduced.
- What are the successes.
- What resistance has been encountered.
- What has been learned.

Each interview was recorded and subsequently transcribed, with the boundaries of confidentiality explicitly contracted and agreed.

The meaning and purpose of coaching in organisations

Organisations have multiple cultures and shifting subcultures within their framework rather than a single culture. Coaching similarly exists in multiple forms; there are multiple definitions and meanings. Each organisation and each individual within an organisation has a different construct of what coaching is, depending on their experience and beliefs. However, it is useful to note that for most internal stakeholders interviewed the coaching construct they were working to embed was explicitly and intentionally non-directive. As one internal stakeholder noted: "we're quite good at the directive, we need to develop people's non-directive capability so that they have more choice about how to respond and more flexibility".

Internal stakeholders pay close attention to the language around coaching. For one, the term 'coaching culture' was purposefully avoided:

> People have been talking about a coaching culture for years and the definition of coaching previously was that you as a manager sit down and tell them what to do . . . the [coaching] culture will happen – but we're not going to advertise this big coaching thing.

For another organisation, the term coaching was not explicitly used in their new leadership competencies, however coaching behaviours were clearly embedded in the framework.

Internal stakeholders recognised the diversity of coaching as a concept and of taking ownership of the specific meaning of coaching within a particular context. As one noted: ". . . we are always clear about what the organisational definition of coaching is, clear about what we mean when we talk about coaching with a new audience". Given the diversity of meaning and organisational legacy, careful attention to terminology on a case by case basis appears to be a very useful principle. It seems particularly important to work from what exists phenomenologically (what is described to be taking place or what is actually happening) rather than attempt to impose a pre-determined idea of coaching and a coaching culture onto an organisational system. Here, using a cognitive behavioural approach as an internal stakeholder may be useful to ensure that any unrealistic or demanding ideas about what 'should' be happening are made explicit, examined and a realistic awareness of the organisational system and the potential options is enabled.

Purpose of introducing a coaching culture

Many reasons for procuring one-to-one coaching support are reported, ranging from developmental/interpersonal requirements to performance coaching and supporting individuals through transition (see Sherin and Caiger, 2004, for a useful summary). Yet one-to-one coaching interventions only capture part of the story; the consultant and internal stakeholders saw multiple applications of coaching in organisations.

Consultants saw coaching as being about promoting learning, at an individual and organisational level, in order to optimise functioning and deliver performance within the context of the organisational system. Coaching was also seen as a way of supporting the organisation to provide an effective performance environment for individuals (see Box 9.1).

Box 9.1 Consultant perspectives

"[It is] more about learning . . . about having a learning conversation, which is not just reliant on individual focus. If we are saying that the ultimate goal of the organisation is to shift their culture or enhance performance or to deliver different values, how you develop that is often by using coaching as a means for delivering that but it is not a panacea. There are multiple methodologies . . . some of which is one on one, some is about having clear coaching conversations, some of it is about shifting the leadership stance to encourage a more coaching style of leadership, some of it is about developing internal coaching cohorts for different interventions. It's not so much the how of coaching, more the outcome of coaching. The coaching is more about shifting organisations."

"Coaching and mentoring are about helping people with the quality of their thinking about issues that matter to them. Within an organisational context what we are trying to do is raise the quality of the learning conversations that people have with the intent that they individually will be more focused, more productive, more fulfilled and that equally this will reflect in the organisation upon the quality of retention of people, the quality of decisions that are made and the quality of reflection. . . ."

"Helping the individual to add value to the organisation . . . The more enlightened businesses want a happy, healthy and engaged employee and they know that

---

> to get that people need to be fully functioning . . . personally and professionally and for [the organisation] to create the right kind of environment for the individual to thrive in . . . bringing on their talent and profiting on this."

For internal stakeholders, key purposes included:

- developing the quality of leadership resources;
- developing innovative and creative approaches;
- providing a safety valve, thus mitigating some of the impact of high pressure environments.

Developing the quality of leadership resources

Leadership development is widely believed to be a key enabler of organisational performance and competitive advantage (e.g. Raelin, 2004). For internal stakeholders coaching was intended to shift leadership styles, to create a "strong leadership base" and "rounded leaders". Coaching as a style of leadership fits the concept of distributed leadership (Bolden, 2007), where the action and influence of people at all levels are integral to the overall direction and functioning of the organisation. This distributed perspective 'puts leadership practice centre stage' (Spillane, 2006: 25). A coaching style of leadership is suggested to support improved performance by enhancing employee engagement, leadership retention and leadership learning.

Enhancing employee engagement

Coaching behaviours among leaders and managers are viewed as contributing to employee engagement, which is agreed to lead to stronger organisational performance (e.g. Barker, 2008; Robertson-Smith and Markwick, 2009). As Barker (2008) comments: 'The war for talent and the fast approaching global labour shortage mean that keeping employees longer and performing to higher levels is crucial to organisational success.' Leader behaviours associated with greater engagement, identified by Robinson and Hayday (2009), include:

- taking an interest in people as individuals, and developing and nurturing their teams;
- tackling difficult issues such as breaking bad news and managing poor performance;
- keeping a focus on performance and an expectation that their teams would deliver to a high standard.

In parallel with these behaviours, leading with a coaching style is frequently about moving away from a command and control structure towards a style where employees feel they have 'contributed', been 'listened to' and 'are valued'. Coaching raises the self-awareness of leaders and the impact of their behaviour on others, changing "how we work interpersonally"; it provides more 'tools and techniques' to support one-to-one development conversations and potentially improves the quality of performance conversations.

From a cognitive behavioural perspective, the consequences of our thinking patterns, the behaviours we exhibit and in particular our interpersonal impact are looked at in detail in multimodal cognitive behavioural frameworks (see Palmer, 2008). A tailored modality profile could be a helpful approach when coaching leaders focused upon enhancing employee engagement.

Enhancing leadership retention

Attrition at senior levels leads to significant loss of resources and investment. Leadership retention was a specific goal for two organisations: "Rather than losing some of our best people – can we keep people by offering coaching to support them." For these organisations a specific, focused one-to-one coaching initiative was designed to support employees through transition into the most senior roles.

Enhancing leadership learning

Coaching initiatives were specifically aligned to embed learning from:

- formal development programmes (e.g. ". . . they might be on an aspirant director or chief executive programme and coaching is very much supporting the learning coming out of that");
- informal experiences (e.g. as noted by one consultant: "Coaching is very much a learning process so if you can support people to learn you can impact upon performance").

Developing innovative and creative approaches

Coaching was seen as a way of enabling new ideas and approaches to emerge and enhancing innovation and creativity. According to Barsh, Capozzi and Davidson (2008) a company's ability to innovate and tap the fresh value-creating ideas of its employees, partners and others is a core driver of growth, performance and valuation. In their survey, 70% of 700 senior executives reported innovation as one of the top three drivers of business growth. In an organisation where creativity is supported, people:

- understand their ideas are valued;
- trust that it is safe to express those ideas, and oversee risk collectively together with their managers;
- believe they can learn from failure – rather than be blamed for failure.

The increased competitiveness of the organisational context – either internal competition for resources or external competition for market and reputation – was a driver for harnessing the creativity of all employees:

> We've got very lean times ahead of us, we may be expected to do a lot more with a lot less. Coaching will help with motivation, but also help people to be innovative and deal with some of the issues that they are going to come up against; helping people to think creatively, strategically, think outside of the box in terms of dealing with some of the changes ahead. . . .

> We have a much more diverse set of competitors. . . to be leading edge, we need to stretch people further. The

competitive landscape through a variety of distribution channels is vast.

Cognitive behavioural techniques are aimed at increasing flexibility of thinking and more choice about how to respond to situations where habitual responses are unhelpful. By enhancing individual awareness of internal thinking processes and their consequences, unhelpful thinking patterns can be highlighted and isolated. More motivational, helpful thinking can be developed through greater self-awareness and the simple act of rehearsal. The habit of examining and intervening with unhelpful thinking is itself a skill that can be developed.

Providing a safety valve

Two organisations explicitly referred to coaching acting as a safety valve. In one company, 'preventing derailers' was specifically highlighted. In this case, as people move into very senior positions, coaching conversations may assist in normalising the experiences that individuals are facing and support them to think about these (and other) issues in a more effective and performance-enhancing way. In a competitive environment, senior people can become very isolated.

Who is involved in driving the coaching agenda?

One seemingly straightforward strategy to facilitate change valued by all interviewees was having senior level sponsorship. Yet, whilst senior sponsorship provided a focus and drive that impacted how coaching initiatives unfolded and embedded, the initial attention and energy that went into building coaching as a viable proposition was less likely to be explicitly sponsored by the board.

Senior level sponsors

The presence of senior level sponsorship was mixed. When absent, an internal stakeholder noted the gap:

We are trying desperately for it not to be an organisational development thing . . . the senior leaders . . . demonstrate very little coaching and mentoring behaviour. . . That's a big barrier to getting coaching out into the business and used by all our leaders and managers.

For a second organisation senior sponsorship was becoming a clear reality, and was described as critical:

We've tasked those two with buying in the rest of the leadership team to make sure that they are genuinely role modelling this from the top . . . taking this forward from a leadership perspective is critical.

Two organisations had very strong sponsorship from the CEO, but the nature and impact of that support appeared to differ. One CEO in particular was very clearly and overtly supportive of the value of coaching and was quoted on every development programme. Here, the coaching initiative across the organisation had received significant levels of financial and people resource.

For the fifth organisation, whose role was to influence thinking and practice in health trusts and strategic health authorities, support for coaching from the Department of Health pushed coaching up the agenda for health organisations and led to resources being targeted to coaching and leadership development.

Our consultant interviewees noted more success where the leadership team conceptually understood what they were buying into, with the best organisations being those that put their senior team through a similar, perhaps shorter process, where they begin to learn coaching skills and where they appreciate that they have to lead by example.

Senior sponsorship then is not necessary for the coaching initiative to get started within an organisation; indeed, there is no 'right' time. Depending on the organisational structure and culture, coaching may get something of a foothold before senior sponsorship becomes a requirement, and a lot can be achieved. As one internal stakeholder noted:

"it's easier to get sponsorship once you have built a viable proposition". However, senior sponsorship is essential for coaching to become embedded in the organisational system and have more chance of being sustained. From a cognitive behavioural perspective, the idea that particular people 'should' (as a demand) be involved is unlikely to be helpful; the question of how they can be involved will potentially yield more options.

Change agents

The internal stakeholders interviewed would be classified in this grouping – individuals or a group of individuals who have the responsibility to make change happen at an operational level (Whybrow and Henderson, 2007). Internal stakeholders described themselves as 'passionate' and 'evangelistic' about the value of coaching, although with varied ability to influence. As one stakeholder described it: "there is an entrepreneurial feel about the development of coaching in the organisation, a collection of individuals who are passionate and driven".

Where change was more emergent, one passionate individual appeared to be central to the initiative, drawing in others with specific responsibilities as coaching gathered momentum. Where the coaching initiative was more focused and at a faster pace, a greater level of people resource was set aside.

Many internal stakeholders held a deep knowledge of coaching, and described the need to "model best practice ourselves, consult with others about what they need and support their agenda". Some had received an accredited level of professional development as a coach practitioner either before or during the current coaching initiative.

External partners

Three of the five organisations had explicitly partnered with one or more external partners on their journey. The external partner could have a highly valuable and highly influential role, for example:

> One of the big things is the partnership with [xx] that has been fundamental to the success. They have helped us get a really good understanding of what coaching is, and have coached us through this change process.

Consultants highlighted the importance of the external partner adopting an exploratory and flexible approach:

> When you go into organisations the key to it is actually finding out what is this organisation . . . you have to understand the organisation's culture, its needs, its challenges.

How is the development of coaching being approached?

Increasing personal and conceptual understanding

Educating people about coaching at a personal and conceptual level was central. As one internal stakeholder described: "It's about clearing the myth for people in the organisation. We're hoping that by educating people about what real coaching actually is – the culture will happen."

Education was taking place at multiple levels, including formal internal development programmes, formal external development programmes, receiving coaching, seeing others role-model coaching behaviours and practising coaching.

Pulling versus pushing

There was explicit attention given to coaching being 'pulled' rather than pushed through the system, although this varied within organisations and across initiatives. Coaching was often developed through many seemingly ad hoc initiatives before the organisation started to want more. As described by an internal stakeholder: "it's about lighting fires around the business, and going where the energy is". Pulling coaching through the organisation, rather than pushing, seemed congruent with the principles of coaching: "it's not quite right being directive about a non-directive approach".

Yet, where the coaching initiative was moving at a faster pace there was a stronger, more coordinated, push of the initiative into the organisational system: ". . . by the end of our financial year all of our managers will have been exposed to the thinking around coaching".

Responsive partnering

Co-creation and co-design were highlighted: "we were prepared to learn, I don't think that we ever came at it from a position of expertise". Reputation and relationship were seen as critical. There was little perceived value in taking an 'expert stance' as a change agent, and the speed and consideration given to requests from coaching programmes such as Continued Professional Development (CPD) was considered a valuable contribution to the outcome.

Informal/distributed initiatives versus formal/ integrated initiatives

In some organisations initiatives were more ad hoc – they were not organised around an explicit strategy, idea or purpose. Yet for each organisation there was a noted event that provided greater momentum, such as a specific management development programme with a significant cohort of managers, or the development of a register for external coaches. All interviewees believed that an integrated, systemic approach with clear direction and vision was necessary for a coaching culture to be sustainable.

What coaching interventions have been introduced?

From our interviews, coaching initiatives can be distinguished into three broad types: coaching as an offering, where a formal one-to-one or team coaching relationship is established; coaching as a style, where coaching principles are integrated into organisational behaviours; and developments that are aimed at embedding coaching into the fabric of the organisation.

Interventions supporting coaching as an offering

The following types of initiatives were introduced to support coaching as a discrete offering to individuals and teams:

- design of specific one-to-one coaching offerings for senior level employees;
- a register for external coaches (one-to-one coaching and team coaching);
- developing an internal coaching pool.

Specific one-to-one offerings

Coaching as a one-to-one offering was more likely to be provided at very senior levels, sometimes as part of leadership development programmes or as part of the support for individuals transitioning into the most senior roles.

Very senior level coaching was offered as a choice and frequently included external coach providers that could be accessed through an organisational register. External coaches were valued at this level because they offered breadth and depth of experience and reduced the challenge of boundary management and confidentiality faced by internal coaches.

At slightly lower levels of seniority, internal coaches were frequently used.

Matching processes were valued for internal and external coaches, as one consultant noted: "Organisations are becoming more and more savvy about what makes a good match." An internal stakeholder commented: "We are certainly going to have control of who's matching up with who. We will have a detailed matching process that we have yet to devise."

Group coaching, and 'coaching clinics' where anyone could turn up and receive coaching on a specific issue, were also offered at more junior management levels.

Developing a register for external coaches

Coaching registers were a popular intervention and were widely used (e.g. many UK Strategic Health Authorities have a coaching register). Just how they were constructed and then used varied across organisations. Two organisations in particular noted that they really started to drive and shift coaching provision in the organisation by getting the external coaching provision 'sorted out'.

Organisations are becoming more sophisticated about when and how to use external coaches. The expected benefits from an external coach included:

- The executive having greater openness to different and new perspectives ("With an external you might be quite courageous in some of the things you think about").
- Greater creativity by being coached from 'outside' the system ("they [external coach] might suggest more innovative, more diverse suggestions perhaps – internal coaches sometimes are influenced by the context – halt the process a little bit").
- Having the opportunity to select a coach from a diverse range of alternatives.

Three of the five organisations interviewed had developed a relatively stringent process for external coach selection, one benefit being that senior executives had more confidence in the coaching available as a result.

Developing a pool of internal coaches

This was a strategy in all organisations, where employees coach colleagues working for the same organisation (Frisch, 2001). Some organisations had already developed a pool of coaching talent to a professional level of qualification; others had clear plans to do so. The benefits of internal coaches included:

- The opportunity to use internal resources (which were viewed as a low cost option).
- Sharing the same context – the value of knowledge and organisational context 'enabling shortcuts'.
- A set of organisational role models, powerfully demonstrating that skilled coaching was not beyond a leader's capability alongside their day job.
- Certain flexibility in meeting the needs of the coachee.

For each benefit there were challenges for internal coaches to manage:

- Multiple relationships between the coach and coachee.
- Balancing full-time job and coaching responsibilities.
- The complexity of working within a system (e.g. boundary management) means that the coach needs to be exceptionally skilled to differentiate what they bring, what impact the system has and what the coachee brings.
- Sharing the same context – perhaps making assumptions and shortcuts that close options too quickly.

However, differences between internal and external coaches in terms of coaching skill and capability are increasingly viewed as artificial.

Creating a supportive infrastructure

A point raised by consultants was the potential limited access of internal coaches to supervision. However, this assumption was not supported by organisational experience. For all internal stakeholders, supervision and CPD were considered important to build, as this quote highlights:

> Part of my role is to ensure that we do in-house supervision and that everyone keeps CPD up to date. We are developing an internal accreditation process; anyone not keeping up to date won't be able to coach in the organisation.

For some organisations, supervisory practices exist in relation to other professional services that can be adapted for the coaching context. Communities of practice are also valued.

Initiatives supporting the development of a coaching style of behaviour

These initiatives were designed to develop leaders with a repertoire of skills, often with a focus on developing stronger non-directive capability. Specific programmes aimed at developing a coaching style were created. For others, coaching skills were embedded in management development programmes, where it was 'stripped back to the basics'. These programmes were often about:

- Raising self-awareness and 'awareness of impact on others'.
- Supporting people to understand the 'inner game'.
- Questioning and listening.
- Building in reflection.

A focus on people understanding the 'inner game' and the concept of interference are core concepts embedded within cognitive behavioural coaching approaches. Rather than individuals unpacking the 'inner game', the purpose was to raise awareness and to notice what happened in relation to the outer game.

Initiatives to embed coaching into the fabric of the organisation

Internal stakeholders commented on a variety of developments aimed at driving and embedding coaching within the organisation, such as creating focused roles or creating an award for leaders who are seen to significantly invest in their people.

What are the successes?

> The ultimate test of successfully developing a coaching culture would be that it would just be the way that we do things around here – we wouldn't call it coaching anymore.

There are significant challenges to measuring the success of coaching and evaluating the return on investment (ROI) (Fillery-Travis and Lane, 2006; Stevens, 2005; Whybrow and Henderson, 2007). One challenge to drawing useful insights about coaching effectiveness at the macro level is that different things happen under the term coaching at different levels in an organisation; reasons for engaging coaches differ and any organisationally sponsored 'programme' of coaching may include unwilling coachees, unready or unable to derive benefit from a coaching-type intervention (Stevens, 2005). Comparing coaching initiatives is a little like comparing apples and oranges, potentially leading researchers to very generic conclusions about the efficacy of coaching.

Consultants noted that effective measurement of coaching was multi-faceted, and that whilst some impact can be measured directly (e.g. increase in sales) the impact of other outcomes was difficult to assess (e.g. number of ideas for an advertising campaign). Typically, consultants reported encouraging organisations to build methods of measurement into existing processes (performance management systems and people surveys), with reflections and stories offering rich insights and greater context to these quantitative approaches.

Internal stakeholders valued evaluation, and were directly facing the challenge of getting clear, hard evidence. In one organisation, the evaluation process had not specifically been articulated, although on reflection there was much data that could be drawn on. For others, some clear outcome measures had been considered. There was a range of evaluation methods used in the organisations we spoke with, including:

- Using an independent third party research institute to evaluate the impact of coaching.
- Gathering rich sources of information, such as stories and case study material.
- Assessing people's access to coaching employee surveys.
- Evaluating individual development programmes.
- Gathering personal impact data – how individuals think the coaching input has developed them as individuals.
- Evaluating impact through changes in 360° feedback completed before and after coaching interventions.

Stories from internal stakeholders

Internal stakeholders noted the personal impact of the coaching development they had gone through on their own awareness and the quality of their own practice (see

Box 9.2). Here a cognitive behavioural framework may be useful for internal stakeholders to work with in order to support the development of self-awareness, the awareness of 'hot buttons' and to unpack and modify 'bad habits'.

Box 9.2 Internal stakeholder stories

"I'm much more self-aware and I know when I'm having a negative impact on other people."

"I think a little bit more before I take action these days."

"Just learning what my core values were and hot buttons and why I reacted in the way I did – you almost feel like you're using muscles you've never used before, they've been there, you've just never used them."

"Coaching has helped me to think more strategically and make sense of lots of things that were happening, taking a more helicopter view of situations – developed my strategic thinking."

"I regarded myself as quite a good coach before I went through this, but I was far far away from where I am now. You have to really understand it."

"I've had to unlearn a lot of bad habits. I was exposed to the grow model – trained in 1992 by Sir John Whitmore, but through the years you learn some bad habits if you don't practise and you're not supervised. . . . I'm now much more formal about my approach to coaching. I'm treating it as something serious and professional as opposed to just a style of how I'd do things."

Stories from the business

Coaching has impacted in a number of ways, as the stories in Box 9.3 testify.

Box 9.3 Business stories sharing the impact of coaching

- **A nurse's story.** "Following the coaching course, one nurse reported a relative was upset about something that hadn't been done and came to the nurses station. The nurse said 'shall we just find an empty office and we can go and sit down and I can listen to you properly'. When she got into the room, the relative said 'this is the first time anyone has really listened to what I've got to say, I really appreciate your time, I realise that you've got a lot to do'. The nurse reported that before the coaching course, she would have normally dealt with a complaint at the nurses station, but the fact that she said she was going to listen to the relative properly had a real impact. It really did help to resolve things quite quickly."
- **What the direct reports say.** "Anecdotally those whose managers have been on the programme report that there has been a real difference – this person listens more, they delegate better, we're having regular team meetings now, we seem to get things done more quickly – there's a better team vibe."
- **Breaking down defences.** "A lot of people have tried using powerful coaching questions with people who are a little bit defensive – and got different consequences from them."
- **Allowing new perspectives to develop.** "I've done some coaching this morning – I just fed back what the person just said – and the response was 'OK that's made me think quite differently', they went quiet for a while – they said 'I'm just recording my thoughts'. Coaching is useful just to help people make sense of what they are already thinking or saying."
- **Shifting senior director behaviour.** "The real success for us has been – that we have trained 150

senior directors in coaching skills, so that there is a practitioner based six day accredited coaching skills programme over three to four months. The impact of that programme has been phenomenal at a personal level and has had some impacts in the organisation. One chief exec that came on a programme completely changing the way they worked – using a coaching style with their staff and using it to engage clinicians in the reform agenda – rather than the old style of leading the clinical medical population. By going on a coaching skills programme and adopting a coaching style, they were looking to make a major change in the culture and the way the business is run."

- **Focusing senior leader thinking.** "One person cited that their external coach had assisted them with the implementation of a new service – generating income for the trust – if they hadn't had that coaching intervention as they moved in to post in a new organisation, they would have not got to that point. They described really focusing in the coaching."

- **Shifting performance.** "One individual who's senior partner described him as 'not very emotionally intelligent, can you fix him'. I started coaching him in October, we've had four to five conversations now – after the third conversation I met his boss, who said 'wow what have you done – he's a changed man – it's working really well – I can see that he's going to come through to partnership' – that's been fantastic . . . it shows that coaching can make a big difference."

What are the elements that were believed to deliver greater success?

A range of ideas and experiences were reflected and shared from both internal stakeholders and consultants, highlighting some of the factors underpinning the success of initiatives.

At the individual level, three ideas were noted as promoting success:

- Explicitly sharing what coaching was through information and personal experience: "we see the light bulb go on".
- Raising individual self-awareness and the skills of reflection.
- Developing confidence.

With issues of confidence in particular, cognitive behavioural frameworks are likely to build capability and interpersonal capacity.

For coaching interventions, clear and explicit contracting contributed to success. As a consultant noted, the contracting phase can help to clarify expectations at multiple levels (line manager as well as the individual coachee).

In order to gain momentum, a tipping point needs to be reached where the concept and value of coaching has been built, leaving a thirst and hunger for the initiative across the organisation. At this point, coaching can be more easily pushed into the system and embedded. Developing a coaching culture is not an end point, but a means to enable an organisation to achieve other outcomes with greater levels of success.

What resistance has been encountered?

> Trying to convince people who've been around for 20–25 years that there is a better way of doing things or a different way to do things is challenging. . . . Change is very scary for many people . . . we make all these changes and expect people to get on with it – and are leaving all these broken people in our wake.
>
> (Internal stakeholder)

Individuals differ in how they react to a shift towards a coaching culture and a coaching style. Some are clearly welcoming but others experience unconscious or conscious resistance. People may not even be aware that they are behaving in a way that is incongruent with what is expected (Whybrow and Henderson, 2007).

Resistance occurs across sectors and is not limited to one particular employee group or level. Certainly, internal stakeholders described coaching as potentially disruptive to established empires and likely to lead to direct reports being more challenging of their managers. Senior level resistance was observed where coaching initiatives were blocked from the agenda, even where resources to develop the coaching agenda were available and individuals were declaring their willingness to lead on coaching.

Contributors to resistance included:

- Aspects that were perceived to be insufficient in some way, for example a lack of resources, ownership and/or evidence of impact.
- Commonly held beliefs that coaching:
  o is 'pink and fluffy' and 'soft', so 'how will it make a difference?';
  o will just take more time;
  o is for poor performers.
- Fear of doing things differently from existing, more comfortable habits.
- Merely tolerating rather than supporting coaching.
- Skill deficits, for example a lack of learning skills.

Consultants viewed resistance as more likely where:

- senior leadership is not aligned or does not buy into the process, creating a lack of clarity;
- reward systems do not match the desired leadership approach. In this situation, the integration of coaching culture may become counterproductive.

Internal stakeholders found that resistance was starting to reduce as personal experience and understanding increased:

Now we've educated people about the value of coaching to improve good performance, some of the resistance the

'I don't need a coach as I'm good at my job' comments have gone away now.

Cognitive behavioural frameworks have been highlighted as useful throughout this chapter. However, it is in dismantling and working with resistance to change where cognitive behavioural approaches can come into their own. For example, the belief that coaching will 'take more time' than a traditional, more directive approach is often heard. When this is explored with individual managers the goal is to enhance performance. Exploring the impact of a directive approach on performance using a cognitive behavioural two-column form technique is highly effective. The cognitive behavioural coaching philosophy is also integrative and as such can 'help to overcome blocks to change' (Palmer and Szymanska, 2007: 86).

What has been learned?

I've been on a hell of a journey really, developing collaborative relationships and using a coaching style – that can be really frustrating. There are times when it would be easier just to make the decision, but you end up alienating people. Edgar Schein's concept of the humble enquirer has really resonated with me, using powerful open questions and building relationships and connections.

(Internal stakeholder)

What had been learned and what advice was there for others? From consultants, lessons included:

- Do not get hooked on coaching – it is not a panacea.
- Clarify your business strategy, what you hope to achieve.
- Clarify your values, what you think are the fundamental principles for your organisation in relation to people and learning.
- Coaching is not just a one-to-one process.
- Embed the practice of learning across your organisation.
- Clarify the outcome you want and design something fit for purpose.

- Do not underestimate the time and resources involved in getting engagement.
- Get senior sponsorship as early as you can.

From internal stakeholders, learning included:

- Do not assume that you know what you need to know.
- Engage an external partner for whom it is their bread and butter.
- Create a register for external coaches. A lot of people say that they coach, but in reality they do not.
- Define what a coaching culture is before you start. Clarify what it is going to do for the business and what it is going to deliver. You can only do things one step at a time, but have a vision of where you are getting to.
- Audit and measure at set points to assess the longevity of impact.
- Manage the expectations of those that you are putting through internal coaching programmes.
- Make selection onto internal coaching programmes tough – and be aware that people may leave to set up their own practice.
- Beware of your own limiting assumptions and ideas (see Box 9.4).

Box 9.4 Internal stakeholders' limiting assumptions and beliefs

"I made some assumptions that the coaching itself – training people in coaching skills – was all you needed to do and very quickly that assumption was shattered. I underestimated the infrastructure and support that needs to be put in place to enable people to have the space to use those skills."

"I underestimated the huge variance of uptake and application across different organisations that we support."

"I underestimated the will to move forward and the timeframe that is needed. It's taken three years to get to this point – I think a couple of the providers in the

> early days didn't think we'd get to this point and they
> said 'it's not worth it, you're not going to do it'. . . . I
> had such a belief in it all – that it was worth it and it
> would work . . . and now we've got lots of fabulous
> evidence about the impact of coaching."

Summary and discussion

In designing this chapter, we were particularly keen to provide some insight into what was happening in organisations in relation to the development of a coaching culture. We are only able to share some of the richness and colour of the stories shared as we draw out the emerging themes and principles that might be learned from and built upon.

The complexity of change processes is borne out in the stories yet there are potentially useful parallels drawn between coaching and individual change, and the application of coaching principles to support organisational change. Partnering, co-creating, being prepared to change your thinking, your approach, following the energy, maintaining focus, raising awareness of and challenging interference and clarifying the goals are phrases used by internal stakeholders to describe how they navigated their organisational context.

Looking across different coaching initiatives to ascertain ROI has limitations (Stevens, 2005). There is no 'paint by numbers' approach to delivering value through coaching. However, more might be gained by exploring the emergent principles from the stories we have heard. These principles include:

- **Language.** Paying close attention to language and being explicit about what is meant is an important starting point to ensure that what is being expressed is clear and meaningful to the listener.
- **Learning.** At all points in bringing coaching into organisations, learning and the skills of learning are evident.
- **Power.** Explicitly, all of us are only ever in a position of influence over others, and coaching as a methodology brings that into sharp focus. Rather than expect that we

have power to control others, it is better to have an open dialogue, enabling us to elicit new understanding and meaning in relation to what has to be achieved and how that might be brought about. Within the context of the organisational system, power and influence are important to attend to.

- **A systems perspective.** This is recognising that, as an individual, you are always working within a system and that system cannot be ignored or removed. Organisational trends influence the shape of coaching interventions. The existing system may support or alternatively undermine coaching as a style (Passmore, 2005); working with that system rather than against it, lighting fires and seeing what sticks may yield greater opportunities than if you approach the system with a view that it should not be as it is. If coaching initiatives remain ad hoc rather than in any way joined up or embedded into the system, individual changes will be transitory at most.

- **Self-awareness.** The concept of self-awareness was embedded at multiple levels in the stories shared in this chapter and included as part of the design of internal development programmes, an aspect of coaching initiatives and important for internal stakeholders.

- **Flexibility.** This emerged strongly as a valuable principle and was important for internal stakeholders in order to support initiatives that were 'fit for purpose', and for consultants so that they could assess and meet the needs of organisations and individual clients. A flexible approach at all stages of the coaching process also helps to counter and reduce resistance.

- **The stories themselves.** Internal stakeholders lament the fact that they mainly have anecdotal evidence rather than hard facts and figures. Pedler (in Burgoyne, Pedler and Boydell, 1994) notes that organisations are in a dynamic process of becoming – existing as a particular entity only in transition. If we believe that stories are something of the fabric and the glue that holds a system together, then these are potentially also a driver and a useful test of change in that system. From this perspective, the many stories about coaching impact and success are critical and useful to support organisations in making sense of the journey they are on.

The journey to developing a coaching culture in an organisation is clearly challenging with the end point being self-determined. There are some similar types of development activities that organisations will adapt and use. Perhaps one way of reviewing whether an organisation has achieved coaching culture is to explore and capture the ways in which organisational change occurs and assessing the congruence between leader behaviours and espoused coaching behaviours.

The value of a cognitive behavioural framework to support the development of a coaching culture

Cognitive behavioural frameworks focus on raising awareness of the thinking habits a person holds and on shifting those habits to bring about change. From the material we have explored for this chapter, the value of a cognitive behavioural framework can be appreciated and has been highlighted throughout. Models of thinking, such as the inner game, draw heavily on self-limiting beliefs or 'interference', both of which are common elements of programmes focused on developing a coaching style. For internal stakeholders, raising awareness of assumptions held led to important shifts in how coaching initiatives were approached. For example:

> I was getting really frustrated, and just could not understand why people didn't 'get it'. My line manager coached me, and highlighted for me that it was my role to help them understand the value of coaching.

In this dialogue, the increased awareness moved the behaviour of others from a frustration that they 'should get it', and clearly did not, to one where the individual removed the 'block' and worked out a more effective solution to the problem.

Some key points of resistance expressed in the stories heard related to unrealistic and unhelpful beliefs. Working through this resistance is likely to involve addressing the beliefs that are held by individuals, and as noted by Palmer and Szymanska the cognitive behavioural approach can 'help to overcome blocks to change' (Palmer and Szymanska, 2007: 86).

At the organisational level, habits of thinking and behaviour were also observed. A 'directive' style of management was more predominant across the organisations interviewed. A core purpose for many organisations was about developing a greater repertoire of responses, thus strengthening the non-directive end of the continuum. This development was intended to provide greater choice to leaders and better outcomes for interactions. Having a different experience of interacting with others, for example through a non-directive coaching approach, can turn on the 'lightbulb'.

A key premise in cognitive behavioural work is that we can become skilled thinkers, becoming aware 'in the moment' of how our beliefs and assumptions are limiting our perspective or choices. Raising the 'quality of thinking' was considered to be part of coaching by consultants, and flexibility was noted as being valuable in supporting the development of a coaching culture.

If we look at how the cognitive behavioural approach has been used within organisations, Palmer and Szymanska (2007: 89) have noted that '. . . within work contexts, the approach often focuses on enhancing or maximising performance under pressure'. However, the popularity of cognitive behavioural coaching seems to be increasing within the workplace, where it is applied in areas such as performance improvement, developmental coaching, executive and leadership coaching, peer and team coaching and career coaching (Williams, Edgerton and Palmer, 2010). The application of cognitive behavioural coaching to support health and well-being has also been documented (e.g. Palmer, Tubbs and Whybrow, 2003). From the stories that we have integrated into this chapter, cognitive behavioural principles and practices also have a key role to play in facilitating and supporting the development of coaching cultures in organisations, thus keeping practitioners focused on the reality of the complex situations that they face and enabling more effective choices and responses.

Discussion issues

Following are some questions to support you to review what *is* happening regarding coaching in your organisation or client organisations (past or present) and what you might learn from these experiences:

- The meaning and purpose of coaching differs across organisations and individuals. What is the intended meaning and purpose of coaching in your organisation and what are the stories that are told about coaching? What differences do you notice?
- What coaching interventions have been introduced and what small fires have been started, successful and/or sustained? What small sparks require support? Who has the energy to be involved?
- What assumptions are you holding about coaching in your organisation that are getting in the way of moving forward? What are you telling yourself 'should' be happening, 'must' happen, 'needs' to happen? Are these assumptions helpful or unhelpful?
- What, if anything, do you notice when you contrast the organisational perspectives with consultant perspectives?

Acknowledgements

In order to write this chapter we were keen to explore what was actually happening in relation to developing a coaching culture in organisations rather than work from a theoretical and philosophical perspective alone. We had great support from a number of organisations and individuals who gave freely of their time, their experience and their learning in this area that was invaluable to us.

We would like to thank the following individuals and organisations for their candid participation in the interviews we conducted, in no particular order:

David Clutterbuck, Director of Clutterbuck Associates.

Dr Caroline Horner, Director of i-coach academy Ltd.

Gladeana McMahon, Director of Gladeana McMahon Associates.

Shirley Ficken, Leadership and Organisational Development, Yorkshire Building Society.

Lisa Gresty, Leadership and Management Development Manager, Mid Cheshire Hospitals NHS Foundation Trust.

Gail Partridge, Talent Development Team, of BSkyB Ltd.

Ian Paterson, Partner – Transaction Advisory Services and Nicki Hickson, Director of Learning and Development, Ernst and Young.

Sue Mortlock, Head of Board Development, NHS Institute of Innovation and Improvement.

References

Allan, J., Fairtlough, G. and Heinzen, B. (2002) *The Power of the Tale: Using Narratives for Organisational Success*. Chichester, UK: Wiley.

Barker, G. (2008) Building the business case for employee engagement. *Personnel Today*. Retrieved on 28 April 2010, from www.personneltoday.com/articles/2008/10/17/47938/employee-engagement-trade-secrets.html

Barsh, J., Capozzi, M. and Davidson, J. (2008) Leadership and innovation. *The McKinsey Quarterly*, *1*: 37–47.

Bolden, R. (2007) Distributed leadership. In A. Marturano and J. Gosling (Eds.), *Leadership: The Key Concepts*. Abingdon: Routledge.

Burgoyne, J., Pedler, M. and Boydell, T. (1994) *Towards the Learning Company: Concepts and Practices*. Maidenhead, UK: McGraw-Hill.

Caldwell, R. (2006) *Agency and Change*. Hove, UK: Routledge.

CIPD (2007) *Learning and Development 2007 Survey Report*. London: Chartered Institute of Personnel and Development.

CIPD (2009) *Taking the Temperature of Coaching*. London: Chartered Institute of Personnel and Development.

Fillery-Travis, A. and Lane, D. (2006) Does coaching work or are we asking the wrong question? *International Coaching Psychology Review*, *1*(1): 23–36.

Frisch, M. (2001) The emerging role of the internal coach. *Consulting Psychology Journal: Practice and Research*, *53*(4): 240–250.

Palmer, S. (2008) Multimodal coaching and its application to workplace, life and health coaching. *The Coaching Psychologist*, *4*(1): 21–29.

Palmer, S. and Szymanska, K. (2007) Cognitive behavioural coaching: An integrative approach. In S. Palmer and A. Whybrow (Eds.), *Handbook of Coaching Psychology: A Guide for Practitioners*. Hove, UK: Routledge.

Palmer, S., Tubbs, I. and Whybrow, W. (2003) Health coaching to facilitate the promotion of healthy behaviour and achievement of health-related goals. *International Journal of Health Promotion and Education*, *41*(3): 91–93.

Passmore, J. (2005) The heart of coaching: Developing a coaching model for managers. *The Coaching Psychologist*, *1*(2): 6–9.

Raelin, J. (2004) Don't bother putting leadership into people. *Academy of Management Executive*, *18*: 131–135.

Robertson-Smith, G. and Markwick, M. (2009) *Employee Engagement: A Review of Current Thinking* (Report 469). Brighton, UK: Institute for Employment Studies.

Robinson, D. and Hayday, S. (2009) *The Engaging Manager* (Report 470). Brighton, UK: Institute for Employment Studies.

Senge, P., Kleiner, A., Roberts, C., Ross, R. and Smith, B. (1994) *The Fifth Discipline Field Book: Strategies and Tools for Building a Learning Organisation*. London: Nicholas Brealey Publishing.

Sherin, J. and Caiger, L. (2004) Rational-emotive behavior therapy: A behavioral change model for executive coaching? *Consulting Psychology Journal: Practice and Research*, *56*(4): 225–233.

Spillane, J. P. (2006) *Distributed Leadership*. San Francisco: Jossey-Bass.

Stevens, Jr, J. H. (2005) Executive coaching from the executive's perspective. *Consulting Psychology Journal: Practice and Research*, *57*(4): 274–285.

Van Oudtshoorn, M. (2002) *Coaching: The catalyst for organisational change?* Professorial Lecture, Middlesex University, UK, 16 October.

Whitmore, J. (1992) *Coaching for Performance*. London: Nicholas Brealey.

Whybrow, A. and Henderson, V. (2007) Concepts to support the integration and sustainability of coaching initiatives within organisations. In S. Palmer and A. Whybrow (Eds.), *Handbook of Coaching Psychology: A Guide for Practitioners*. Hove, UK: Routledge.

Williams, H., Edgerton, N. and Palmer, S. (2010) Cognitive behavioural coaching. In E. Cox, T. Bachkirova and D. Clutterbuck (Eds.), *The Complete Handbook of Coaching*. London: Sage.

Afterword

In editing this book we have enjoyed working with experienced colleagues who have provided insight into different aspects of cognitive behavioural coaching. From the 1980s we were enthusiastic about the application of the cognitive behavioural approach to the field of training, management and human resources, and in the 1990s to the field of coaching, but there was a lack of research to underpin our practice. We soon realised that we had to modify the therapeutic language as it was unsuitable for the workplace and we thank the many employees we worked with for their frank and useful feedback on our adapted approach. We were informed by therapy research, which had investigated a wide range of clinical disorders, and we applied this knowledge to the area of enhancing performance and reducing stress at work. Understandably, this was not totally satisfactory. However, the situation changed as more research into the effectiveness of cognitive behavioural coaching and coaching in general was published during the last decade. We hope that this book has been at the cutting edge of the approach and look forward to receiving your feedback and suggestions for the next edition.

Michael Neenan
Stephen Palmer

Appendices

Appendix 1: Performance-Enhancing Form

Target problem	Performance-interfering thinking (PIT)	Emotional/behavioural reaction	Performance-enhancing thinking (PET)	Effective and new approach to problem
(A)	(B)	(C)	(D)	(E)

© Centre for Coaching, 2011.

Appendix 2: Enhancing performance

State problem: Goal:	
Performance-interfering thinking (PIT)	Performance-enhancing thinking (PET)

Appendix 3:   Stress Thought Record

State problem:	
Goal:	
Stress-inducing thinking (SIT)	**Stress-alleviating thinking (SAT)**

Appendix 4: Stress Management Form

Target problem (A)	Stress-inducing thinking (SIT) (B)	Emotional/behavioural reaction (C)	Stress-alleviating thinking (SAT) (D)	Effective and new approach to problem (E)

Web resources and training institutes

- **adSapiens, Swedish Centre for Work Based Learning**
  Runs a range of cognitive coaching and therapy courses in Göteborg, Sweden.
  www.adsapiens.se

- **Albert Ellis Institute**
  Provides a range of courses in the rational emotive behavioural approach. Sells books, training DVDs and other material online.
  www.rebt.org

- **Association for Coaching**
  An established professional body. Publishes an international journal and a newsletter.
  www.associationforcoaching.com

- **Association for Professional Executive Coaching and Supervision**
  A professional body specialising in executive coaching.
  www.apecs.org

- **Association for Rational Emotive Behavioural Therapy**
  A professional body that runs conferences, publishes a journal and accredits REB coaches, therapists, trainers and supervisors.
  www.arebt.org

- **British Association for Behavioural and Cognitive Psychotherapies**
  A professional body that runs conferences and workshops, publishes journals and accredits cognitive behavioural therapists.
  www.babcp.com

- **Centre of Applied Positive Psychology**
  Provides training and resources in positive psychology.
  www.cappeu.com

- **Centre for Coaching and Faculty of Coaching Psychology**
  Based in London, UK. Offers professional body recognised and university accredited coaching courses at Certificate, Diploma and Postgraduate levels. Specialises in cognitive behavioural and rational coaching.
  www.centreforcoaching.com

- **Centre for Stress Management**
  Based in London, UK. Its Faculty of Cognitive Behavioural and Rational Emotive Therapy provides a range of cognitive behavioural and rational emotive behavioural therapy courses at Certificate and Diploma levels recognised by professional bodies. It also runs a Certificate and Diploma programme in stress management.
  www.managingstress.com

- **Coaching and Mentoring Relationship Research**
  This website maintains a list of coach–coachee and mentor–mentee publications that are relevant to Chapter 3.
  www.coachingrelationshipresearch.webs.com

- *Coaching at Work*
  Bi-monthly magazine that publishes articles on a range of coaching subjects associated with the workplace. Online resources, coach listing and articles.
  www.coaching-at-work.com

- **Coaching Psychology Unit, City University London, UK**
  Undertakes research into coaching, coaching psychology, the client–coach/therapist relationship, cognitive behavioural and rational coaching and leadership, stress, health and well-being. It was the first Coaching Psychology Unit to be established in the UK. Offers DPsych and PhD research programmes.
  www.city.ac.uk/social-sciences/psychology/research/coaching-psychology-unit

- **Coaching Psychology Unit, University of East London, UK**
  Runs a range of postgraduate coaching and coaching psychology programmes.
  www.uel.ac.uk/psychology/coaching

- **International Academy for Professional Development**
  Provides distance learning courses in coaching and coaching psychology, with online courses in cognitive behavioural and rational coaching and university accredited professional development programmes.
  www.iafpd.com

- **International Coach Federation**
  A professional coaching body. Website has a link to Code of Ethics.
  www.coachfederation.org

- **International Society for Coaching Psychology**
  A professional body for coaching psychologists. Website has a link to Code of Ethics.
  www.isfcp.net

- **Society for Intercultural Education, Training and Research (SIETAR)**
  SIETAR is the world's largest interdisciplinary network for professionals working in the intercultural field.
  www.sietar-europa.org

Index